Schriften des Europa-Instituts der Universität des Saarlandes – Rechtswissenschaft

Herausgegeben von

Professor Dr. Werner Meng
Professor Dr. Dr. Dr. h.c. mult. Georg Ress
Professor Dr. Torsten Stein

Band 89

Prof. Dr. Christos Gortsos

Fundamentals of Public International Financial Law

International Banking Law within the system of Public International Financial Law

Nomos

Die Deutsche Nationalbibliothek verzeichnet diese Publikation in der Deutschen Nationalbibliografie; detaillierte bibliografische Daten sind im Internet über http://dnb.d-nb.de abrufbar.

Die Deutsche Nationalbibliothek lists this publication in the Deutsche Nationalbibliografie; detailed bibliographic data is available in the Internet at http://dnb.d-nb.de.

ISBN 978-3-8329-7180-9

1. Auflage 2012

To my beloved son Nikiforos

Foreword

This book aims to offer an integral overview of public international banking law, as part of the system of international financial law, which is one of the three (3) branches of public international economic law – alongside with public international monetary law. This branch of public international economic law has developed gradually over the course of just the last thirty years and has been further evolving following the recent (2007-2009) international financial crisis, which, *inter alia*, brought the need for its rules to be readjusted.

In the period between the outbreak of the crisis and the completion of this study, I tried to take stock of and analyse systematically different aspects of this readjustment in various academic articles. The present study contains many of the positions and views presented in my articles during that period. However, the study is not simply an attempt to reproduce this work, but a synthesis into a new unified, coherent text, taking into account the relevant literature.

I am fully aware of the dynamics underlying the formation of public international banking (and, in general, financial) law. When this study was being finalised, several regulatory developments were in the making that could not be covered in it. I am certain that in due time, sooner rather than later, the study will be revised in the hope that its main premises still apply.

I owe special thanks to my colleague, Lecturer Dr. Christina Livada, for her mostly valuable comments and remarks on each and every section of this study, as well as to Vassilis Panagiotidis for his crucial comments on the subject-area of payment services and systems on which he is an expert. Decisive has been the contribution of PhD candidate Katerina Lagaria through the outstanding editing of the English text. The elaboration of this study has also received substantial input from Dr. Sophia Ziakou.

Last but not least, very warm thanks go to Professor Werner Meng, whose strong encouragement was of invaluable help to me, to Professor Torsten Stein, who also supported my initiative, and to my publisher, Nomos Verlagsgesellschaft, for accepting this book for publication under their imprint.

Athens, May 2012 *Professor Christos Gortsos*

Table of Contents

CHAPTER THREE
THE SOURCES OF PUBLIC INTERNATIONAL BANKING LAW 197

SECTION FIVE
AN OVERVIEW OF THE SOURCES OF PUBLIC INTERNATIONAL FINANCIAL LAW 199

TABLES INCLUDED IN THE TEXT

INTRODUCTION

This study aims at introducing its readers into public international banking law, as this has gradually developed since 1974 and is still evolving rapidly. Public international banking law is discussed within the context of public international financial law, since it constitutes one of its branches (and potentially its most significant). Accordingly, there are several references to public international financial law in general (where deemed appropriate), but the main focus is on public international banking law.

In order to achieve this goal, the author has structured the study in six (6) sections organized under three (3) Chapters as follows:

1. Chapter One, entitled *"Regulatory intervention in the financial system as the basis of the rules of public international financial law"*, contains the first two sections of the study, which can be viewed as an introduction to financial economics for non-economists:

(a) Section One (*"The financial system"*) is a brief presentation of:

- the functions of the financial system (under A),
- the infrastructures of the financial system (under B),
- the services provided in the financial system (under C), and
- the categories of financial services providers (hereinafter 'financial firms', under D).

(b) Section Two (*"The case for regulatory intervention in the financial system: financial policy objectives and instruments"*) is devoted to the analysis of:

- the concept and content of regulatory intervention in the financial system (see under A and B below), and
- in particular, the instruments for ensuring the stability of the banking system (under C).

2. Chapter Two, entitled *"The making of public international financial law"*, contains the sections three and four of the study:

(a) In Section Three (*"Definition, historical evolution and levels of making and enforcement of public international financial law"*) the author is presenting:

- the definition of public international financial law, its delimitation *vis-á-vis* other branches of international law, as well as its branches based on the analysis in section two (under A),
- the historical evolution of the institutions of public international financial law from 1971 until today (under B), and
- the four levels in the making and enforcement of public international financial law (under C).

(b) Section Four (*"In particular: the international fora"*) is studying:

- in detail, the international fora adopting international financial standards, as well as the Committee on the Global Financial System (under A), and
- in more detail, the Basel Committee on Banking Supervision, which is the main forum for the adoption of rules of public international banking law (under B).

3. Finally, Chapter Three, entitled *"The sources of public international financial law"*, contains the last two sections of the study:

(a) Section Five (*"An overview of the sources of public international financial law"*) contains (as indicated by its title) a general overview of the main sources of public international financial law, with particular attention to:

- the reports included in the *"Compendium of Standards and Codes*" of the Financial Stability Board (under A 2),
- the initiatives undertaken by the G-20 during its most important recent summits with a view to re-adjusting the public international financial law after the recent (2007-2009) international financial crisis (under B), and
- the progress report of the Financial Stability Board with regard to current supervisory and regulatory developments at international level (under C).

(b) The provisions of two main blocks of sources of public international banking law are then analysed in Section Six. These are reports of the Basel Committee on Banking Supervision which refer to:

- the conduct of micro-prudential supervision to international banks and the cross-border cooperation between supervisory authorities (under A), and
- the micro-prudential and macro-prudential regulation of international banks (under B).

In the concluding remarks of the study ('An Overall Assessment') the author presents briefly his own personal views on:

- the extent and scope of adequate regulatory intervention in the financial system, since (to his view) the possibility cannot be excluded that in our days, mainly as a result of the recent international financial crisis, the international community will resort to a 'regulatory over-shooting' (under A), and
- the future of public international financial law (under B).

References to primary sources can be found in the footnotes. There is also a rather extensive list of secondary sources at the end of the study, albeit selective, given the vast plethora of sources on this topic that could not be covered entirely in this study. Some are not even mentioned in the main text (or references are, for the most part, merely indicative). This is the author's choice, based on his view that this is an introductory study mainly aimed at students interested in this field and more exhaustive references to secondary sources in the main text would definitely have compromised its character. Those interested are nevertheless given the opportunity to resort to them.

Finally, the interested reader can find a list of useful internet addresses of all international organisations and fora referred to in this study. Access to those will allow him/her the necessary updating with regard to recent developments that could not be covered in it.

The cut-off date for data included in this study was end-May 2012.

CHAPTER ONE

REGULATORY INTERVENTION IN THE FINANCIAL SYSTEM AS THE BASIS FOR THE RULES OF PUBLIC INTERNATIONAL FINANCIAL LAW

SECTION ONE THE FINANCIAL SYSTEM

A. The functions of the financial system[1]

1. Introduction

In market economies, the financial system is one of the systems set up for the provision of services, within which the following two functions are performed through a complex nexus of markets, services providers and infrastructures:

(a) The first function is channelling funds from the economy's positive savers to the negative savers (for more details, see 2 below).

Here, it is necessary to make a semantic clarification (aa) and an important note (ab).

(αα) The term 'channelling of funds'[2] is used in a dual manner comprising two individual parts:

- funds provided by positive savers, in the form of bank deposits and insurance premiums, for the purchase of debt instruments issued by negative savers and traded in financial markets (constituting borrowed funds for negative savers), and
- funds provided for the purchase of equities issued by negative savers/ companies and traded in financial markets (constituting own funds for negative savers).

In this context:

- 'positive savers' shall mean the economic units (households, enterprises, and the government) offering their available income or property for saving, and
- 'negative savers' shall mean the economic units that seek either borrowed funds to meet their investment, mortgage or consumer needs or (in the case of enterprises with the legal form of a public limited liability company (société anonyme), a stake in their own funds).

In open economies (i.e. economies where there are no restrictions on the international movement of capital), positive and negative savers may also be foreign natural or legal persons.

1 This chapter provides an introduction to the functions and infrastructures of the financial system, as well as to financial services. In this respect, the following should be pointed out:
(a) There is quite extensive literature on the issues discussed in this study and it would thus be impossible to cite it exhaustively. Consequently, all bibliographical references are mere indications.
(b) It is the author's intention to distance himself from any legal regime governing the operation of the financial system, as this would lead to restrictive results.

2 See **Mishkin (2007)**, p. 23, and **Allen and Gale (2001)**.

(ab) In every economy, the amount of funds channelled through the financial system is merely a subset of the funds generally channelled from positive to negative savers. Borrowed funds are also channelled to negative savers through private lending, while a large part of own funds of public limited liability companies (sociétés anonymes) and funds of other corporate forms is drawn from natural and legal persons outside the financial system. Consequently, households and enterprises, as negative savers, can draw funds from positive savers directly without the intermediation of the financial system. The financial system brings added value to the economy by, inter alia, offering businesses the opportunity to draw own and/or borrowed funds from a pool of positive savers to which they either have no access or they have access at a disproportionately high cost.

(b) The second function of the financial system consists in enabling natural and legal persons (including positive and negative savers) to make payments without using cash, namely coins and banknotes (see under 3 below).

For the most part, the literature on the functions of the financial system focuses on the channelling of funds from positive to negative savers (first function) and does not address cashless payments as a second function. The author is of the view that this approach is restrictive based on the following arguments:

(i) Payment instruments and fund transfer services, through which this function is performed, are principally offered by financial firms, most of all banks, in the context of the first function.

(ii) In every economy, payment instruments and fund transfer services providers, i.e. payment services providers, are authorised and supervised by those authorities that also supervise financial firms in performing the first function of the financial system. This also applies mainly to banks.

(iii) As discussed below with regard to the infrastructures of the financial system, it is impossible to make a distinction between the securities clearing and settlement systems and the payment systems used to finally settle the payments for the purchase of securities.

(iv) Finally, it should be noted that certain legal acts that form the sources of international, European and national financial law explicitly treat the provision of payment instruments and fund transfer services as financial services (see under C 3 below).

In this respect, it is the author's view that the function of contributing to cashless payments is an integral part of the financial system.[3]

3 See **Stillhart (2002)**, pp. 105-121.

2. The first function: channelling funds from positive to negative savers

2.1 Introductory remarks

As mentioned above, the first function of the financial system consists in the channelling of funds from the economy's positive savers to the negative savers. This function is performed via two channels:

- direct financing of negative savers by positive savers (see under 2.2 below), and
- indirect financing of negative savers by positive savers or financial intermediation (under 2.3).[4]

2.2 Direct financing

2.2.1 The concepts of financial markets and capital markets

The channel of direct financing from positive to negative savers is activated through financial markets, defined as the markets where:

- debt instruments and equities are issued and traded (under 2.2.2.1 below), and
- derivatives are traded (under 2.2.2.2).

Financial markets are also referred to as money and capital markets.[5] The distinction between money markets and capital markets is made on the basis of the maturity of financial instruments[6] traded therein:

- short-term debt instruments (with an initial term of up to one year), issued by businesses and governments, are traded in money markets, whereas
- long-term debt instruments (with an initial term of more than one year), issued by businesses and governments, are traded in capital markets along with equities of listed companies.[7]

For the sake of brevity, the terms 'financial markets' or 'capital markets' will be used hereinafter to describe both money and capital markets – unless otherwise specified.

4 See **Mishkin (2007)**, pp. 23-32 and 35-42, respectively.
5 Ibid., pp. 23-25.
6 'Financial instruments' is a general term (also widely used in legislation), which includes debt instruments, equities, and derivative financial instruments.
7 See **Mishkin (2007)**, pp. 27-28.

2.2.2 Categories of financial markets

2.2.2.1 Markets for debt instruments and equities

Markets for debt instruments[8] and equities (often collectively referred to as 'transferable securities') are divided into separate categories according to the following criteria:

- the function performed in the market (under a below), and
- the way the market is organised (under b).

(a) Depending on the function performed, debt instruments and equities markets are divided into primary markets (under (aa)), and secondary markets (under (ab)):

(aa) A 'primary market' is a financial market to which certain classes of negative savers[9] can turn in order to draw either borrowed and/or own funds from positive savers through the issuance of debt instruments and equities, respectively.[10] Debt instruments and equities can be sold to positive savers either by private placement, or by a public offer procedure (which entails enhanced regulatory intervention requirements for investor protection).[11]

(ab) A 'secondary market' is a financial market where debt instruments and equities issued by negative savers are traded. This is the market where the current market value of financial instruments is fixed so as to ensure, *inter alia,* their liquidity.

(b) Depending on the way in which they are organised, debt instrument and equity financial markets are divided into regulated markets (see under (ba) below) and non-regulated markets or over-the-counter markets (OTC) (under (bb)):[12]

(ba) A 'regulated market' is a financial market authorised in a state by the competent supervisory authorities of the capital markets and operating in accordance with the

8 The definition of the term 'debt instruments' includes all types of instruments (now mostly dematerialised) incorporating a usually interest-bearing claim of the bearer (the positive saver) against the issuer (the negative saver) (such as bonds and bills). For more details, see **Mishkin (2007)**, pp. 25-26.

9 The classes of negative savers with access to capital markets are limited in relation to those with access to the banking system. More specifically, access to capital markets is limited to:
- governments when issuing debt instruments, and
- as regards enterprises, to public limited liability companies (*sociétés anonymes*) drawing funds through the issuance of equities and debt instruments.

10 For enterprises/negative savers, issuing debt instruments in the markets is an alternative to borrowing funds through the banking sector. On the contrary, choosing between a loan (in general) and the issuance of equities depends on the amount of leverage they wish to be exposed to.

11 See under 3.3 in Section Two below.

12 On this distinction, see **Mishkin (2007)**, pp. 27. Traditionally, regulated markets were known as 'organised markets', a term falling gradually out of use.

specific rules laid down by the legislation of that state. Stock exchanges are a typical example of this.[13]

(bb) A non-regulated market is initially a financial market that does not fulfil the above-mentioned conditions and in which investment services providers buy and sell financial instruments in the name and on behalf of their clients at prices fixed according to the given demand and supply.[14] At the same time, in the past few years, rapid technological advances and novel applications have made it possible for banks, investment firms and the markets themselves, *inter alia*, to develop alternative trading mechanisms enabling the execution of buy/sell orders for debt instruments and equities outside regulated markets, in particular:

- through multilateral systems operated by a bank, an investment firm, or a market operator and called multilateral trading facilities, also known as 'MTFs', and
- internally within the bank or the investment firm ('internalisation').[15]

2.2.2.2 Markets for derivative financial instruments

Derivative financial instruments are instruments available in financial markets allowing:

- on the one hand, to hedge the risks that economic units assume in their commercial (and also financial) transactions, given the price volatility of various parameters (e.g. interest rates, bonds, equities, foreign exchange rates), and
- on the other hand, to take advantage of speculative opportunities regarding the future price fluctuation of those parameters.[16]

13 Traditionally, stock exchanges were either bodies managed by their members ('mutualisation') or legal persons of public law. Currently, as a rule, they are being managed and operated by public limited liability companies (*sociétés anonymes*), which may be listed in regulated markets, and are known as 'market operators'. For more information on the 'demutualisation' process, see **Aggarwal (2002)**, and **Steil (2002)**.

14 Consequently, this market also has a market price fixing mechanism (albeit often inadequate, especially in terms of transparency), which constitutes a condition determining the liquid nature of financial instruments traded therein.

15 The terms 'multilateral trading facility' and 'internalisation' are also found in **Directive 2004/39/EC** of the European Parliament and of the Council on markets in financial instruments *"amending Council Directives 85/611/EEC and 93/6/EEC and Directive 2000/12/EC of the European Parliament and of the Council and repealing Council Directive 93/22/EEC"*, commonly known as MiFID (OJ L 145, 30.4.2004, pp. 1-42). For a more precise definition of these terms, and their distinction from the term 'regulated market' under EU capital market law, see **Binning and Willey (2008)**, pp. 73-100.

16 For more details on these financial instruments, see the seminal works of **Cox and Rubinstein (1985)**, and **Hull (1997)**, as well as **Benjamin (2007)**, pp. 64-79, and **McKnight (2008)**, pp. 559-572. See also **Zerey (2010, Hrsg.)**, a study which extensively covers the relevant legal aspects.

Derivative financial instruments are divided into two categories, depending on the way that markets in which they are traded are organised:

(a) The first category includes instruments traded in regulated markets ('exchange-traded derivative instruments'), i.e. exchange-traded contracts such as futures and options contracts.

(b) The second category includes derivative financial instruments developed and valued outside regulated markets, and, as a rule, through the banking system ('over-the-counter derivative instruments') such as forwards, options and swaps. Derivative financial instruments may also be traded in multilateral trading facilities, as already mentioned (under 2.2.2.1).

Table 1: Categorisation of financial markets

Markets for debt instruments and equities		**Markets for derivative financial instruments**
Categorisation depending on market function	Categorisation depending on market organisation	Categorisation depending on market organisation
primary markets	regulated markets	regulated markets
secondary markets	non-regulated markets	non-regulated markets

2.2.3 Categories of financial firms

Various categories of financial firms operate in direct financing and can be categorised from a systematic point of view as follows:[17]

(a) The first category includes those providing services on a professional basis, known as 'investment services',[18] to both positive and negative savers on an individual basis. These providers are cumulatively called 'investment firms'.[19] This category includes:

- banks, to the extent that they are allowed by law to provide investment services,[20]
- 'securities firms', which are allowed by law to provide the entire range of investment services, including the execution of orders for the purchase or sale of financial instruments in the name, and on behalf, of their clients, and
- other categories of investment undertakings that have the right to provide certain investment services alone.

17 The mix of providers that can operate professionally by providing investment services in a given state, the terms applicable to the provision of such services and the extent of the investment services provided, are determined by the legislation in force. More often than not, it is legally stipulated that these providers must be authorised and be subject to micro-prudential regulation and supervision.

18 For more details on these services, see below under C 2.1 of this Section.

19 These providers are often referred to as 'market intermediaries'.

20 See on this below under C 2.2.3 of this Section.

The latter subcategory comprises 'investment banks' under US federal financial law. It should be noted that this term often leads to the false impression that these are banks in the traditional meaning of the term, namely financial firms that have the right to accept deposits from the public (as will be discussed below under 2.3.2 of this subsection). This is why in accordance with European financial law, pursuant to the provisions of the above-mentioned Directive 2004/39/EC of the European Parliament and of the Council, the use of this term is not allowed. Under European law, companies offering the services provided by 'investment banks' in the US fall into the category of 'investment firms'.[21]

(b) The second category of market intermediaries in financial markets includes the 'undertakings for collective investment in transferable securities' (e.g. mutual funds and portfolio investment companies).[22] As a rule, these providers have the legal monopoly of providing financial instruments' portfolio management services on a collective basis, without being precluded from providing at least certain investment services on an individual basis as well.

It is worth mentioning that a type of investment vehicle, known as 'hedge funds', has emerged over the last decades. Its operation has only recently, after the recent (2007-2009) international financial crisis, been subject to micro-prudential regulation and supervision, as a collective investment undertaking. This is an asset pool consisting of borrowed funds from (usually high-income) private and institutional investors, placed in various financial instruments, primarily derivatives, with a view to capitalising on the imperfections of the markets and operating at high leverage.[23]

Private equity funds are different from hedge funds in terms of their investment strategy, which consists in buying equities of non-listed companies, restructuring such companies, and re-selling them at a higher price (usually also aiming at subsequently listing them on a regulated market). The managers of these funds have also been subject to micro-prudential regulation and supervision, just after the recent (2007-2009) international financial crisis.

21 Ibid.

22 Despite being called undertakings for collective investment in transferable securities (namely equities and bonds), these organisations also make placements in financial derivative instruments.

23 With regard to the operation of hedge funds and the policy objective to regulate them as financial firms, see **Garbaravicius and Dierick (2005)**, **Chan, Getmansky, Haas and Andrew (2006)**, **Crocket (2007)**, **Ferguson, Hartmann, Panetta and Portes (2007)**, pp. 119-130, and **Athanassiou (2012)**.

2.3 Indirect financing or financial intermediation

2.3.1 The rationale for developing financial intermediation

The second category of channelling funds[24] from positive to negative savers is indirect financing or financial intermediation. According to financial theory, the indirect financing channel has emerged as a result of:

- the (relatively high) cost of transactions in financial markets,
- the (relatively high) credit risk that investments in debt instruments and equities entail for positive savers ('risk sharing'), and
- information asymmetries arising in the relationship between positive and negative savers in the context of direct financing. [25]

These arguments are strong from a theoretical-systematic point of view but have limited practical relevance taking into account that:

- *banks historically operated as intermediaries before the development of financial markets, and*
- *banks and other categories of intermediaries which provide indirect financing services offer the possibility to draw borrowed funds to many categories of negative savers (mainly households and various categories of enterprises) with no access to financial markets, as already mentioned.*

It is nonetheless true that in most national financial systems, indirect financing mainly through banks ('bank-based' systems) is more extensive than direct financing, even in the United States and Canada that are traditionally considered to have more advanced financial markets ('market-based' systems).[26]

In order to address the above-mentioned problems, it is necessary to have different categories of financial intermediaries[27] that can be systematically classified into three categories:

- banks (see under 2.3.2 below),
- companies providing credit (under 2.3.3), and
- insurance undertakings and pension funds (under 2.3.4).

24 It is worth noting that, contrary to direct financing, funds are always borrowed in indirect financing.

25 On this see **Mishkin (2007)**, pp. 35-39 and 184-198. Specifically regarding the meaning of information asymmetry and the problems that it causes to transactions, see **Rasmusen (1989)**, pp. 181-203 as to 'adverse selection', and pp. 133-179 as to 'moral hazard'.

26 For more details see **Mishkin (2007)**, p. 36.

27 The term 'financial intermediaries' refers to all categories of financial firms providing services in the financial system in the context of indirect intermediation. For a detailed presentation of the functions that financial intermediaries are performing in the financial system according to the above, see **Allen and Santomero (1999)**, **Allen (2001)**, **Allen and Gale (2001)**, and **Gorton and Winton (2002)**.

2.3.2 Banking intermediation

The first (and most important) category of financial intermediaries consists of banks.[28] In banking intermediation:

- positive savers offer their borrowed funds in the form of bank deposits[29] and
- subsequently banks finance negative savers by providing loans and other credit facilities.

The indirect nature of this form of financing lies in the fact that, as opposed to financial markets, no legal or economic relationship develops between positive and negative savers, since positive savers obtain receivables against banks and, for their part, banks obtain receivables against the negative savers that they are financing.[30]

Here, it is necessary to make four (4) remarks:

(a) *Positive savers resorting to bank intermediation services include households, enterprises and governments. On the contrary, negative savers include, as a rule, households and (private and state-owned) companies alone, because in developed economies governments draw borrowed funds exclusively from capital markets in order to cover their expenditure (unless they are 'excluded' from these markets as a result of credit rating downgrades, as in the case of Greece, Ireland and Portugal recently).*

However, there is regulatory intervention in many developing economies, on the basis of which banks are forced to place an (often high) percentage of their deposits in short-term and long-term government bonds not issued in the primary market.[31]

(b) *Given their function, banks are one of the most highly leveraged categories of companies, since their borrowed funds are significantly higher than their own funds.*

(c) *Banks draw borrowed funds not only from depositors, but also from their central bank, from other banks as part of interbank market operations, and also through the issuance of debt securities in financial markets.*

(d) *Banks do not channel the entirety of their deposits into loans or other credit facilities. Apart from retaining liquid and promptly cashable assets in order to meet de-*

28 The most characteristic (and in most states the larger in terms of size) category of banks is 'commercial banks'. However in various economies there are also special bank categories, such as cooperative, mortgage, development and savings banks. Enactment of such special banks (often called 'special credit organisations') is usually the result of the legislator's regulatory intervention, notably in developing or less developed economies.

29 A deposit is not just a loan to the bank, but also a consignment. The level of the interest rate of a deposit is the best indicator of the aspect which prevails (obviously, a higher interest rate reflects a bank's need to attract deposits).

30 In banking economics, many theoretical models have been created in an effort to identify and analyse the reasons why banks are in a position to offer such services and make the transformations mentioned below. For an overview of these models from the existing extensive literature, see, *inter alia*, **Allen and Santomero (1999)**, and **Gorton and Winton (2002)**, pp. 5-20.

31 On the contrary, in every economy banks are free to buy government bonds on the secondary market in the context of their asset management.

positors' demand for cash withdrawals, banks also invest in financial instruments traded in financial markets in the context of their portfolio management:

- *either long-term (included in the 'investment book'), or*
- *aimed at capitalising on the short-term market conditions (included in the 'trading book').*[32]

In their capacity as financial intermediaries, banks make a set of transformations:

- credit risk transformation, as they assume the credit risk of the economic units they finance, transferring the risk of their own solvency to positive savers,
- size transformation, since they convert liabilities of usually small nominal value (e.g. deposits) to large-value receivables (e.g. industrial loans), and
- maturity transformation, since they convert short-term liabilities (e.g. sight deposits) into long-term receivables (e.g. housing loans).

The ability of banks to make these transformations is concurrently the main cause of their (structural) exposure to credit risk, interest-rate income risk and liquidity risk, respectively, and, as a result, the main reason behind the need:

- on the one hand, to manage these risks,[33] and
- on the other, for regulatory intervention aimed at ensuring the stability of the banking system, which can be threatened due to excessive exposure to these risks.[34]

2.3.3 Intermediation through non-bank companies providing credit

Companies providing credit constitute the second category of financial intermediaries in the context of indirect financing. Although in every economy, taking deposits from the public is a legal monopoly of the banks, as mentioned above, the service of providing credit on a professional basis may also be offered by other companies, which finance this activity by drawing own or borrowed funds either from the financial system or outside of it, with the exception of taking deposits from the public, *inter alia*: leasing companies, factoring companies, and credit companies.[35]

32 For a detailed overview of the structure of assets and liabilities in banks' balance sheets along with their off-balance sheet items, see, *inter alia*, **Sinkey (1992)** and **Meyer (1996)**.

33 In order to control their exposure to these risks, banks transfer part of their loans to special purpose vehicles ('SPVs') through 'asset securitisation' in the context of the 'originate and distribute' model. The significant extent to which banks used this practice is considered to be one of the causes of the recent financial crisis. On this see **Borio (2008)**, pp. 1-13.

34 For more details, see under B in Section Two below.

35 It should be noted that the intermediation function of these financial institutions is incomplete, in that they only deal with negative savers and not with positive savers.

To the extent that credit intermediation is provided by non-bank unregulated entities, reference is made to the 'shadow banking system'. This is defined "as credit intermediation involving entities and activities outside the regular banking system".[36]

2.3.4 Intermediation by insurance undertakings and pension funds

The third category of financial intermediaries operating in indirect financing are insurance undertakings (see under (a) below)[37] and pension funds (under (b)).[38]

(a) Insurance intermediation is divided into two categories:[39]

(i) The first category is the 'benefit policy' under which the insurance undertaking assumes the obligation to:
  - pay the insured a predefined lump sum or annuity (life-insurance and private pension schemes), or
  - compensate the insured person for any financial loss incurred as a result of accident or illness ('accident and illness insurance').

(ii) The second category is 'non-life insurance', which comprises assets insurance, liabilities insurance and maritime insurance. In this case, the insurance undertaking assumes the obligation to restore a specific loss suffered by the insured.

(b) Respectively, pension funds collect funds from contributing employers and employees and then invest them in the financial system, on the one hand, and, on the other hand, collect other assets so that the total generated assets make it possible to pay benefits, following retirement or in the event of death or disability.[40]

3. The second function: contributing to making cashless payments[41]

3.1 Introductory remarks

The second function of financial systems is to contribute to making cashless payments. This function enables the transfer of funds between households, enterprises and the

36 See **Financial Stability Board (2011)**: *"Shadow Banking: Strengthening Oversight and Regulation, Recommendations of the Financial Stability Board"*, October, available at: http://www.financialstabilityboard.org/publications/r_111027a.pdf).

37 Similar to the service of accepting deposits (as already mentioned), insurance (and reinsurance) services are, for the most part, a legal monopoly as well, in the sense that only undertakings authorised as insurance undertakings may provide these services.

38 Here as well (as in the case of credit companies), intermediation is incomplete, since insurance undertakings and pension funds deal directly only with positive and not with negative savers, but invest their available funds in financial instruments and deposits.

39 See details in **Mishkin (2006)**, pp. 40-41.

40 Ibid.

41 See details in **Kokkola (2010)**, pp. 25-37.

government, from the payer to the beneficiary (or payee) – indicatively, but not limited – to paying off debts from private and commercial transactions (including financial transactions),[42] and from monetary obligations under applicable legislation or as a result of a court ruling, on condition that there is an agreement not to use cash, namely coins and banknotes.[43] This function is performed:

- either through the issuance and acceptance, from various categories of financial firms, of physical (and in an individual case, digital) payment instruments (see under 3.2 below), or
- through the provision, of fund transfer services by these providers, on the basis of payment orders (under 3.3).

Here, it is necessary to make a semantic clarification (under a) and an important note (under b).

(a) Consistently with the position that money, i.e. coins and banknotes, is the only means of payment, the term 'means of payment', albeit often used in legislation, should not be used to describe the means enabling the performance of cashless payments such as cheques and cards. This is the reason why in this study, the author has opted for the term 'payment instruments'. Furthermore, it would be a paradox to describe both cheques (being one of the 'payment instruments') and sight deposits required for cheques to be issued as means of payment.

(b) Payment services are mainly provided by banks, but also by various other categories of financial firms, such as payment card companies, fund transfer companies, postal cheques bureaus and other categories of payment institutions pursuant to the provisions *of legislation applicable at a given time in a given state*. However, the use of payment instruments normally presupposes a bank deposit and, therefore, a bank account, and particularly in the case of fund transfers usually at least one such account.

In this context, it should be pointed out that bank deposits are of material importance to the operation of both the monetary and the financial system, given that:

- they constitute money in the context of the operation of the monetary system (either simply sight deposits under the narrow definition of money or also other categories of deposits under the broader definition of money),
- taking such deposits is one of the core services offered in the context of banking intermediation, and
- the existence of a sufficient balance in a deposit account is usually a condition prior to the use of payment instruments and the activation of fund transfer services.

42 Funds may also be transferred in view of a donation (for example, a parent placing an order to credit the bank account of his/her child studying abroad).

43 There is controversy over whether the use of payment instruments or the transfer of funds by order, without the lender's consent, constitutes due payment against monetary obligations.

3.2 Payment instruments

A 'payment instrument' is any device and/or set of procedures agreed between the payment services user and the payment services provider and used by the payment services user in order to initiate a payment order.[44] The concept of payment instruments, which can be either tangible or digital, includes the following:[45]

(a) The first category of payment instruments includes cheques.[46]

(b) The second category of payment instruments are payment cards. Debit cards and credit cards are just two, albeit more frequently used, card types that constitute a payment instrument. Other types include:

- charge cards or travel and entertainment cards,
- retailer cards, and
- limited-purpose prepaid cards.[47]

(c) The third category of payment instrument includes electronic money. Electronic money means any value stored electronically in a device,[48] such as:

- a chip card ('hardware-based' or 'card-based' product, a typical example of which is the 'multi-purpose, prepaid, reloadable or not, card' or 'electronic purse'), and
- a hard drive in a personal computer ('software-based' or 'network-based products', a typical example being digital cash).

44 In this regard, see **Committee on Payment and Settlement Systems (2003a):** *"A glossary of terms used in payments and settlement systems"*, Bank for International Settlements, March, available at: http://www.bis.org/publ/cpss00b.htm, p. 38. In this CPSS glossary of terms used in payment and settlement systems, the definition of every payment instrument is accompanied by a reference to other studies of the Committee on special issues relating to payment instruments.

45 With the exception of cheques, payment instruments are usually also called 'electronic payment instruments'. Note also that over the past few years there has been a great increase in the volume of payments made for the purchase of goods and services via the Internet ('internet payments' or 'e-payments') and mobile applications ('mobile payments' or 'm-payments'). Normally, in these cases, there are no new payment instruments (since the relevant payments are performed either with the use of credit cards or by credit transfer or direct debit), but new channels which are used to direct payment orders to the payment systems.
A striking example is the execution of payment transactions, where the payer gives his/her consent to execute a payment transaction via a telecommunications, digital or IT device, and payment is made to the operator of the telecommunications or IT system/network, who then acts exclusively as intermediary between the payment systems user and the provider of the goods and services.

46 For a definition of this payment instrument ('cheque') according to international standards, see **Committee on Payment and Settlement Systems (2003a)**, op. cit., p. 12.

47 For a definition of these payment instruments, see ibid., pp. 19, 16, 50, 42 and 39, respectively. On this particular point, note that cash cards and cheque guarantee cards do not constitute payment instruments (ibid., p. 11 and p. 12, respectively), while the multi-purpose prepaid card (ibid., p. 39) falls under the term 'electronic money'.

48 Ibid., p. 22. For more details on electronic money, see **Weber (1999)**.

3.3 Payment order-based fund transfer services

The concept of payment order-based fund transfer services includes:

- remittances, and
- services for the execution of payment transactions, notably the execution of credit transfers, direct debits and payment transactions with payment cards.[49]

B. The infrastructures of the financial system[50]

1. Introductory remarks

In order to implement the above-mentioned functions of the financial system, two infrastructures are absolutely necessary:

- payment systems (see under 2 below), and
- clearing and settlement systems for transactions in transferable securities (under 3).

There are also other important infrastructures which operate in the financial system, usually on an interbank basis, albeit not as significant as the ones mentioned above:

(a) A category of infrastructure are interbank systems used to collect and process data on the behaviour of negative savers/borrowers across the entire banking system, which banks can then use to perform credit ratings of their borrowers and subsequently:

- adjust their pricing policy accordingly (in favour of 'creditworthy' borrowers), and/or
- avoid providing loans to borrowers with inappropriate credit ratings.

(b) Another category of infrastructure are interbank systems aimed at establishing a register of businesses whose contracts on the use of credit cards as payment instruments have been terminated, following a breach of the terms of transaction (e.g. acceptance of cards that have been reported stolen or lost, fictitious transactions). This file usually does not include any information concerning card purchases (e.g. product, price) or card holders.

49 On these services, see below under C 3 of this Section.

50 From the relatively limited literature on this subject, see **De Haan, Oosterloo, and Schoenmaker (2009)**, pp. 136-163, and **Kokkola (2010),** pp. 37-47.

2. Payment systems – clearing and settlements systems

2.1 Definitions

2.1.1 Payment systems

Payment system means the set of instruments, services and procedures and, typically, interbank systems that ensure the transfer of funds between bodies participating therein.[51] In order to specify this definition, the following clarifications are needed:

(a) Funds transfer means any transfer of funds conducted using all available payment instruments and order-based fund transfer services, according to subsection A above (under 3).

(b) Participants in payment systems are mostly banks (without excluding other categories of financial firms authorised to provide payment services). This is the reason why payment systems are usually called 'interbank'.

(c) As regards payment systems management, there is no prevailing standard. A payment system may be managed:

- by central banks,[52]
- by central banks along with banks and other categories of financial firms,
- or by financial firms alone.

2.1.2 Clearing and settlement systems

One of the components of a payment system is the clearing and settlement process for payments carried out in the system. Specifically:

(a) Clearing system means a set of procedures whereby system participants present and exchange data and/or documents relating to fund transfers to other participants at a single location, the 'clearing house', with a view to determining the beneficiaries of payments and the amount of each payment.[53]

(b) Settlement system means a system used to facilitate the settlement of transfers of funds or financial instruments.[54] Settlement of payments is usually made in accounts that the system participants keep in the central bank, through which the bank accounts

51 In this regard, see **Committee on Payment and Settlement Systems (2003a)**, op. cit., p. 38.
52 This is the first function that central banks perform on payment and settlement systems.
53 See **Committee on Payment and Settlement Systems (2003a)**, op. cit., p. 14. Clearing often includes a mechanism for offsetting receivables.
54 Ibid., p. 46.

of those ordering the payment – or in case of direct debits, the debtors – are debited, and subsequently the bank accounts of the final beneficiaries are credited.[55]

2.2 Classification of payment systems and clearing and settlement systems

2.2.1 Payment systems

Payment systems are classified into the following categories, on the basis of six criteria:[56]

(a) Depending on the payment instrument or service used to transfer funds, a distinction is made between cheque systems, credit transfer systems,[57] direct debit systems,[58] payment card systems, and electronic money systems.

(b) Depending on the way in which the system processes payment orders, a distinction is made between electronically and manually managed systems.[59]

(c) Depending on the value of capitals transferred per transaction through the system, the following distinction is made:

55 This is the second function that central banks perform on payment and settlement systems. The third function is the oversight of payment systems to ensure the stability and effectiveness thereof. See **Committee on Payment and Settlement Systems (2003b):** *"Policy issues for central banks in retail payments"*, Bank for International Settlements, March, available at: http://www.bis.org/publ/cpss52.htm, pp. 8-15.

56 See **Committee on Payment and Settlement Systems (2006):** *"General guidance for national payment system development"*, Bank for International Settlements, January, available at: http://www.bis.org/publ/cpss70.htm.

57 In this field, three different cases can be established depending on the number of payers and beneficiaries:
(a) In the first case, the payer orders his/her bank to transfer funds to the bank account of a single beneficiary.
(b) In the second case, the payer orders his/her bank to transfer funds to the bank account of more than one beneficiaries (e.g. payment of pensions by an organisation to beneficiary pensioners).
(c) In the third case, more than one payers order their banks to transfer funds to the bank account of a single beneficiary (e.g. payment of employer contributions to an insurance organisation).

58 In this field, two different cases can be distinguished, depending on the flow of authorisation by the payer to the beneficiary:
(a) In the first case, the payer authorises the beneficiary or the beneficiary's bank, either once or with a standing payment order, to withdraw funds from his/her bank account and credit them to the beneficiary's bank account upon fulfilment of a monetary obligation by the payer to the beneficiary (e.g. single or standing direct debit order for the payment of public utility bills).
(b) In the second case, the payer authorises his/her bank.

59 Manual management still exists only for certain cheque systems which, as already mentioned, are the only systems processing paper-based instruments.

- large-value payment systems, and
- small-value payment systems or 'retail payment systems'.[60]

(d) Depending on the netting of instructions in a payment system, a distinction is made between bilateral and multilateral netting payment systems. After bilateral netting has been performed in a payment system, a participant has a net position towards each of the other participants in the system. After multilateral netting has been performed, the participant has an overall net position towards each of the other participants in the system.[61]

(e) A distinction is also made between:

- systemically important payment systems,[62] i.e. systems in which the occurrence of a malfunction may potentially activate or spread additional malfunctions between participants or systemic malfunctions across the entire financial system,[63] and
- non-systemically important payment systems, i.e. systems that do not have the above-mentioned potential.

(f) Finally, a distinction is made between 'pure' payment systems used exclusively for the transfer of funds between participants and payment systems operating in the context of a transferable securities payment and settlement system for the clearing and settlement of the part that concerns payments for the purchase or sale of transferable securities.[64]

2.2.2 Clearing and settlement systems

Clearing and settlement systems are divided into three categories, depending on the manner in which the orders for the transfer of funds are to be settled. Specifically:

(a) Net settlement systems are the systems whose settlement operations are completed by offsetting and clearing all the participants' receivables at one or more discrete, predefined times during the processing day (known as 'settlement cycles') when settlement takes place.[65]

60 The criterion that differentiates between these systems is conventional. Typically, retail payment systems are credit transfer systems used to transfer payments between various consumers, businesses and governments of relatively low value and urgency. See **Committee on Payment and Settlement Systems (2006),** op. cit., pp. 70-71.

61 See **Committee on Payment and Settlement Systems (2006),** op.cit., pp. 68 and 70.

62 Large-value payment systems are an indicative example of such systems.

63 See **Committee on Payment and Settlement Systems (2001):** "*Core Principles for Systemically Important Payment Systems*", Bank for International Settlements, January, available at: http://www.bis.org/publ/cpss43.htm, p. 5, and **Committee on Payment and Settlement Systems and IOSCO Technical Committee (2012):** "*Principles for financial markets infrastructures*", Bank for International Settlements, April, available at: http://www.bis.org/publ/cpss101a.pdf, p. 12.

64 See below under 3 of this subsection.

65 See **Committee on Payment and Settlement Systems (2003a)**, op. cit., p. 34.

(b) Gross settlement systems are systems where settlement takes place separately for each payment, on an instruction-by-instruction basis, at one or more prescribed times during the processing day.[66]

(c) Real-time gross settlement systems are systems where settlement occurs not only separately for each and every payment, but also in real time and in the order that the relevant payment orders are given.[67]

A typical example of such a system is the TARGET2 system (Trans-European Automated Real-time Gross settlement Express Transfer system), used, inter alia, to settle payments resulting from open-market transactions in the context of implementing the single monetary policy of the European System of Central Banks in the eurozone.[68]

3. Securities clearing and settlement systems[69]

The second infrastructure of the financial system comprises clearing and settlement systems for transactions in securities.[70]

(a) Similarly to what applies to payments, the securities clearing and settlement system is the set of procedures whereby system participants present and exchange data and/or documents relating to transfers of securities to other participants at a single clearing house, so as to define the beneficiaries of the securities traded.[71]

(b) The settlement system is the set of means and procedures enabling the settlement of transactions in securities, by crediting securities to the end-beneficiaries' accounts, as well as the safekeeping of securities.[72] The above-mentioned triple classification of payment settlement systems, depending on the manner in which fund transfer orders are to be settled, also applies to securities settlement systems.

66 Ibid., p. 25.

67 Ibid., p. 41 (see also details in **Committee on Payment and Settlement Systems (1997)** *Real-time Gross Settlement Systems*, March, available at: http://www.bis.org/publ/cpss22.htm).

68 On this system, see **Geva (2008), pp. 113-123.**

69 See in detail **Kokkola (2010)**, pp. 75-90, and 106-113 (for derivative financial instruments).

70 See **Committee on Payment and Settlement Systems and IOSCO Technical Committee (2001):** *"Recommendations for securities settlement systems"*, Bank for International Settlements, November (available at: http://www.bis.org/publ/cpss46.htm), and **Committee on Payment and Settlement Systems and IOSCO Technical Committee (2012):** "*Principles for financial markets infrastructures*", Bank for International Settlements, April (available at: http://www.bis.org/publ/cpss101a.pdf).
Most studies refer to securities clearing and settlement systems. Note, however, that clearing and settlement procedures also occur for derivatives, both in stock exchange and OTC markets. For more details, see **Committee on Payment and Settlement Systems (2007):** "*New developments in clearing and settlement arrangements for OTC derivatives*", Bank for International Settlements, March, available at: http://www.bis.org/publ/cpss77.htm.

71 See **Committee on Payment and Settlement Systems (2003a)**, op. cit., p. 14. As in the case of payments, clearing often (and usually) includes a mechanism for offsetting receivables.

72 Ibid., p. 44.

The operational framework of these systems also includes a payments clearing and settlement system in view of the clearing and settlement of the part of the transaction that is relevant to the transfer of funds, whereby the monetary obligation generated by the purchase or sale of the securities is fulfilled and the bank accounts of the end-beneficiaries are credited with the amounts due from the transaction.

In view of the above, it is necessary to make the following clarifications:

(a) The term 'payment systems' also includes payment clearing and settlement systems.

(b) Consequently 'payment clearing and settlement systems' constitute a subset of clearing and settlement systems in general.

(c) The semantically more appropriate term would be 'payment and settlement system' which includes:

- on the one hand, payment systems, including payment clearing and settlement systems, and
- on the other hand, securities clearing and settlement systems, used in the clearing and settlement of both securities and payments related to the purchase and sale of securities.

C. Classification of services provided in the financial system

1. Introductory remarks – classification approaches

The various categories of firms operating in the context of the financial system and its infrastructures, as defined above, provide services. These are designated as 'financial services'.

To the author's knowledge, neither the existing literature nor any legal acts provide a systematic recording of all financial services. The single exception would perhaps be Annex 1 to the General Agreement on Trade in Services (GATS).[73] *This legal act of international economic law defines the concept of 'financial service' in the broadest possible way, and, as a result, covers sixteen (16) categories of services provided in the financial system.*[74]

For the purposes of classifying financial services, it is possible to adopt one of two approaches:

(a) According to the first approach, services are classified on the basis of their providers. In this context, a distinction is made between services provided, *inter alia,*

73 See under C 3.2.2 in Section Three below.

74 See **World Trade Organisation (1994):** *"General Agreement on Trade in Services, Annex on Financial Services"*, paragraph 5(a).

by banks ('banking services'), investment firms ('investment services'), insurance and re-insurance undertakings ('insurance and re-insurance services') or payment institutions ('payment services'). However, this approach stumbles upon two inherent weaknesses:

(i) The first lies in the fact that, if we exclude those services that are provided almost uniformly by one single category of providers (such as deposit-taking by banks), there are many services provided concurrently by more than one categories of firms and, as a result, there is extensive overlapping.[75]
(ii) The second weakness of this approach lies in the fact that this classification can be used only in conjunction with the legislation of a given state (or in the case of the European Union (hereinafter the ('EU'), in conjunction with the provisions of European financial law) given that the range of services that individual categories of providers can supply is laid down in such legislation.

In cases where this approach is adopted, usually services are further classified according to the rules governing the accounting for the transactions conducted by financial firms. In this context, balance-sheet items (assets-liabilities) may be differentiated from off-balance sheet items.[76] It is also common practice, especially in the case of private banking law (being the law governing banking transactions), for a distinction to be made between commercial banking services and investment services.[77]

(b) In accordance with the above and taking into account the functions performed in the financial system, as well as its infrastructures, it seems more appropriate to adopt the operational approach. This approach groups financial services into the following three categories:[78]

- services offered in the context of the first function of the financial system, differentiating between services provided in the framework of direct intermediation between positive and negative savers (see under 2.1 below), and services provided in the framework of indirect intermediation (under 2.2),
- services provided in the context of the second function of the financial system relating to the contribution to making cashless payments (under 3), and
- services provided in the context of the infrastructures of the financial system (under 4).

75 Investment services are a striking example as they are usually provided by both banks and investment firms (depending on the limitations set by legislation). Another example are payment services which may be offered by banks and other specialised payment institutions.
76 As regards banks' off-balance sheet services, see **Äberli (1989)** (still accurate).
77 For more details, see **Schwintowski/Schäfer (2004)** and **Einsele (2006)**.
78 An exhaustive reference to the typology of transactions per individual service goes beyond the scope of this study and therefore transactions are categorised on the basis of their common characteristics.

2. Services provided in the context of the financial system's first function

2.1 Services provided in the context of direct financing: investment services and collective portfolio management

The category of services provided as part of direct financing of negative savers by positive savers, includes all services provided in capital markets. These services can be broken down into two broad categories:

(a) The first category includes services provided by financial firms in capital markets on an individual basis; these are called investment services. Investment services are provided both to negative savers (see under (i) below) and to positive savers (under (ii)). Investment services are also provided by financial firms on their own behalf, while the operation of a multilateral trading facility constitutes an investment activity.

(i) The category of investment services to positive savers includes:
- reception and transmission of orders on behalf of clients for transactions in relation to one or more financial instruments (securities and derivatives),
- execution of orders on behalf of clients, which consists in acting to conclude agreements to buy or sell one or more financial instruments on behalf of clients,
- portfolio management, which consists in managing clients' portfolios, at the clients' discretion and in the context of their mandate in relation to one or more financial instruments,
- investment advice, which consists in providing personal recommendations to a client, either upon the client's request or upon the initiative of the provider, in respect of one or more transactions relating to financial instruments,
- safe-keeping and administration of financial instruments for the account of clients, including custodianship and related services such as cash/collateral management,
- granting credits or loans to an investor to allow him to carry out a transaction in one or more financial instruments, where the supplier granting the credit or loan is involved in the transaction,
- foreign exchange services where these are connected with the provision of investment services, and
- investment research and financial analysis or other forms of general recommendation relating to transactions in financial instruments.

(ii) Accordingly, the category of investment services to negative savers includes:
- underwriting and/or placing of financial instruments on a firm commitment basis,
- placing of financial instruments without a firm commitment basis,
- provision of underwriting-related services, and
- advice to undertakings on capital structure, industrial strategy and related matters, and advice and services relating to mergers and acquisitions of undertakings.

(b) The second category includes collective (securities) portfolio management, a service provided by financial firms known as 'undertakings for collective investment in transferable securities' ('UCITS').

2.2 Services provided in the context of indirect financing

2.2.1 Introductory remarks

The category of services provided in the context of indirect financing (or financial intermediation) includes:

- services provided by banks in the context of this intermediation,[79]
- services provided by insurance undertakings, and
- services provided by credit companies, which form a subset of the services provided by banks.

Only services provided by banks will be discussed below, without any reference to those provided by insurance undertakings.[80]

2.2.2 Services provided by banks in the context of indirect financing (financial intermediation)

The category of services provided by banks in the context of financial intermediation includes the following services provided either to positive savers (see under (a) below) or negative savers (under (b)):

(a) The category of services to positive savers includes taking deposits or other repayable funds from the public, a service that (according to EU banking law,[81] and the law of most states in the world) can only be provided by institutions authorised as banks.

79 The author has opted not to use the term 'banking services' given that, for the most part, banks are allowed to provide a broader range of services, covering investment and payment services. In view of the above, the meaning of the term 'banking services' encompasses all the services that banks may provide in a given state in accordance with applicable legislation.

80 As a rule, the insurance services category includes direct insurance services, both in life and other branches, reinsurance services, insurance mediation services (e.g. agents), and ancillary services, such as consultancy.

81 **Directive 2006/48/EC** of the European Parliament and of the Council relating to the taking up and pursuit of the business of credit institutions (recast) (OJ L 177, 30.6.2006, p. 1-200), Article 5(a).

(b) The category of services provided to negative savers includes:

(i) lending for own account,[82] including, *inter alia*, financing of commercial transactions, consumer and mortgage (mostly housing) credit and factoring,
(ii) financial leasing, and
(iii) guarantees and commitments (off-balance sheet services).

2.2.3 Other services provided by banks

Banks are often allowed to also offer other services which are not directly connected to financial intermediation. This category includes:

- payment services, as above (see under 3 below),
- services provided on own account,
- money brokerage (interbank services),
- insurance intermediation services,
- safety deposit boxes, and
- certain 'ancillary services' such as credit reference services, IT services and consultancy services.

It is up to national legislators (and in the European Union, the European Parliament and the Council which adopt the main provisions of EU financial law),[83] to determine the exact range of services that banks are allowed to provide based on assessments performed, particularly with regard to possible conflicts of interest and the rationale for safeguarding the stability of the financial system. As a rule, however, banks are not allowed to provide insurance and re-insurance services and other commercial or industrial activities. On the contrary, they are allowed (albeit with quantitative restrictions in certain states) to hold equity in such undertakings.[84]

The issue whether banks should be allowed to provide investment services, and to what extent, has been and still remains the source of major debate.[85] In some states (such as the EU member states),[86] these services can be provided by banks unconditionally,

82 It is worth noting that banks are designated by the term 'credit institutions' under EU banking law, and 'depository institutions' under US banking law. According to EU banking law (**Directive 2006/48/EC**, Article 4, point (1)), the services of receiving deposits or other repayable funds from the public and granting credit for its own account cumulatively form the basis for an undertaking to be designated as a 'credit institution'.
83 See on this **Gortsos (2012b)**, Chapters 2 and 3.
84 See below the Excursus of this Section.
85 See **Santos (1998)**.
86 According to the provisions of Article 15, paragraph 3, of **Council Directive 93/22/EEC** *"on investment services in the securities field"* (OJ L 141, 11.6.93, pp. 27-46), member states were prohibited, since 1996, to impose on EU credit institutions limitations with regard to the provision of investment services. See **Mauerhofer (1998)**, p. 92.

according to the so-called 'universal banking system',[87] while in others limitations are put in place.[88]

This issue has re-emerged in the wake of the recent (2007-2009) international financial crisis[89] *and the United States have already enacted legislation limiting the power of banks to provide investment services, according to the provisions of the 'Volcker Rule'. Similar initiatives are underway in the United Kingdom, based on the 'Vickers Report',*[90] *and the EU, upon the proposals of the 'Liikanen Group' to be submitted in autumn 2012. More specifically:*

(a) *The Volcker Rule, which is implemented by Title VI of the 2010 Dodd-Frank Wall Street Reform and Consumer Protection Act,*[91] *prohibits an insured 'depository institution' (the term for banks used in US financial law) and its affiliates from:*

- *engaging in 'proprietary trading',*
- *acquiring or retaining any equity, partnership or other ownership interest in a hedge fund or private equity fund, and*
- *sponsoring a hedge fund or a private equity fund.*

(b) *The Vickers Report contains the recommendations submitted in September 2011 by the Independent Commission on Banking, chaired by Sir John Vickers ("Independent Commission on Banking: Final Report, Recommendations"). The mandate of this Commission is to consider structural and relevant non-structural reforms in the UK banking sector to promote financial stability and competition, and making recommendations to the Government.*[92]

(c) *The Liikanen Group ("High-level Expert Group on structural aspects of the EU banking sector") was set up in November 2011 by the European Commission. Its mandate consists in "determining whether, in addition to ongoing regulatory reforms, structural reforms of EU banks would strengthen financial stability and improve efficiency and consumer protection, and if that is the case make any relevant proposals as appropriate".*

87 On this model, see **Saunders and Walter (1994)**, pp. 3-9 and 84-126.
88 *In extremis*, under US federal financial law, banks were, since 1933, not allowed either to provide investment services or to have subsidiaries that offer investment services pursuant to the provisions of the *Glass-Steagall Act* (see **Jackson and Symons (1999)**, pp. 1033-1035 and 1043-1070), and **Liechtenstein (2010)**, pp. 217-224). This law was partly repealed in 1999 with the *Financial Services Modernisation Act* (widely known as 'Gramm-Leach-Bliley Act', Public Law 106-102, 113 Stat. 1338). On this act, see briefly **Mishkin ((2007)**, pp. 268-269.
89 See **Chow and Surti (2011)**, including further references.
90 See at: http://ec.europa.eu/commission_2010-2014/barnier/headlines/news/2012/01/20120116.
91 Public Law 111-203, 124 Stat. 1376-2223.
92 The Report is available at: http://bankingcommission.independent.gov.uk.

3. Services provided in the context of the financial system's second function: payment services

3.1 Introductory remarks

The category of services provided in the context of the second function of the financial system relating to its contribution to making cashless payments, namely the 'payment services', includes the following two service categories:

- services relating to the issuance and acceptance of payment instruments (see under 3.2 below), and
- payment order-based fund transfer services[93] (under 3.3).

Here, it should be pointed out that according to a broad definition of the term, also taking into account services provided mostly to facilitate the use of cash in the financial system, payment services include:

- *services allowing cash to be placed in a payments account,[94] as well as all activities required to keep a payments account, and*
- *services allowing cash withdrawals from a payments account.*

3.2 Services relating to the issuance and acceptance of payment instruments

This subcategory of payment services includes the following:

- issuing and accepting cheques,
- issuing credit and debit cards and accepting credit and debit cards' transactions, and
- issuing electronic money and accepting electronic money transactions.[95]

In the case of credit and debit cards, as well as electronic money in the form of multipurpose prepaid cards, the issuance service is provided to the payer, while the acceptance service to the beneficiary, usually a commercial enterprise.

93 The term 'funds' includes banknotes and coins, deposits and electronic money.
94 A 'payments account', namely an account kept in the name of one or more payment services users and used to perform payments, may be kept either with a bank or with another payment services supplier, provided this is allowed under applicable legislation.
95 On electronic money, see **Weber (1999)**.

3.3 Payment order-based fund transfer services

This subcategory of payment services includes the following:

(a) Remittances are the first service. In this case, a sum is collected from the payer, without the existence or opening of a payments account in the name of the payer or the beneficiary, with the sole purpose of transferring this sum to a beneficiary or other payment services provider acting on the beneficiary's behalf and/or in which, this sum is collected on the beneficiary's behalf and made available to him.

(b) The second service is the performance of payment transactions, namely transactions activated either by the payer or by the beneficiary, relating to the placement, transfer or withdrawal of funds. Three individual services are identified in the context of this service:

(i) The first service is the execution of credit transfers, including standing orders.

(ii) The second service is the execution of direct debits, including one-off direct debits. This is a payment service whereby the payer's payment account is debited when the beneficiary initiates the payment transaction, based on the payer's consent granted either to the beneficiary or to the beneficiary's payment services provider or the payer's payment services provider.

(iii) Finally, the third individual service is the execution of payment transactions by means of payment cards.

In all cases, funds may be covered by a credit exposure for the payment services user.

4. Services provided in the context of the operation of the financial system infrastructures

Finally, in the context of the infrastructures of the financial system, the following two services are provided:

- clearing and settlement of payments and financial instruments, and
- safe-keeping and administration of financial instruments for the account of clients, including custodianship and related services such as cash/collateral management.

Table 2: Classification of financial services

Classification criterion	Service categories
I. Services provided in the context of the financial system's first function	
A. Services provided in the context of direct financing	**1. Individual investment services** • Services to negative savers • Services to positive savers • Services for own account • Multilateral trading facility management **2. Collective portfolio management**
B. Services provided in the context of indirect financing	**1. Services provided by banks (subset of 'banking services')** • Services to negative savers • Services to positive savers • Interbank services • Insurance intermediation services • Safe custody services (safety deposit boxes) • Ancillary services **2. Services provided by insurance undertakings (insurance services)** **3. Services provided by credit companies**
II. Services provided in the context of the financial system's second function	**Payment services** • Services relating to the issuance and acceptance of payment instruments • Payment order-based fund transfer services
III. Services provided in the context of the infrastructures of the financial system	• Clearing and settlement of payments and financial instruments • Safekeeping and administration of financial instruments for the account of clients

Excursus: Groups of financial firms

In view of the above, there are many categories of financial firms allowed to provide all of the financial services stipulated by the law of a given state. Irrespective of the approach adopted at a given time and at a given state, a general rule applies: in all states a legal monopoly has been established in three cases:

- only banks are allowed to take deposits,
- only insurance undertakings are allowed to provide insurance and re-insurance services, and
- mutual funds can only be managed by mutual fund management companies (most of which are exclusive scope companies).

Financial firms are often organised into 'financial groups'. A financial group usually consists of (at least) one bank, one insurance undertaking and one investment firm. As a result of the different regulatory conditions in place,[96] financial groups are usually distinguished into two categories:

(a) The first category is 'groups with homogeneous financial activities'. These groups comprise either financial firms that are similar in nature (i.e. only banks or only insurance undertakings or only investment firms) or banks and investment firms. In such cases, the standard corporate structure is typically based on the parent company's relationship with its subsidiaries.

(b) The second category, which has expanded rapidly over the past decades encompasses 'financial conglomerates'.[97] A group is a financial conglomerate when at least one of its undertakings is an insurance company and at least another one is a bank or investment firm.[98]

There are three (3) corporate structure standards for groups in this class:

- parent-to-subsidiary corporation,
- a holding company at the top of the group,
- a horizontal group with joint management of all the participating companies.[99]

In the first case, the parent company is usually a bank ('banking group') or (rarely) an insurance undertaking ('insurance group'). The subsidiaries can be other financial firms in order for the group to effectively cover the entire spectrum of financial services, always taking into account restrictions laid down by domestic law.[100]

96 Regarding the risk arising from a financial group's operation, see **Dierick (2004)**, pp. 15-16.

97 For more details, see **OECD (1993)**, pp. 7-28, **Dierick (2004)**, pp. 6-9, and **Herring and Carmassi (2010)**, pp.195-201.

98 With reference to the reasons that led to the creation of such groups **Dierick (2004)**pAs regards the risk arising from a financial group's operation, see i.p

99 Ibid., pp. 17-19.

100 For instance, a banking group wishing to provide insurance services will need to establish (or acquire) a subsidiary insurance undertaking. If it wishes to manage mutual funds, it will need to establish (or acquire) a subsidiary mutual funds management firm, since the bank cannot offer those services *in-house.* The same applies to the provision of leasing services, investment services (mainly execution of orders) and the issuance and acquisition of cards, if the legislation does not permit their provision by a bank.

SECTION TWO THE CASE FOR REGULATORY INTERVENTION IN THE FINANCIAL SYSTEM: FINANCIAL POLICY OBJECTIVES AND INSTRUMENTS

A. Introductory remarks

1. General overview

The financial system (and definitely some of its sectors, mainly the banking sector) is one of the branches of the economy that are subject, in almost every state all over the world, to heavy 'sector-specific' regulatory intervention and supervision.[101] The extent of this intervention is graduated and there are significant differences between economically less-developed and developing states, on the one hand (see under 2 below), and economically developed states, on the other (under 3), mainly on account of different policy objectives.[102]

The following analysis is based on the 'public interest approach' to regulatory intervention, according to which financial regulation is intended to promote the common good by calling upon individuals and firms to change their preferred behaviour in ways that will benefit others.[103] *This is opposed to:*

- *the 'public choice theory approach', according to which regulation is the outcome of efforts by interest groups, politicians and bureaucrats to use the political process for their own personal gain,*[104] *and*
- *the 'industrial organisation theory approach', according to which financial regulation is a response to the demand of financial firms and their customers for cer-*

101 According to **Kane (1987)**, p. 111: *"On average, across the world, the financial sector (and in particular the banking industry) is probably more closely regulated than any other segment of the private economy"*. A notable exception to this statement are 'offshore financial centers', which are characterised by the substantial lack of regulatory intervention in the monetary and the financial systems, coupled with favourable corporate taxation ('tax havens').

102 As a rule, the classification of the International Monetary Fund can be followed in this respect. See on this **Nielsen (2011)**.
The author avoids the use of the vague term 'emerging markets', which was introduced by the World Bank in the 1980s to replace the term 'third world countries' with regard to states whose financial markets are illiquid and small in terms of capitalisation (currently, with the exception of the G20 member states).

103 See **Herring and Litan (1995)**, pp. 79-82.

104 Ibid., pp. 82-83.

tification of soundness and facilitation of the clearing and settlement of transactions.[105]

Financial firms are also subject to regulatory intervention in all states for reasons that apply equally to other categories of services providers, as reflected in the provisions of the following (indicative) areas of law: company law, competition law, data protection law, taxation law, as well as labour and social law.

Here, it is useful to delineate the content of the three concepts examined at length below:

- *regulation,*
- *supervision, and*
- *oversight.*

(a) *Regulation is the adoption of legislative or administrative provisions that prescribe or prohibit behaviour on the part of financial firms and markets, which is aimed at meeting a specific policy objective. The outcome of regulatory intervention consists in (administrative law) regulations which comprise the regulatory (or normative) framework.*

(b) *Supervision means monitoring of financial firms and markets by the competent authorities, in accordance with regulatory framework provisions. Such monitoring is carried out on a preventive basis and is known as 'micro-prudential supervision'.*

(c) *Oversight is monitoring by the competent authorities with a view to ensuring the sound operation of a market or a subsystem of the financial system.*[106]

2. Regulatory intervention in economically less-developed and developing states

In economically less-developed states, regulatory intervention in the financial system, notably in the banking sector, is mainly aimed at achieving specific economic and broader social objectives.[107] Taking into account that the financial system and banks, in particular, act as intermediaries for the channelling of borrowed funds (or own funds in the case of listed companies) from positive to negative savers, regulations are imposed on them in order to ensure that these funds are channelled:

105 Ibid., pp. 83-84. For an overall review of regulatory intervention in the financial system, see ibid., pp. 49-64, and **Herring and Santomero (2000)**.

106 Taking road traffic as an example:
- regulation means laying down rules on the maximum speed limit,
- supervision of compliance with these rules is carried out by traffic wardens, who issue speed tickets to the offenders, and
- oversight is conducted by traffic police helicopters that look for congestion problems in given roads, in order to smooth the traffic with appropriate instructions.

107 See **World Bank (1989)**, pp. 54-69.

- either to the government for financing its expenditures under favourable terms (by administratively fixed interest rates), or
- to enterprises which are considered by the political system to be eligible for financing under the applicable development policy (without due assessment of the credit risk involved).

Some examples of such regulatory intervention include:

(i) Imposing restrictions on banks relating to:
  - the provision of non-purely banking services (e.g. not allowing them to provide investment services and/or non-financial services), and/or
  - the geographical range of their activity.[108]

(ii) Imposing maximum limits on loan rates (in order to subsidise bank financing) and minimum limits on deposit rates (in order to make bank deposits attractive).

(iii) Imposing an obligation on banks to invest a significant percentage of their deposits:
  - in specific segments of the real sector of the economy, usually with preferential terms and subsidised interest rates, and
  - in government (short-term and long-term) bonds, thus ensuring the subsidised financing of public expenditures.

(iv) State ownership of commercial banks, either directly or through state-controlled entities (mainly pension funds).

(v) Setting-up by law 'specific', typically state-owned banks, such as agricultural, mortgage and development banks.

3. Regulatory intervention in economically developed states

3.1 Introductory remarks

In economically developed states, the above-mentioned objectives of regulatory intervention – particularly the first three – are not common, since most of the measures taken to achieve relevant regulatory objectives are not compatible with the principle of an open market economy with free competition. Therefore, given that this principle is applied in such states as a model for an economy's organisation and functioning, the adoption and implementation of these measures is prohibited.

On the other hand, in economically developed states, there is also intense regulatory intervention in the financial system and, over the past three (3) decades, this interven-

108 However, a striking example of an economically developed state which had resorted to this measure was that of the United States, not allowing banks, for a long period of time, to operate beyond the border of the state where their headquarters were seated.

tion was greatly expanded mainly because of the extensive laxity of other regulatory measures (a process known as 'financial deregulation').[109] However, as a rule:

- the policy objectives of regulatory intervention are primarily associated with the sound operation of the financial system, and
- their main (albeit not sole) task is to address 'market failures' emerging in the financial system.[110]

These aspects of financial regulatory intervention will be examined in more detail below. More specifically, apart from ensuring free competition in the financial system, which is the prevailing objective in the entire market, regulation is also aimed at meeting the following objectives:

- ensuring the stability of the financial system (see under 3.2 below),
- ensuring investor protection and capitals market integrity, efficiency and transparency (under 3.3),
- compensating investors in the event of an investment firm's insolvency (under 3.4),
- safeguarding the efficiency of payment systems (under 3.5),
- protecting the economic interests of consumers trading with financial firms (under 3.6), and
- combating the use of the financial system for the commitment of economic crimes, such as money laundering, terrorist financing and fraud in payment instruments and systems (under 3.7).

It should be pointed out, however, that the policy objectives justifying regulatory intervention in the financial system at any given time cannot be exhaustive, given that the prevailing economic and social conditions may call for new objectives in future. The dynamics of this variability are clearly demonstrated by the fact that certain policy objectives which stand today, did not stand a few years ago. In particular:

(a) The rationale for regulatory intervention in the financial system with a view to tackling consumer over-indebtedness emerged in the late 1990s as a result of the full liberalisation of consumer credit and the subsequent extensive exposure of households to debt.

(b) The rationale for combating terrorist financing through the financial system emerged mostly following the terrorist attacks in the United States on 11 September 2001.

(c) The debate on the need to deal with the adverse impact on public finances of exposure to insolvency of banks and other financial firms, which have grown 'too big to be left to fail' or are 'too interconnected to be left to fail' (currently referred to as

109 See on this in more detail under A in the Section 'An Overall Assessment' below.

110 As regards market failures, and, in particular, negative externalities and information asymmetries, see **Mercuro and Medema (2006)**, pp. 60-67 and, in more detail, **Ippolito (2005)**, pp. 153-379.

'systemically important financial institutions' or 'SIFI's), especially those operating internationally, is currently predominant in the financial policy agenda after the recent (2007-2009) international financial crisis. By default, the main concern is to ensure that:

- these entities will not be exposed to insolvency, or
- if otherwise exposed, their resolution will be feasible without becoming a charge on the public finances.

This problem, associated with the policy objective of ensuring financial stability, is definitely not new, but has become more acute during the recent crisis owing to large-scale government bailouts of financial firms and the ensuing negative impact on public finances (see, for example, the case of Ireland).

3.2 Ensuring the stability of the financial system

The first (and primary) policy objective justifying regulatory intervention in the financial system of economically developed states is ensuring the financial system's stability, which may be threatened by the occurrence of 'systemic crises'. Within this framework, there are five individual, yet closely linked, financial policy objectives (based on the distinct sectors and infrastructures of the financial system):

(a) The first objective is to ensure the stability of the banking sector by preventing the evolution of negative externalities in the form of contagious bank failures (i.e. by preventing a chain reaction of bank failures or 'bank failure spillover effects').[111] The policy instruments employed to attain this objective comprise the 'bank safety net' and are materialised through the adoption of rules concerning:

- the authorisation of banks by competent authorities,
- the micro-prudential regulation and supervision of banks,
- the application of macro-prudential policies,
- the reorganisation of troubled banks, as well as the resolution and winding-up of insolvent banks, and
- the operation of deposit guarantee systems.

Last-resort lending by the central bank (in its capacity as monetary authority) to solvent banks exposed to temporary illiquidity and monetary authority measures to neutralise a shift in public demand for cash – which is excessive in periods of crisis – aimed at preventing the cumulative collapse of the financial system, constitute the last components of the bank safety net. Recourse to these components is usually not premised on legislative rules but on discretionary decisions of central banks.

111 From the very extensive literature on this financial policy objective, see **Herring and Litan (1995)**, pp. 50-61. Regarding the synergies between the stability and effectiveness of the financial system, see **Barth, Caprio and Levine (2006)**, pp. 307-309.

It is worth mentioning that the first three (3) components of the bank safety net are preventive, whereas the others are considered protective ('crisis management') financial policy instruments. See a detailed overview below, under B. 2 of this Section.

(b) The second objective is ensuring capital market stability, which may be disrupted owing to either an abrupt and large-scale price fluctuation of financial instruments traded therein[112] or to the bankruptcy of a financial intermediary offering investment services.[113]

The latter argument has, however, been criticised by those who are of the view that the risk of spillover effects, i.e. of more investment firms becoming insolvent, is extremely limited.[114] *Within this framework, it may be reasonably argued that provisions are adopted mainly to ensure a level-playing field between investment undertakings and banks in terms of conditions for their authorisation, operation and supervision (in the case of banks such conditions are aimed at safeguarding the banking system's stability, given the palpable systemic risk of a ripple of successive bank authorisation withdrawals), to the extent that the former provide the same type of services and are exposed to the same kind of risks as the latter.*[115]

This objective is pursued through the adoption of rules concerning:[116]

- the sound operation of trading mechanisms for primary and derivative financial instruments,
- the authorisation, oversight and ongoing supervision by competent (administrative) authorities of securities exchanges and other markets for trading in financial instruments, and
- the authorisation and micro-prudential supervision by these authorities of financial firms providing investment services in capital markets, the micro- and macro-prudential regulation of these firms, as well as the macro-prudential oversight of markets.

(c) The third objective is ensuring stability in the insurance (and re-insurance) sector of the financial system against the risk of bankruptcy of insurance and reinsurance undertakings.[117] It is achieved with the adoption of rules on the authorisation and mi-

112 This risk is associated with market operation and cannot be addressed in principle with regulatory interventions. But what is needed is to prevent the emergence of inefficient institutional infrastructures that accentuate any problems caused by strong market fluctuations.

113 See **IOSCO (2008)**: *"Objectives and Principles of Securities Regulation"*, pp. 6-7, available at: http://www.iosco.org/library/index.cfm?section=pubdocs.

114 See **Haberman (1987)**, and **Herring and Litan (1995)**, pp. 72-73.

115 As regards differences between banks and investment undertakings in terms of a potential ripple of failures, see **Haberman (1987)**, **Herring and Litan (1995)**, pp. 72-73, and **Allen and Herring (2001).**

116 On the best international practices with regard to this aspect, see **IOSCO (2010):** *"Objectives and Principles of Securities Regulation"*, available at: http://www.compliance-exchange.com/governance/library/ioscoprinciples2010.pdf, principles 10-12, 29-34, and 37-38.

117 See **Herring and Litan (1995)**, pp. 73-74.

cro-prudential regulation and supervision of these undertakings by competent (administrative) authorities.[118]

(d) The fourth objective (which has become topical of late) concerns safeguarding the stability of the entire financial system against the emergence of widespread financial crises in the economy as a result of excessive risk-taking by financial conglomerates, comprising banks, insurance undertakings and investment firms (in accordance with what was mentioned under D in Section 1 above). This objective is sought through the adoption of rules concerning the 'supplementary' micro-prudential regulation and supervision of such conglomerates by competent (administrative) authorities.[119]

(e) Finally, the fifth objective consists in ensuring the normal and smooth operation of payment and settlement systems. The risk to such systems consists in the contagion of liquidity and/or solvency problems from one member of the system to another, with all the adverse systemic consequences that this may potentially have on the functioning of the financial system.[120] Exposure to this risk is controlled through proper oversight of payment and settlement systems.[121]

3.3. Ensuring investor protection and capital markets integrity, efficiency and transparency

3.3.1 The content of the objective

The second policy objective for regulatory intervention in the financial system is related to:

- ensuring the protection of investors that wish to invest, or already invest, in primary and derivative financial instruments, that are either going to be listed in a

118 On the best international practices with regard to this aspect, see **International Association of Insurance Supervisors (2011)**: *"Insurance Core Principles and Methodology"*, principles 1-23, available at: http://www.iaisweb.org/temp/Insurance_Core_Principles_Standards_Guidance_and_Assessment_Methodology_October_2011.pdf.

119 The supervision exercised on such conglomerates is supplementary in nature. Namely it is exercised additionally to the supervision exercised on the participating financial firms on an individual and on a consolidated basis within homogeneous activity groups. See **Dierick (2004)**, pp. 20-26, and **Herring and Carmassi (2010)**, pp. 214-226.

120 See **Committee on Payment and Settlement Systems and IOSCO (2012)**: *"Principles for Financial Market Infrastructures"*, April, available at: http://www.bis.org/publ/cpss101a.pdf, section 2.

121 See **Committee on Payment and Settlement Systems (2005)**: *"Central Bank Oversight of payment and settlement systems"*, Bank for International Settlements, May, available at: http://www.bis.org/publ/cpss68.htm.

regulated market (the 'primary market'), or are already being traded therein (the 'secondary market'),[122] as well as
- safeguarding the integrity, efficiency and transparency of capital markets.[123]

The 'closeness' of the connection between these two financial policy objectives with regard to capital markets can be explained by the fact that they share, to a large extent, the same financial policy instruments, making their distinction often difficult.[124]

A detailed examination of these two policy objectives exceeds the scope of this study.[125] Nevertheless, it is worth making three (3) remarks:

(a) Investors need special protection given their participation in the process of direct financing of companies and governments in capital markets where financial instruments – in which they invested or will invest – are traded. Fostering and bolstering investor confidence in a capital market's efficient operation is in any event crucial, as it is a necessary condition for investor participation in such a market. This dictates the adoption of special measures on the basis of the given market's characteristics and mechanisms governing its operation.

(b) In line with the above, obligations set and dictated by the need to protect investors – as those persons who invest in a market with specific characteristics and risks – to make sure that they trust and invest in a market's efficiency, respond to special requirements under capital markets law, which are independent of those arising from consumer protection law (see below, under 3.6). Of course, it is possible for an investor to be a consumer as well depending on the transactions conducted with the investment undertaking.

In this respect, investors/consumers are usually subjected to information asymmetry and have limited negotiating capacity vis-à-vis providers, i.e. financial firms, which is why, as a result, consumer protection provisions are put into effect. Here it should be noted, however, that investor protection measures are also sometimes aimed at redressing information asymmetries which, manifestly, go at the expense of investors. But such information asymmetries differ from those under consumer protection law, given that:

- *information asymmetry under capital markets law is a function of the investor's knowledge regarding the profile and financial condition of the undertaking that issues the instruments on which he/she will invest his/her savings or regarding the price formation mechanism in the markets where trading takes place, and*
- *information asymmetry may also exist among investors themselves, such as in the case of insider trading.*

(c) With regard to the extent of protection afforded to recipients of investment services under capital markets law, it should be noted that a distinction is made between pro-

122 See **IOSCO (2008)**, pp. 5-6.
123 Ibid., p. 6.
124 Ibid., p. 5.
125 Ibid., pp. 5-6.

fessional (institutional) and existing or potential private customers. It has been rightly pointed out that the distinction between private and institutional [investors] does not serve an abstract need to categorise investors, but is inextricably linked with the realisation that the need to protect investors – as subjects of capital markets law – is not as strong across all categories.

3.3.2 Policy instruments

Meeting the objective for safeguarding investor protection, as well as capital market integrity, efficiency and transparency, justifies strong regulatory intervention in the capital markets. This is pursued by adopting certain regulations, which can be systematically divided into five (5) categories, depending on their recipients, i.e.: issuers of transferable securities (see under (a) below), investment firms and banks providing investment services (under b), undertakings for collective investment in transferable securities (hereinafter the 'UCITS') and hedge funds (under c), secondary markets' operation (under d), and credit rating agencies as well as auditors (under e).[126]

(a) The first set of rules applies to issuers of transferable securities in capital markets, i.e. listed companies and firms planning their transferable securities' admission to trading in regulated markets, and refers to:

- the obligation of firms intending to raise own or borrowed funds through the capital market to report information to their investors that is key to their decision on whether to invest in the transferable securities of such companies/firms,
- corporate governance (including internal audit mechanisms) of listed companies,
- listing particulars for issuers,
- prospectus requirements for issuers,
- the periodical dissemination of information by listed companies,
- the protection of rights and interests of minority shareholders in the case of takeover bids, and
- accounting and auditing standards for listed companies.

(b) The second set of rules applies to investment firms and banks providing investment services and refers to:

- adequate internal organisation with regard to the provision of investment services mainly aimed at avoiding conflict of interests, and
- the *stricto sensu* investor protection ensured, *inter alia*, by imposing a code of conduct on the provision of investment services to customers, an obligation to execute orders in the most favourable terms for customers, and also rules on equal treatment of customer orders.

126 This categorisation is based on **IOSCO**'s **2008 report**. On the best international practices with regard to this aspect, see **IOSCO (2010)**, principles 16-18, 31, 24-28, 33 and 35-38 and 19-22, respectively.

(c) The third set of rules applies to UCITS and hedge funds management companies. With respect to UCITS the relevant rules refer to:

- the authorisation and supervision of UCITS management companies,
- the segregation and protection of investor assets,
- the dissemination of information, essentially addressed to investors as part of their decision-making, by UCITS management companies,
- criteria for the evaluation of UCITS assets and redemption of UCITS units, and
- rules concerning the investment policies of UCITS.

The rules concerning hedge funds management companies set out the following:

- the conditions for the authorisation and supervision of hedge fund managers,
- the conditions that must govern the conduct of their business, and
- the transparency requirements with which both investors and supervisors need to comply.

(d) The fourth set of rules relates to the sound operation of secondary markets and refers to:

- the conditions for authorisation and conduct of business, and the supervision and oversight of regulated markets,
- the transparency of transactions conducted in secondary markets (i.e. equity, bond and derivative markets),
- combating (i.e. preventing and containing) market abuse (market manipulation and insider trading),
- oversight of systems for the clearing and settlement of transactions in securities and derivative instruments, and
- the obligation to clear OTC derivatives that meet certain criteria (e.g. highly liquid OTC derivatives) through a central counterparty (CCP) and report them to trade repositories, in view of bolstering transparency and identifying and addressing systemic risk.

(e) Finally, the fifth set of rules relates to the operation of credit rating agencies and auditors. With respect to credit rating agencies, the relevant rules lay down obligations for their supervision and registration, and the necessary conditions for the issuance of credit ratings. Rules relating to auditors concern:

- their supervision,
- the quality requirements of audit standards, and
- the independence of auditors.

3.4 Compensation of investors

3.4.1 The content of the objective

The third policy objective for regulatory intervention also concerns the capital markets. It refers to the compensation of investors trading with an investment undertaking or bank that provides investment services (i.e. investment services provider), if both of the following conditions are met:

- supervisory or judicial authorities decide to suspend the investment services provider's operation, normally in the event of insolvency, and
- if the investment services provider cannot return funds or financial assets to their owners, i.e. the investors.

3.4.2 Policy instruments

The appropriate policy instrument in this case is the establishment of explicit investor compensation systems to offer 'explicit coverage' to investors (usually up to a certain amount).[127]

3.5 Safeguarding the efficiency of payment and settlement systems

The fourth policy objective of regulatory intervention in the financial system concerns safeguarding the efficiency of payment and settlement systems, which is the second policy objective associated with these systems.[128] Proper oversight of payment and settlement systems is the appropriate policy instrument in this case as well.[129]

Here, the significant role played by central banks should be highlighted. The assignment of this power to central banks is a corollary of the operational synergies that exist between the tasks of conducting monetary policy, safeguarding the stability of the financial system and overseeing payment systems.

127 The term 'explicit coverage' is used to incorporate all those arrangements that are not based on the premise that investor coverage should be *ex post*, at the discretion of supervisory authorities or the State, and solely conducted on an *ad hoc* basis, i.e. after a 'politically', 'socially' or 'systemically' important investment services provider becomes insolvent ('implicit coverage'). On the best international practices with regard to this aspect, see **IOSCO (2010)**, principle 32. The operation of investor compensation systems is another protective financial policy instrument.

128 See **Committee on Payment and Settlement Systems and IOSCO (2012)**, Section 1. Regarding the synergies between the stability and efficiency of payment and settlement systems, see ibid., para. 1.15, and **Committee on Payment and Settlement Systems (2005)**, paragraph 60.

129 See **Committee on Payment and Settlement Systems (2005)**.

The scope of the relevant power covers, first of all, large-value payment and settlement systems – given the interest in the smooth execution of monetary policy operations. With regard to small-value payment systems, the scope of the relevant power varies across different states and it may include:

- *low-value payment systems,*
- *systemically important small-value payment systems, and*
- *systems involving ad hoc systemic risk.*[130]

3.6. Protection of the economic interests of financial services consumers

3.6.1 The content of the objective

The fifth policy objective relative to regulatory intervention in the financial system is the protection of the economic interests of financial services consumers, namely consumers contracting with financial firms.[131] Policy concerns in this area are, first of all, based on generally accepted assumptions in the context of financial services provision that apply across the board in relation to the protection of consumers' economic interests[132] and have to do with the following two aspects:

(a) Reducing the information asymmetry that exists between consumers and financial firms[133] with regard to available information on a product or service that may become the object of a transaction between them. Such information asymmetry can be attributed to:

- the provider's typically greater expertise and knowledge on the provided financial service's features, function and characteristics, and
- the consumer's lack of experience and acquaintance with financial transactions.

This information asymmetry – accentuated in the case of specialised and complex financial services – and the consumer's typical lack of the resources necessary to fill the information gap upset the balance between the two parties given that the con-

130 See **Committee on Payment and Settlement Systems (2003b)**, and **European Central Bank (2011)**: *"Eurosystem oversight policy framework"*, July, available at: http://www.ecb.int/pub/pdf/other/eurosystemoversightpolicyframework2011en.pdf?ab6bddb77fd53f6acfff742adc24f4ef.

131 See **Herring and Litan (1995)**, pp. 61-62.

132 These policy objectives and policy instruments refer to the precontractual period and the contractual relationship that develops between the provider and the consumer in terms of a service's promotion and provision. That is, they are associated *lato sensu* with the consumption of a product or service.

133 With regard to this form of information asymmetry, see **Cartwright (2004)**, pp. 49-84, **Calais-Aulois and Steinmetz (2006)**, pp. 53-67 and **Rasmusen (1989)**, pp. 133-153.

sumer[134] cannot opt for the financial service of his/her choice based on an accurate assessment of its features. The policy objective for regulatory intervention consists in redressing this information asymmetry, so that the consumer may understand the financial service's nature and characteristics, and make informed and conscious choices that respond not only to his/her needs but also to his/her economic profile.

(b) Addressing the problem of consumers' limited negotiating capacity vis-à-vis financial firms, mainly owing to the broad use of general terms of transactions.[135]

The recourse to general terms of transactions, as a result of the standardisation of modern transactions, is aimed at ensuring predictability, security, equal treatment and also save providers and customers time and money. But the absence of a genuine negotiating equity between the parties, given the use of general terms of transactions, results in upsetting their contractual balance, particularly to the extent that abusive terms are used, while it is anyway agreed that the parties do not have the same level of influence on the elaboration of contractual terms.

Consequently, the policy objective in this case is to address this limited negotiating capacity which is presumed to consist in the contractual relationship between the consumer and the provider for the reasons mentioned above.

(c) More specifically, with regard to the extension of credit to consumers, over the last decade (at least) households have shown an increased tendency towards over-indebtedness. The liberalisation of consumer credit, consumers' increasingly easier access to financial services, certain households' resort to multiple borrowing, and sometimes consumers' inability to assess their financial capacity objectively and accurately are simply some of the main causes of consumer over-indebtedness.

The term 'over-indebtedness' refers to a consumer's inability to meet his/her financial obligations (default) arising from a loan contract he/she has signed or his/her current household financial obligations (i.e. payment of utility bills). However, there are quite different approaches with regard to:

- *the notion of such a default (for example genuine inability to repay loans or inability considered to be unbearable?),*
- *the default's timing (after how long is there default?), and*
- *the criteria based on which it is calculated (on the basis of the person's total assets or net income).*

The policy objective for regulatory intervention in this case is to prevent consumer over-indebtedness and avoid the negative consequences that this phenomenon might have from a social and economic point of view.

134 For example, through the assistance of a legal or technical consultant, available to business people, who either have the necessary infrastructure within the framework of their business or are able to afford such assistance.

135 With regard to this issue, see **Calais-Aulois and Steinmetz (2006)**, pp. 188-203, and **Howells and Weatherill (2005)**, p. 261 ff. General transaction terms are meant as the terms set *a priori* by the provider for an undefined number of future contracts.

3.6.2 Policy instruments

The policy instruments employed in order to achieve the above-mentioned objectives include rules pertaining to the following:

(a) The provision of adequate information to consumers ensuring the provision of sufficient information to consumers (prior to the contract, upon the conclusion of the contract and in the course of its duration) in respect of the nature, characteristics and risks entailed by the provided service, the content of concluded contracts, as well as the ensuing rights and obligations of the parties. Furthermore, unfair commercial practices which might either be misleading for consumers in terms of a given service's properties and features or exert pressure on consumers to accept a service that they would not have accepted, had they not been misled or pressured, are prohibited.

Despite the latest trend of legislative provisions on very extensive information obligations for service providers aimed at achieving the above-mentioned objective, it is the author's view that over-information cannot achieve this objective, since it is equally harmful to 'dis-information', 'under-information' or 'mis-information' and weakens the consumer's position by not allowing him/her to concentrate on, and understand, the vital characteristics of the provided financial service, which should affect his/her choice. In this context, the role of financial education could be particularly useful, as it may help consumers understand financial risks and make informed decisions. Financial education has taken on an increasingly broader sense.

(b) Provisions are also set in order to address the problem of consumers' limited negotiating capacity, aiming at:

- the control and prohibition of abusive terms, so that the consumer is not bound by any abusive general terms of financial services contracts (see under (i) below),
- the safeguarding of certain consumers' contractual rights, which are considered as crucial for the consumer (e.g. the right of withdrawal), in order to ensure that the consumer executes them under certain circumstances (under (ii)), and
- the possibility for consumers to have recourse to judicial proceedings through collective actions or to out-of-court dispute settlement systems (under (iii)).

(i) The prohibition of abusive general terms of transactions is the most direct manifestation of the protection of consumers given their limited negotiating capacity vis-à-vis the providers. This limited ability to shape the content of contractual terms can result in binding consumers to abusive terms, presenting an immediate risk to be dealt with through regulatory intervention.

A contractual term which has not been individually negotiated shall be regarded as abusive if, contrary to the requirement of good faith, it causes a significant imbalance in the parties' rights and obligations arising under the contract, to the detriment of the consumer. The abusive nature of a contractual term is assessed by a court of law.

(ii) Concurrently, the consumer's limited negotiating capacity justifies, to a certain extent, further intervention by the legislator on the principle of private autonomy which governs all contractual relations aimed at safeguarding certain consumer rights concerning the content of contracts concluded, but not negotiated on equal terms, with providers. Particularly with regard to financial services, such regulation consists indicatively in establishing consumers' right for early loan repayment under certain conditions, as well as their right to withdraw from a contract within a specific deadline and with specific legal effects.

(iii) Finally, within the same framework, measures are taken to facilitate the settlement of disputes between consumers and providers, either by encouraging out-of-court dispute settlement systems, which save consumers both time and money or by establishing measures to facilitate consumer access to the courts.[136] In this case, the means to meet the policy objective for regulatory intervention are legally premised solely on the limited negotiating capacity of the consumer, i.e. facilitate consumer access to the courts for *ex post* settlement of disputes with the provider.

These measures are also adopted bearing in mind that the – usually small – amounts associated with relevant disputes, the time-consuming processes and the comparatively elevated cost of court action discourage consumers from effectively asserting their rights.

(c) As already mentioned, especially in relation to consumer lending, in recent years the combating (i.e. prevention and containing) of consumer over-indebtedness has been elevated to a separate rationale for regulatory intervention, with a view to avoiding the potential negative social and economic consequences of consumers' excessive exposure to debt.[137] The adequate policy instruments in this case are the adoption of rules on 'responsible lending' and consumer bankruptcy.[138]

As regards the relatively recent phenomenon of over-indebtedness in modern economies, there is still no convergence of opinion on optimum intervention to prevent or address this phenomenon effectively. In the current conjuncture, five (5) measures are being implemented:

- imposing an obligation on banks to develop internal credit risk management systems (already available in most banks), in order to be able to detect (and therefore refuse to finance) existing or potential customers with an increased probability of default,
- establishing rules providing for increased capital requirements if doubtful loans are included in a bank's portfolio,[139]
- indirectly limiting 'financial pressure' on consumers by imposing an obligation on banks not to grant loans to consumers whose debt servicing absorbs more than a reasonable amount (i.e. 40%) of their monthly income,

136 An illustrative example of the latter case is the establishment of collective court action.

137 See **Finlay (2009)**, pp. 73-76, **Rosenthal (2002)**, p. 150 ff., and **Barret-Barney (2002)**.

138 See **Bouteiller (2004)**, p. 155, **Ramsay (1997)** and **Piedelièvre (2008)**, p. 475 ff. The latter is also a protective financial policy instrument.

139 The regulatory framework on banks' capital adequacy under the Basel Committee's rules on capital adequacy moves in this direction. See under B 2 in Section 6 below.

- establishing the principle of responsible lending, and
- adopting rules on 'consumer bankruptcy'.

It should be noted that the first three (3) categories of measures have not been put in place exclusively for the prevention of household over-indebtedness, but also in view of safeguarding the stability of the banking system. Furthermore, the first four (4) categories of measures refer to the prevention of over-indebtedness, and the fifth to addressing its consequences.

3.7 Combating the use of the financial system for the commitment of economic crimes

Finally, the sixth policy objective for regulatory intervention in the financial system consists in combating (i.e. preventing and containing) the use of the financial system for the commitment of economic crimes, such as money laundering, terrorist financing and payment instruments fraud).[140] In order to achieve this policy objective, rules are adopted with regard to:

- the prevention and containment of money laundering through the control of transactions carried out (with a view to identifying 'suspicious transactions') and the forwarding of information to the competent authorities,
- the prevention and containment of terrorist financing, and
- the prevention and containment of fraud in the use of payment instruments (in particular cards).

Table 3: Financial policy objectives and instruments

Policy objectives	Policy instruments
1. Ensuring financial system stability	
1.1 Ensuring banking sector stability	Components of the 'bank safety net' (for more details see under B below) • Rules on the authorisation of banks • Rules on the micro- and macro-prudential regulation of banks • Rules on the micro-prudential supervision of banks • Macro-prudential financial oversight • Reorganisation, resolution and winding-up of banks • Establishment of deposit guarantee systems • Lending of last resort

140 See **Dupuis-Danon (2005)** and **Blair, Walker and Purves (2009)**, pp. 487-488.

Policy objectives	Policy instruments
1.2 Ensuring capital market stability	• Rules on the authorisation of investment firms • Rules on the micro- and macro-prudential regulation of investment firms • Rules on the micro-prudential supervision of investment firms • Macro-prudential financial oversight • Rules on the sound operation of markets and infrastructures for trading in financial instruments
1.3 Ensuring insurance and reinsurance sector stability	• Rules on the authorisation of insurance and reinsurance undertakings • Rules on the micro- and macro-prudential regulation of insurance and reinsurance undertakings • Rules on the micro-prudential supervision of insurance and reinsurance undertakings • Macro-prudential financial oversight
1.4 Ensuring financial stability *in globo*, as regards financial conglomerate activities	• Rules on the supplementary micro-prudential supervision of financial conglomerates • Ancillary micro-prudential regulation of financial conglomerates
1.5 Ensuring the stability of payment and settlement systems	• Oversight • Functional interventions
2. Ensuring investor protection and capital markets integrity, efficiency and transparency	
2.1 Rules addressed to issuers of transferable securities	• Reporting of information to investors • Corporate governance rules for listed companies • Listing particulars for issuers • Prospectus requirements for issuers • Periodical dissemination of information by listed companies • Protection of rights and interests of minority shareholders in the case of takeover bids • Accounting and auditing standards for listed companies
2.2 Rules addressed to investment firms and banks providing investment services	• Adequate internal organisation with regard to the provision of investment services • *Stricto sensu* investor protection
2.3 Rules addressed to UCITS and hedge funds management companies 2.3.1 Rules addressed to UCITS management companies	• Authorisation and supervision of UCITS management companies • Segregation and protection of investors' assets • Dissemination of information by UCITS management companies • Criteria for the evaluation of UCITS assets and redemption of UCITS units • Rules on the investment policies of UCITS

Policy objectives	Policy instruments
2.3.2 Rules concerning hedge funds management companies	• Authorisation and supervision of hedge funds management companies • Rules on the conduct of their business • Transparency requirements
2.4 Rules on the sound operation of secondary markets	• Authorisation, conduct of business, supervision and oversight of regulated markets • Transparency of transactions conducted in secondary markets • Combating market abuse (market manipulation and insider trading) • Oversight of systems for the clearing and settlement of transactions • Obligation to carry out clearing of OTC derivatives through central counterparties (CCPs) and obligation to record transactions in these derivatives in central databases
2.5 Rules concerning credit rating agencies and auditors 2.5.1 Rules concerning credit rating agencies	• Supervision and registration in a register of CRAs • Conditions for the issuing of credit ratings
2.5.2 Rules relating to auditors	• Supervision of auditors • Quality requirements of audit standards • Independence of auditors
3. Compensation of investors in case of suspension of the operation of firms providing investment services	Establishment of explicit investor compensation systems
4. Safeguarding the efficiency of payment and settlement systems	Oversight
5. Protection of the economic interests of financial services consumers	
5.1 Reducing information asymmetry	• Provision of adequate information to consumers • Prohibition of unfair commercial practices • Financial education
5.2 Addressing the problem of consumers' limited negotiating capacity vis-à-vis financial firms	• Rules on the control and prohibition of abusive general terms of transactions • Rules on safeguarding of specific consumer rights after the conclusion of a contract • Rules on facilitating consumer access to justice (in-court/out-of-court)
5.3 Combating consumer over-indebtedness	• Rules on responsible lending • Rules on consumers' bankruptcy
6. Combating the use of the financial system for the commitment of economic crimes	Rules on the prevention and containment of: • money laundering • terrorist financing • fraud in the use of payment instruments

B. *More specifically: instruments to achieve the policy objective of ensuring banking stability: the 'bank safety net'*[141]

1. The channels for negative externalities in banking

1.1 Introduction

Traditionally, the main channel for spillover effects in the banking sector with the potential to lead to generalised crises is panic on the part of depositors (the 'informational channel'). However, 'real channels' of contagion also exist as a result of the interconnectedness of banks with other banks (and financial firms, in general), e.g. through the interbank market,[142] the markets for OTC derivatives (forwards, OTC options, swaps), or the holding of assets (equity and debt). The recent (2007-2009) international financial crisis provides the most important evidence in this respect.[143]

As already mentioned, the main policy objective for regulatory intervention in banks' operation is safeguarding the stability of the banking system, which may be put at risk by simultaneous or successive bank authorisation withdrawals. The depletion of a bank's equity and its insolvency does not have a negative impact on depositors and other creditor categories alone. A key specificity that sets the banking market apart in the whole economic system lies in the risk of the entire banking system's destabilisation by an individual bank's insolvency.,[144, 145]

141 See **Guttentag and Herring (1986b), Herring and Litan (1995)**, pp. 50-61, and **Yokoi-Arai (2002)**, pp. 3-25.

142 See **Saunders (1987)**, as early as in the 1980s.

143 See, in particular, **International Monetary Fund (2010)**, Chapter 2.

144 The theory on banking crises and their transmission channels is discussed in detail in **Guttentag and Herring (1986b), Saunders (1987), Calomiris and Gorton (1990), Herring and Litan (1995)**, pp. 50-61, and **Caprio and Klingebiel (1996)**.

145 The comparative advantage of banks vis-à-vis other financial services providers lies in the structure of their portfolio, i.e. the fact that not immediately payable claims (credits and loans) can be converted to immediately redeemable obligations (deposits). The capacity of banks to offer these two services concurrently is what sets them apart in the financial system, but it is also the source of their structural weaknesses. Banks collect and process data as part of the management of credit contracts, the content of which is known only to investors. As a result, the cost of transfer of credit claims is high, because each transferee has to collect all the necessary investor information again. In light of this, bank financing is characterised by a low degree of liquidity and imperfect negotiability.

As evidenced by the recent (2007-2009) international financial crisis, the real sector of the economy may be adversely impacted amidst a financial crisis owing to the decline in, or lack of, bank financing to households and enterprises and the fall in total demand in the economy.[146]

1.2 Risks to which banks may be exposed

1.2.1 Introductory remarks

Banks are exposed to three categories of risk (apart from reputation risk, which, as shown in the recent international financial crisis, is the most severe and may lead to detrimental outcomes for the economy):[147]

(a) Financial risks, which can be subdivided as follows:

- risks arising from the transformation function of banks: credit risk, liquidity risk, and interest-rate income risk, and
- market risks to the extent that banks operate also in capital, foreign exchange and commodities markets (position risk, foreign exchange risk and risk from open positions in commodities).

(b) Risks arising from payment, clearing and settlement systems.

(c) Finally, operational risk, the definition of which also encompasses legal risk.[148]

Thus the lack of a secondary market constantly reflecting their market value has two significant consequences:
(a) The first consequence is the inability of depositors to discipline the banking market effectively. A bank, just like any other enterprise with an information advantage over its creditors, has an incentive to take greater risks when investing the funds it has been entrusted with, without risking to be punished for its choices with an obligation to introduce higher interest rates that reflect its riskier portfolio.
See in detail below under 1.3.3.2.
(b) The second consequence is banks' structural exposure to liquidity risk. If, for whatever reason, a significant number of depositors withdraw their deposits at the same time, their bank may not be able to meet its obligations if it immediately liquidates its claims at fair value, although it would have been able to cash them in at market value.
See in detail below under 1.3.3.3.

146 Fore a more detailed review of transmission channels between the financial system and the real sector of the economy, see on the secondary sources **Basel Committee on Banking Supervision (2011)**, and **Galati and Moessner (2011)**, section 5.2.

147 With regard to all these risks, apart from the extensive literature, reference should be made to the relevant work of the Basel Committee on Banking Supervision (http://www.bis.org/bcbs), and the Committee on Payment and Settlement Systems (http://www.bis.org/cpss/index.htm).

148 On legal risk, see also **McCormick (2006)**.

1.2.2 Risks arising from the transformation function of banks

1.2.2.1 Credit risk

(a) Credit risk is, in principle, a bank's risk of loss following a borrower's default or, in the case of undertakings, credit rating downgrade, which puts borrower debt-servicing ability at risk. Banks' exposure to credit risk arises from their main function, i.e. transformation related to the allocation of liquidity risk according to the above. When managing this risk, banks calculate specific parameters for each exposure such as:

- a borrower's probability of default (PD),
- loss given default (LGD), which refers to the calculation of a bank's (average) expected loss per claim (a function of accepted collateral) in the event of a borrower's inability to meet liabilities (a concept which incorporates capital losses, loss of earnings (in the form of interest income) and operating expenses),
- exposure at default (EAD), which is exposure upon default of a borrower, and
- the loan contract's maturity (M).[149]

(b) Banks' exposure to credit risk does not only arise from granted loans and credit, but also from the total sum of claims, both on- and off-balance sheet (e.g. bonds or positions in OTC derivatives).[150] Of particular importance within this framework is the credit risk to which banks are exposed as a result of positions in tradable debt securities, equities and financial derivative instruments, held in their trading book.

(c) A special dimension of credit risk is 'country risk', which refers to the probability of adverse, and normally unforeseen, economic, political or social circumstances in a given state, which do not allow borrowers to repay their foreign currency-denominated debt when due, in accordance with the contractual terms laid down.[151] The most significant and frequent manifestation of this risk is 'transfer risk', which relates to the probability of a borrower's reduced ability or limited willingness to secure foreign currency to repay debt denominated in foreign currency.

149 These parameters are also particularly important for the calculation of banks' capital requirements in accordance with the 'internal ratings-based approach'. See **Gleeson (2010)**, pp. 75-77, and **Hills (2004)**, pp. 39-42.

150 As regards credit risk to which banks are exposed as a result of off-balance sheet items, see **Äberli (1989)**.

151 See **Siegwart, Caytas, and Mahari (1989)**.

1.2.2.2 Liquidity risk

Liquidity is the ability to fund assets and to settle obligations when due.[152] Liquidity risk refers to the likelihood of a bank's liquidity position drying up following an unforeseen increase in liquidity needs. This risk arises from maturity transformation.

Liquidity risk has two aspects:

(a) The first aspect is the 'funding (or liability) liquidity risk', which refers to the probability of loss as a result of a bank's inability to borrow funds at an acceptable cost in order to refinance its debt. Examples of this aspect are:

- a rapid, mass withdrawal of deposits,
- a crisis in the interbank market not allowing fund-raising through this market,[153] and
- inability to issue or refinance debt instruments in money and capital markets.[154]

(b) The second aspect is 'asset (or market) liquidity risk', i.e. the risk of loss resulting from the inability to liquidate assets at prices that do not deviate significantly from their nominal value, in order to meet obligations when due. The lowering of asset value due to haircuts or, in the most extreme case, the complete inability to liquidate, as shown during the recent (2007-2009) international financial crisis, are some of the most indicative examples.

1.2.2.3 Income risk

Income risk refers to the likelihood of a decline in bank interest rate income following an unexpected rise/fall of nominal rates. Banks are vulnerable to this risk due to the structure of their portfolio, given that on-balance sheet assets typically have longer maturities than liabilities and, as a result, are less vulnerable to interest rate fluctuations. The greater the short-term repricing gap – defined as the ratio of assets to liabilities, repriced within one year to own funds – and the stronger the fluctuation of interest rates, the more vulnerable banks are to this risk (and thus the greater the decline/increase in its prospective interest income as a result of higher/lower interest rates).

152 Liquidity risk and the alternative measures for its assessment, management and supervision are discussed in detail in **Basel Committee on Banking Supervision (2008):** *"Principles for Sound Liquidity Risk Management and Supervision"*, September, available at: http://www.bis.org/publ/bcbs144.htm.

153 An indicative example is the 2008 crisis in the interbank market as a result of the recent (2007-2009) international financial crisis.

154 For example, Greek banks have been exposed to this risk since 2010 due to the considerable downgrading in the credit rating of Greece's government bonds, which brought about the downgrades of their own credit ratings as well.

1.2.3 Market risks

1.2.3.1 Position risk

Position risk is defined as the probability of loss associated with open positions in debt instruments, equities and derivative instruments (or foreign currency) due to changes in various market parameters, to the extent that these positions are held for the purpose of resale or speculation. From a systematic point of view, the concept of risk arising from positions in primary instruments should be presented separately from risk arising from positions in derivative instruments (analysed below, under (I) and (II), respectively).

(I) *Risk arising from open positions in debt securities and equities*

According to the prevalent 'building-blocks approach', position risk arising from open positions in debt securities and equities can be broken down in two components: specific (see under (a) below) and general (under (b)):

(a) *Specific position risk*: this is defined as the probability of loss due to a negative change in a debt security's price, mainly as a result of parameters associated with its issuer. The notion of this component of position risk encompasses:

- 'non-systematic risk', defined as a debt security's volatility (of returns) relative to the market rate of return,
- 'event risk', i.e. the risk of a negative change in the price of debt securities in the case of exceptional events, including issuer default (default risk),
- the risk of inability to liquidate an open position in the market, and
- execution risk in arbitrage transactions.[155]

(b) *General position risk*: General position risk is defined as the risk of loss as a result of unfavourable price changes. This component of position risk refers to the probability of loss arising from open positions in tradable debt securities and equities following an abrupt change in their market value as a result of:

- either (unfavourable) changes in nominal rates (in the case of debt instruments),[156] or
- a strong price fluctuation in the markets where equities are traded, which is not attributed to specific issuers' characteristics.

155 See **Basel Committee on Banking Supervision (2006)**: International Convergence of Capital Measurement and Capital Standards, A Revised Framework – Comprehensive Version, June 2006, paragraph 701(iii).

156 General position risk arising from open positions in debt instruments, also known as 'investment risk', is the first of two components of interest rate risk. The second component of interest rate risk is 'income risk', for which see above under 1.2.2.3.

(II) *Risk arising from open positions in derivative instruments*

The 'building-blocks approach' is also used for derivative instruments included in trading books:

(a) Specific position risk is the result of an abrupt change in the derivative instrument's market value for reasons associated with the underlying security's issuer.

(b) By contrast, general position risk arises from open positions in derivative instruments or derivative portfolios taken on various forms, which can be divided into two systematic categories:

(i) The first category encompasses those forms of market risk that arise from open positions in all derivative instruments, be they based on forward or option contracts, such as 'delta risk'/'absolute price risk,[fn] 'rho risk'/'discount rate risk',[157] 'basis risk' and 'spread risk'.[158]

(ii) The second category includes forms of market risk arising exclusively from open positions in option derivatives, such as 'gamma risk'/'convexity risk',[159] 'vega risk'/'volatility risk',[160] and 'theta risk'.[161]

The market value of option derivatives is thus not only affected by changes in the underlying instruments' prices (as is the case with derivative instruments based on forward contracts), but also by other parameters such as the volatility of yields of underlying instruments and the time dimension.

1.2.3.2 Foreign exchange risk

Foreign exchange risk relates to a bank's possible loss as a result of unpredictable, unfavourable revaluation of the currencies in which on- and off-balance sheet items

157 This risk relates to the probability of loss incurred by the holder of an open position in an option derivative as a result of changes in discount rate levels. Particularly with regard to currency call options there are two rhos, one for each currency's interest rate.

158 Basis risk is the risk arising from a shift in rate relationships between two similar (but not identical) financial instruments with comparable maturities. This risk emerges in the event of imperfect hedging, i.e. when an open position in a primary financial instrument is hedged by a derivative instrument, the underlying security of which is another financial instrument. Exposure risk is a special aspect of basis risk, where the risk of a shift in the rate relationship between two similar instruments is consciously undertaken by the bank which holds the open positions.

159 This risk relates to the probability of loss incurred by the holder of an open position in an option derivative as a result of a change in the option's delta. Gamma is thus the second 'derivative' (in the mathematical notion of the term) of such a derivative instrument's value with regard to the underlying instrument's price.

160 Vega risk refers to the probability of loss due to the negative impact on a derivative instrument's price of the underlying instrument's volatility (of returns). The vega of a derivative instrument is also called lambda (λ), kappa (κ) or sigma (σ).

161 Theta risk refers to the probability of loss due to a change in the derivative instrument's value with regard to the length of time until its expiry. Theta is only expressed in negative values, because the value of an option contract drops as it nears its expiration date.

are denominated vis-à-vis the currency of the bank's financial statements.[162] In the context of a variable exchange-rate system, in effect internationally since 1971,[163] the risk arising from foreign exchange open positions is a result of the fluctuation of nominal exchange rates. In fact, as a result of the frequency and intensity of foreign exchange fluctuations, supervisory authorities are not only interested in the eventuality of loss, but also in the extent to which banks' open position portfolios could be affected in such an eventuality, as a function of three (3) factors:

- exchange-rate volatility,[164]
- possible correlation between currency pairs,[165] and
- the duration of foreign exchange open positions.[166]

1.2.3.3 Risk arising from open positions in commodities

This risk is associated with the probability of loss from open positions in commodities held in a bank's trading book, as a result of changes in commodity prices.

1.2.4 Operational risk

Operational risk refers to the probability of loss attributed either to inappropriate or incorrect internal processes/systems or human error, or to external causes. This risk also covers legal, but not strategic or reputation risk.[167] As pointed out by **Kokkola (2010)**:

> "*This definition has a broader focus and, in addition to technology, also includes organizational aspects and other relevant factors. It creates an awareness that operational failures are not caused by the malfunctioning of technical components alone, but can also be the product of errors, fraud, inaccessibility of key staff, unavailability of external stakeholders, etc.*".[168]

162 This definition refers to the first aspect of foreign exchange risk, i.e. transaction risk, and delineates it vis-à-vis the other two aspects of foreign exchange risk, i.e. translation risk and economic risk.

163 See under B 2.1.1 (b) in Section Three below.

164 Experience of how international foreign exchange markets work so far suggests that certain foreign exchange positions are more risky than others, as certain currency pairs present relatively stronger volatility.

165 Market experience and institutional restrictions (e.g. the Exchange Rate Mechanism of the European Monetary System) have also shown that exchange rates for certain currencies tend to move in parallel with one another, i.e. have a high degree of correlation.

166 The probability of incurring a loss as a result of a foreign exchange open position is a positive parameter for its duration.

167 See **Basel Committee on Banking Supervision (2011)**: Principles for the Sound Management of Operational Risk, June, available at: http://www.bis.org/publ/bcbs144.htm. For a detailed definition of legal risk, see **McCormick (2006)**.

168 See **Kokkola (2010)**, p. 125.

1.3 Channels of contagion among banks

1.3.1 Introductory remarks

The channels of contagion among banks are divided into two (2) categories:

(a) *The information channel*

The first channel of contagion is the information channel and is associated with the emergence of panic, either a run on an individual bank or a bank run in the entire banking system (literally a "banking panic").[169] A banking panic is an occurrence whereby depositors' demand to be paid in cash for their claims to such an extent that the banking system is only able to respond through a suspension of convertibility or by issuing clearing-house loan certificates.

This issue will be examined in detail under 1.3.2 below.

(b) *The real channel*

The second channel of contagion is real and refers to the transmission of problems from one market segment to another following the emergence of systemic risk. Systemic risk is defined as the risk of:

- a disruption in the provision of (and/or inability to provide) financial services due to the weakening of a given sector or of the entire financial system,
- with the likelihood of serious negative impacts in the real sector of the economy.[170]

Systemic risk has two dimensions:[171]

- on the one hand, the time dimension, i.e. the development of systemic risk in the course of time, and
- on the other, the cross-sectional dimension, i.e. how risk is distributed in the financial system at a given point in time.

1.3.2 More specifically: panics as the main channel for negative externalities in banking

1.3.2.1 Introduction

Panics occur when *"bank debtholders at all, or many, banks in the banking system suddenly demand that banks convert their debt into cash at par to such an extent that*

169 See **Calomiris and Gorton (1990)**.

170 See **Committee on the Global Financial System (2010a)**, Section 2.1. See also **Schwarcz (2008)**, Chapter II, and **Brunnermeier et. al. (2009)**, Chapter 2.

171 See **Committee on the Global Financial System (2010a)**, Annex 1, Section 2, and **FSB, IMF and BIS (2011)**, Section 2.

banks suspend convertibility of their debt into cash".[172] Panic is the cause of failure in the banking market to the extent that as the panic evolves even solvent banks can face a heavy liquidity strain, which in turn may cause their insolvency.[173]

There are several models explaining banking panics.[174] All of them view panics as caused by imperfect information to depositors about the quality of bank asset portfolios and bank viability. This makes depositors unable to distinguish between 'good' and 'bad' banks and, under certain circumstances, induces them to withdraw funds from the banking system massively. Depending on the economic event triggering depositors' sudden demand for convertibility, the models on banking panics are classified in accordance with two theories:

- the non-fundamental theory (see under 1.3.2.2 below), and
- the fundamental theory (under 1.3.2.3).

1.3.2.2 The non-fundamental theory

The non-fundamental theory considers bank panics to be caused by random large fund withdrawals from the banking system. According to the 'sunspot' or 'random withdrawal hypothesis', panics can be triggered by *"anything that causes depositors to anticipate a run such as a bad earnings report, a negative government forecast or even a sunspot."*[175]

1.3.2.3 The fundamental theory

According to this theory, bank panics are caused by any economic event that can induce depositors to change perceptions about bank risk exposure: *"if depositors change, on a rational basis, their perception of asset riskiness they will not be able to discern which bank is underperforming. They will be induced to withdraw from the banking system as a whole, leading the system into panic."*[176] **Gorton (1988a)** presents three different versions of the fundamental theory analysed just below.

(a) *The recession hypothesis*

The 'recession hypothesis' maintains that depositors withdraw funds from the banking system after the dissemination of information about a looming severe recession. When an economic variable predicting recession (e.g. unemployment rate, sales) reaches a

172 This definition of panics is given by **Calomiris and Gorton (1990).**

173 A bank becomes insolvent when either its liquidity is so low that it cannot repay its outstanding debt or the market value of its non-equity liabilities exceeds that of its assets.

174 These models are reviewed in **Carisano (1992)**, pp. 32-56.

175 See **Diamond and Dybvig (1983)**, p. 410.

176 See **Carisano (1992)**, p. 48.

critical value, depositors hurry to convert their deposits into cash in the anticipation of several bank failures.[177]

(b) *The seasonal hypothesis*

According to the 'seasonal hypothesis', the origin of panics lies in the existence of stringent money market conditions such as the failure of specific firms, depressed stock prices or high interest rates.[178]

(c) *The failure hypothesis*

The 'failure hypothesis' maintains that panics are generated by the unexpected failure of a usually, but not necessarily, large credit institution.[179] The failure of a large bank, or even the anticipation thereof, can change depositor risk perceptions with regard to the entire market and induce domino effects. Because of its relevance to further analysis, this hypothesis will be examined more closely.

The lack of market information on the market value of banks' portfolio does not allow for correct assessment of banks' exposure to an individual insolvent bank, whereas depositors may also think that banks of 'similar type' to the insolvent bank are also exposed to similar risks. Therefore, depositors' inability to judge whether the withdrawal of a bank's authorisation is attributed to specific reasons or to factors that concern all banks alike (as a result of information asymmetry), coupled with the demand for payment in full of the nominal value of their claims – if they manage to withdraw their deposits in time – leads to panic in the absence of a reliable deposit guarantee system.

1.3.3 More specifically: the failure hypothesis of banking panics

1.3.3.1 Introduction

Any bank can be exposed to insolvency, which is a positive function of two factors: the intensity of potential risks and the extent of its vulnerability to risks:

- risk intensity depends on the insolvency's frequency and predictability, as well as the extent of losses that could be caused if it were to occur, while
- risk vulnerability depends on both the current exposure of a bank to each individual risk as well as its capacity to absorb losses, if risks occur.[180]

177 See **Gorton (1988a)**, p. 225 with references to **Michell (1941)** and **Fels (1959)**.
178 Ibid., p. 224, with references to **Kemmerer (1910)** and **Miron (1985)**.
179 Ibid., pp. 224-225.
180 See **Guttentag and Herring (1988)**, p. 27.

Banks are subject to runs because they promise liquidity, i.e. redemption of deposits at nominal value.[181] During a run, many depositors simultaneously demand convertibility of their deposits into cash. The development of runs, like that of panics, is facilitated by two structural features of the banking sector:

- information asymmetries (see under 1.3.3.2 below) and
- the structural vulnerability of banks to liquidity risk, arising from the features of bank loans and deposits (under 1.3.3.3).

1.3.3.2 Information asymmetries in banking

Business loans which account for a large part of banks' asset portfolios are non-marketable and illiquid. This is due to the fact that *"banks are observing information about each loan which is exclusively shared between the borrower and itself. If the intermediary were to sell the loan and transfer the monitoring and the enforcement to someone else, the new claimant would have to incur the monitoring cost again, duplicating the effort of the first intermediary."*[182]

To the extent that there is no secondary market for business and other bank loans (which exists, in practice, only in the case of asset securitisation), these financial assets cannot be marked to market and thus cannot be precisely valued.[183] This makes it difficult for depositors to determine the current value of the bank asset portfolio and evaluate a bank's net worth. The problem of information asymmetry, present in money and capital markets, also emerges in the banking system. The asymmetric division of information between depositors and the bank has several implications:

(a) It is the main cause of the reduced discipline exerted by depositors in the market.[184]

(b) It creates moral hazard problems.[185] Bank insiders with superior information about the expected performance of the loan portfolio are tempted, as would any agent exercising control over information, to assume higher risk exposure, because the level of their effort cannot be observed by the principals (i.e. depositors).[186]

181 According to **Dybvig (1983),** p. 172, not all financial institutions offering liquid claims are subject to runs. If the assets of the firm are also liquid, as is the case with money-market mutual funds, withdrawals are always covered by these assets and the claimants do not have the incentive to be 'first in line' to withdraw their funds.

182 See **Diamond (1984)**, p. 410.

183 Marking-to-market is an accounting principle requiring the valuation of tradable financial instruments according to market prices. Usually such a valuation must be effected on a daily basis.

184 The 'market discipline test' refers to whether or not the market value of a firm's liabilities responds to individual risk-taking activity.

185 **Rasmusen (1989)**, pp. 133 ff., distinguishes between games of moral hazard with hidden action and games of moral hazard with hidden information. In both cases the principal offers a contract, the agent accepts, and then noise is added to the task to be performed.

186 Ibid., p. 140.

(c) Since there is not enough information in the market, reputation and trust play a proportionally more important role in banking than in most other sectors of the economy. Imprudent banks can free-ride and benefit from the reputation established by other banks which have managed risks prudently.[187]

(d) From the perspective of public policy, the most serious consequence of information asymmetries in banking is that depositors are tempted to participate in banking panics.[188] Since bank managers and depositors do not share the same information about a banking firm's financial performance, concerns about its solvency may trigger withdrawals. Uninformed depositors, and especially those who are insured, do not have the time, the competence or even the incentive to monitor and control their bank.

Conversion may be required even from creditors who would have preferred to leave their savings with the bank, but decide to monitor the bank by withdrawing deposits, as they cannot adequately assess its net worth.[189] This process is facilitated by the fact that the claim of bank depositors has a fixed nominal value, which does not vary with changes in the market value of the bank portfolio in assets.[190] Uncertain and unable to coordinate with others, each depositor wants to collect his/her claim before reimbursement is suspended.[191]

1.3.3.3 Structural vulnerability of banks to liquidity risk

Bank runs can create extensive liquidity problems; they can even induce solvency problems in the bank hit by the run, resulting from a bank's structural vulnerability to liquidity risk.[192] An illiquidity-caused insolvency occurs when a bank is unable to service deposit withdrawals. As already mentioned, the structural vulnerability of banks to liquidity risk and their subsequent susceptibility to insolvency is caused by their ability to transform liquid liabilities into illiquid assets, which concurrently constitutes the *raison d'être* of banking intermediation.

To the extent that bank assets are marketable, it can overcome a sudden exposure to liquidity risk by selling such assets in the secondary market. However, since business and consumer loans are illiquid,[193] a bank is unable to satisfy its depositors if they all choose to exercise their withdrawal option. In principle then, banks with a substantial portfolio of illiquid and non-marketable assets are vulnerable to losses incurred either as a result of the liquidation of loans at emergency prices, or because of the need to be

187 This important argument was raised by **Goodhart (1988)**.
188 See **Gorton (1988a)**, p. 225.
189 This arises from the non-marketability of a large portion of bank assets; see **Diamond and Dybvig (1983)**, p. 402.
190 See **Freedman (1987)**, p. 189.
191 In this case the money supply is also affected due to the increase in the liquidity ratio of the public, which affects the multiplier of the monetary basis.
192 See **Guttentag and Herring (1988)**, p. 3.
193 These financial assets are not eligible for rediscounting at the central bank. The theory of the discount policy of central banks is discussed in **Barro (1990)**, p. 431.

funded in the money or interbank market at a high premium. In other words, a bank hit by a run and finding it impossible either to borrow at market rates or to sell marketable assets at market prices is exposed to illiquidity-caused insolvency.

Whether liquidity problems are transformed into solvency problems depends on the behaviour of depositors after they have exercised their withdrawal option. If they do not redeposit with other banks or if they do not purchase other securities issued by banks, but rather hold their funds in the form of currency outside the banking system, it is more likely that liquidity problems will be transformed into solvency problems.[194]

1.3.3.4 Channels for risk transmission among banks

Whereas a bank run need not always lead to a generalised panic, the financial troubles and the potential failure of one bank can become contagious and affect others for two reasons:

- either because depositors assume that their bank is or may soon become exposed to the same risks as an insolvent bank (pure information contagion), or
- because they place it in the same class of riskiness as others exposed to a troubled bank regardless of whether or not a failure has occurred (signal information contagion).[195]

In either case, the catalyst for the interbank transmission of risks is the behaviour of depositors and the existence of information asymmetries. Depositors lack the information necessary to determine whether the run on a bank or even its insolvency was caused by excessive risk vulnerability, or whether the bank was simply the first victim of adverse conditions prevailing throughout the banking system.

The failure or the prospective failure of large banks may induce depositors to panic. Whereas it is impossible to prevent runs on individual institutions, runs should not be contagious because during a generalised withdrawal of funds from the banking system, caused by a sudden and significant increase in depositors' demand for cash, even solvent banks can fail due to their structural vulnerability to liquidity risk.[196] This can have a cumulative impact on several other banks with the spillover effect of illiquidity-caused failures. Under such circumstances, business firms are forced to interrupt their productive investments, leading the economy into a sudden recession.

The impact on the transaction balances of depositors (known as the 'macro-domino' effect) and the implications on the functioning of the payment system and the conduct of monetary policy are grave as well.[197]

194 See **Carisano (1992)**, p. 15.
195 See **Saunders (1987)**, p. 205.
196 See **Carisano (1992)**, p. 14.
197 See **Guttentag and Herring (1987a)**, pp. 158-159.

2. The components of the 'bank safety net'

2.1 Introductory remarks

As already mentioned in the preceding subsection, the need for regulatory intervention in the banking system is aimed at ensuring its stability against the risk of simultaneous or successive bank authorisation withdrawals. Ensuring the stability of the banking system, by preventing the above-mentioned spillover effects between banks, renders necessary the adoption of various preventative measures, and also protective (or 'crisis management') policies.

Public authorities are greatly concerned about the vulnerability of the banking system to economic and financial shocks, and the preservation of its stability and soundness. In order to prevent the evolution of negative externalities in the form of contagious bank failures, they command a broad range of instruments which comprise the 'bank safety net'. According to **Guttentag and Herring (1988)**, the components of the bank safety net can be viewed as *"a series of circuit breakers designed to prevent a shock to one part of the financial system from surging through the financial network to damage the rest of the system"*.[198] Even though the various components of this 'crisis prevention and crisis management system' are somewhat complementary,[199] each has a specific contribution to the safeguarding of the banking system's stability.

Apart from the components to be analysed below, the bank safety net also includes measures by monetary authorities to eliminate any tendencies on the part of depositors for excessive cash withdrawals in periods of crisis. This measure is inextricably linked with the conduct of monetary policy and is a manifestation of the close relationship between the operation of the banking and the monetary system.

2.2 Authorisation requirements

The first component of the bank safety net consists in laying down certain conditions, whose fulfilment is a *sine qua non* for the taking up of banking activity. Authorisation requirements serve a screening function. They are aimed at preventing market entry by private or legal persons whose management could lead to heavy losses in a bank and impair the reputation of the banking system as a whole.[200] Authorisation requirements also assure that the banking firm has sufficient financial resources to finance its initial investments and withstand temporary losses.

198 See **Guttentag and Herring (1988)**, p. 9.
199 Ibid., p. 8.
200 Ibid., pp. 12-13.

Standard requirements imposed by supervisory authorities in the context of the licensing procedure are the following:

- a minimum initial capital requirement,[201]
- requirements on the organisational structure of the bank,
- specific fit-and-proper criteria for major shareholders, and
- similar criteria for the bank management (the 'four-eyes principle').[202]

2.3 Micro-prudential banking regulation and supervision

2.3.1 Micro-prudential regulation

2.3.1.1 Content

Micro-prudential banking regulation seeks to enforce the safety and soundness of banks by limiting their exposure either to insolvency or to liquidity risk (which might lead to insolvency under certain circumstances)[203] and by curbing their risk vulnerability through:

- limiting their exposure to various categories of financial risks, and all other risks associated with the conduct of their business to which they might be exposed, and
- increasing their capacity to absorb losses incurred in the event of such risks.[204]

Hence, micro-prudential regulation serves a failure-preventing function, by preventing the failure of individual banks, the risk of contagion and subsequent negative externalities in terms of confidence in the financial system as a whole.

2.3.1.2 Policy instruments

Micro-prudential banking regulation is mainly performed by laying down rules on:

- banks' capital adequacy against exposure to risks associated with the conduct of their business,
- provisions for future exposure to risks,

201 This is the first function of bank capital, the second being its loss-buffer function.

202 See **OECD (1987)**, pp. 46-49.

203 See **Guttentag and Herring (1988**, pp. 34-45) are of the view that supervisors should focus more on the potential exposure of banks to insolvency, because it is such banks that seriously threaten the stability of the system.

204 In this respect, it should be pointed out that the measures taken by banks themselves in managing the risks involved with their portfolio are aimed at the same objective. Indeed, quite often, supervisory authorities issue guidelines to banks regarding the management of their risk exposure.

- portfolio diversification (namely rules on 'large exposures'),
- a leverage ratio,
- liquidity ratios,
- rules on the organisation and operation of in-house risk management units, and
- rules for imposing limits on banks' holdings in other companies, mainly outside the financial system.[205]

2.3.2 Micro-prudential supervision

2.3.2.1 General remarks

Micro-prudential banking regulation can only be effective if coupled with micro-prudential supervision by competent authorities, with a view to:

- assessing the quality of banks' portfolios, and
- ascertaining compliance with the applicable regulatory framework, in order to prevent banks' exposure to exceptional, unmanageable risk levels.

Micro-prudential supervision is conducted by means of:

- regular and extraordinary examinations performed by supervisory authorities themselves, and
- the audit of annual accounts and other financial and organisational aspects by external auditors on behalf of supervisory authorities.

Supervisory authorities may also require banks to draw up recovery and resolution plans on how to deal with financial stress.[206]

2.3.2.2 Institutional aspects

There are three (3) alternative approaches to the institutional structure of micro-prudential banking (and, more generally, financial) supervision.[207] Irrespective of the approach opted for, the established authorities have the competence to supervise and

205 Micro-prudential banking regulation and its policy instruments (as well as its correlation with micro-prudential supervision) are discussed in greater detail in **Barth, Caprio and Levine (2006)**, pp. 110-132 (a study published before the outbreak of the recent (2007-2009) international financial crisis). On the concept and necessity of introducing a leverage ratio, see **Hildebrand (2008)**.

206 See on this **Avgouleas, Goodhart, and Schoenmaker (2010)**.

207 For an overview of these approaches, see **Lastra (2006)**, pp. 324-328, **Group of Thirty (2008)** and, more recently, **Central Bank Governance Group (2011)**. As regards the different governance practices of the financial regulatory and supervisory agencies in 103 IMF member states before the recent (2007-2009) international financial crisis, see **Seelig and Novoa (2009).**

impose sanctions, but also to regulate to a certain extent.[208] Hence, supervisory authorities are also regulatory authorities.

(a) In accordance with the 'sectoral approach', a different supervisory authority is entrusted with the authorisation and micro-prudential supervision of financial firms for each of the three main sectors of the financial system (banking sector, capital markets, and private insurance sector).[209] One of the three is also responsible for conducting ancillary micro-prudential supervision of financial conglomerates.[210]

The task of checking compliance with rules on ensuring capital market efficiency is assigned to the supervisory authority responsible for the authorisation and micro-prudential supervision of investment firms. If the 'sectoral' approach is adopted, an issue arises regarding the competence for the micro-prudential supervision of banks providing investment services in terms of their compliance with rules on ensuring capital market efficiency and investor protection, given that such supervision can be carried out either by the supervisory authority responsible for the authorisation and micro-prudential supervision of banks, or by the capital market supervisory authority.

As regards banks, the supervisory authority may be:

- either the central bank, namely the monetary authority,[211] or
- an administrative authority.

Historically, micro-prudential supervision of banks is the main competence of central banks (with the exception of certain central European states), but over the past twenty pre-crisis years, an increasing amount of states around the world have entrusted independent authorities, apart from central banks, with the (exclusive or concurrent) competence on this supervision.[212] However, following the outbreak of the recent (2007-2009) international financial crisis, many independent supervisory authorities were found to have failed in effectively discharging their tasks and it was ascertained that micro-prudential supervision of banks is closely intertwined with the competence of central banks to ensure the stability of the financial system, thus leading many states (such as Germany and the United Kingdom) to review their practices and take initia-

208 Regulatory competence may be legislatively assigned to supervisory authorities on the basis of a general procurement or on an *ad hoc* basis.

209 As already mentioned under B in Section One above, payment and settlement systems are the fourth main sector of the financial system.

210 Typically, this competence is assigned to the supervisory authority responsible for the supervision of a group's parent company or, in the case of horizontal groups, the supervisory authority responsible for the micro-prudential supervision of the group's largest company.

211 In the majority of economically developed states, central banks are independent authorities (in personal, institutional, financial, and operational terms). For more details on the concept and extent of central bank independence, see **Amtenbrik (1999)** and **Central Bank Governance Group (2009)**, chapters 5 and 6.

212 For a more detailed analysis of arguments for and against the separation of monetary and supervisory competencies of central banks, see – from an extensive literature – **Goodhart and Schoenmaker (1993)**, and **Goodhart (2000a)**. As regards trends in the 1990s and 2000s, up until the onset of the recent crisis, see **Herring and Carmassi (2008)**.

tives to include micro-prudential supervision of banks in the tasks assigned to their central banks.[213]

Under a 'modified sectoral approach', there may be only two supervisory authorities:

- the first for the two main sectors of the financial system (usually the banking sector and capital markets), and
- the second for the third sector.

(b) If the 'full integration approach' is adopted, a single supervisory authority is exclusively competent for the micro-prudential supervision of financial firms operating in the three main sectors of the financial system. Usually, this supervisory authority is an administrative authority, even though in certain countries (such as Ireland) the task is assigned to the central bank.

(c) Finally, under the 'functional approach', responsibilities are allocated between two supervisory authorities, as follows:

- the first is competent for the authorisation and micro-prudential supervision of financial firms operating in the three main sectors of the financial system, as well as for ancillary supervision of financial conglomerates, and
- the second is competent for checking compliance with provisions on ensuring capital market efficiency and investor protection.

In this case, the former may be either the central bank or an administrative authority, and the latter is always an administrative authority.

2.4 Macro-prudential policies[214]

2.4.1 Content

The term 'financial macro-prudential policies' includes the set of (mainly preventive) policies adopted and implemented to limit the financial system's exposure to 'systemic risk' arising from factors not associated with individual financial firms or individual markets and structures of the financial system, but of a more general nature.[215] Macro-

213 See **Davies and Green (2008)**, pp. 187-213, with extensive bibliographical references.

214 As regards this issue, which came to the forefront particularly in the wake of the recent (2007-2009) international financial crisis, see **Committee on the Global Financial System (2010a)**, **Financial Stability Board, International Monetary Fund and Bank for International Settlements (2011)** *Macro-prudential policy tools and frameworks*, February, available at: http://www.financialstabilityboard.org/publications/r_1103.pdf, and **Galati and Moessner (2011)**.

215 See **Financial Stability Board, International Monetary Fund and Bank for International Settlements (2011)**, section 2.

prudential policies seek to address the two above-mentioned dimensions of systemic risk:[216]

(a) The first is the 'time dimension', namely the systemic risk's evolution through time. In this context, macro-prudential policies seek to strengthen the resilience of the financial system at times of economic downturn by limiting procyclicality, which can accentuate systemic risk because of the interactions developed either within the financial system, or between the financial system and the real sector of the economy.[217]

The objective is to 'lean against the financial cycle',[218] bearing in mind that it has been proven historically that failures caused by credit expansion are generated on the upside of the economic cycle, but become apparent on the downside, especially when the economic cycle is in a downturn. More specifically, on the upside of the economic cycle there is typically large credit expansion (with increased numbers of extended loans and credits), significant rises in real property, security and other asset prices, significant leveraging of banks [219] and money and capital markets, as well as maturity mismatches of assets and liabilities in the balance sheet of banks.

In the absence of a proper protection of the financial system, when the economic cycle is in a downturn, problems may emerge for financial firms and they can be aggravated by the need for deleveraging. Usually, under such circumstances the capacity to extend loans and credits is limited, impacting negatively on the real sector of the economy.

(b) The second dimension is the 'cross-sectional dimension', namely allocation of risk in the financial system at any given point in time. In this case, macro-prudential policies are aimed at limiting systemic risk concentration, which could result:

- either from the concurrent exposure of multiple financial institutions to risks arising from similar exposures, or
- from the interconnectedness of such institutions (and the contagion of problems among them), especially if they are systemically important financial institutions ('SIFIs').[220]

216 See **Committee on the Global Financial System (2010a)**, Annex 1, section 2, and **Financial Stability Board, International Monetary Fund and Bank for International Settlements (2011)**, section 2.

217 For a detailed overview of contagion channels between the financial system and the real sector of the economy, see, in the secondary sources, **Basel Committee on Banking Supervision (2011)**, and **Galati and Moessner (2011)**, section 5.2.

218 See **Committee on the Global Financial System (2010a)**, section 2.1.

219 'Leverage' is the (non-risk based) ratio of a bank's total assets (including off-balance sheet items) to its regulatory capital.

220 Regarding the delineation of the definition of SIFIs, see **Huertas and Lastra (2011)**, pp. 255-258 (who use the term 'systemically significant financial institutions' or SSFIs).

2.4.2 Policy instruments

2.4.2.1 Introductory remarks

A mix of instruments is adopted in order to meet the objective for addressing these two dimensions of systemic risk. Specifically:

(a) First of all, it is necessary to set up institutions and procedures for ensuring macro-prudential financial oversight, thus enabling the identification, measurement and assessment of systemic risk.[221]

Macro-prudential oversight of the financial system by central banks is gradually becoming a common instrument for achieving financial stability. The objective of macro-prudential oversight is to limit the distress of the financial system as a whole in order to protect the overall economy against significant losses in real output.

While risks to the financial system may in principle stem from the failure of an individual financial institution – if it is large enough in relation to the state concerned and/or if it has multiple branches/subsidiaries in other states – the much more important international systemic risk arises from exposure of several financial institutions to the same risk factors.[222] *Macro-prudential analysis must therefore pay particular attention to common or correlated shocks and shocks to those segments of the financial system that trigger spillover effects.*

Macro-prudential oversight cannot be meaningful, unless it can somehow impact on supervision at the micro-level, whilst micro-prudential regulation and supervision cannot effectively safeguard financial stability without adequately taking account of macro-level developments.

(b) Moreover, it is necessary to adopt macro-prudential regulations, which:

- are addressed to banks and/or other financial firms, as well as money and capital markets, and
- are differentiated depending on the systemic risk dimension they are called upon to address.[223]

221 See **Financial Stability Board, International Monetary Fund and Bank for International Settlements (2011)**, section 3.
Regarding this issue in the European Union, the European Systemic Risk Board was instituted and started operating on 1 January 2011 (Regulation (EU) no. 1092/2010 of the European Parliament and of the Council of 24 November 2010 *"on European Union macro-prudential oversight of the financial system and establishing a European Systemic Risk Board"* (OJ L 331, 15.12.2010, p. 1-11), and Council Regulation (EU) No 1096/2010 of 17 November 2010 *"conferring specific tasks upon the European Central Bank concerning the functioning of the European Systemic Risk Board"* (OJ L 331, 15.12.2010, p. 162-164).

222 On the content of macro-prudential financial oversight see, *inter alia*, **Borio (2003)** and **Clement (2010).**

223 See **Committee on the Global Financial System (2010a)**, section 3, and **Galati and Moessner (2011)**, section 4. For an overall review of how these measures were adopted, both at a national and international level, see **Financial Stability Board, International Monetary Fund and Bank for International Settlements (2011)**, pp. 5-9.

(c) Finally, it should be noted that oversight of payment and settlement systems has now been formally established as a necessary instrument for addressing the systemic risk's cross-sectional dimension.[224]

2.4.2.2 Macro-prudential regulations to address the systemic risk's time dimension

The policy instruments used in order to achieve the objective of addressing the systemic risk's time dimension, and notably the financial system's procyclicality issue, mainly include the following macro-prudential regulations:

(a) First of all, it is necessary to adopt rules imposing an obligation on banks to set:

- capital conservation buffers,
- countercyclical buffers, and
- forward-looking provisions.[225]

(b) The second, ancillary measure, concerns the development of appropriate micro-prudential regulations such as requiring banks to maintain leverage and liquidity ratios (as mentioned under 2.3.1.2 above), thus making it possible to address the systemic risk's time dimension.

(c) Also included are other prudential measures which:

- either affect the prices of services provided by banks ('price-based prudential tools') such as introducing, when the economic cycle is on the upside, stricter risk weights for calculating the capital adequacy ratio on specific exposures (e.g. loans denominated in foreign exchange, mortgage loans or loans for the purchase of securities and positions in derivatives), or
- affect the quantity of services provided ('quantity-based prudential tools'), such as time-variation, depending on the phase of the economic cycle, the loan-to-value ratios of mortgage loans, and the debt-to-income ratios in mortgage and consumer loans.

(d) Finally, the systemic risk's time dimension (and notably the procyclicality caused by leveraging capital markets) can be addressed by stricter rules imposing margins and haircuts on positions in securities and derivatives during economic upturns.[226]

224 See **Committee on Payment and Settlement Systems (2005)** *"Central bank oversight of payment and settlement systems"*, May, available at: http://www.bis.org/publ/cpss68.htm.
225 See **Brunnenmeier et al. (2009)**, chapter 4.
226 See **Committee on the Global Financial System (2010b)**.

2.4.2.3 Macro-prudential regulations to address the systemic risk's cross-sectional dimension

The policy instruments used in order to achieve the objective of addressing the systemic risk's cross-sectional dimension mainly include the following macro-prudential regulations:

(a) The key measure is to adopt rules on the resolution of systemically important banks (and other category of financial firms) exposed to insolvency, that will enable (in part or in whole) the suspension of their operations without:

- jeopardising the stability of the banking (and, more generally, the financial) system,
- or making state intervention necessary for their bailout, invoking the argument that they are too-big-to-fail.

(b) The second measure is ancillary and consists in adopting appropriate specific micro-prudential regulations (such as rules to cover banks against exposure to credit risk from specific portfolio items, included within the regulatory framework on capital adequacy), thus making it possible to address the systemic risk's cross-sectional dimension.

(c) Measures are also taken to strengthen infrastructures in relation to over-the-counter (OTC) derivatives, notably the obligation for clearing OTC transactions through central counterparties.[227]

(d) Finally, addressing the systemic risk's cross-sectional dimension can also be achieved with the introduction of restrictions on the range of services provided by systemically important financial institutions (especially banks).[228]

2.5 Reorganisation, resolution and winding-up of troubled banks

In light of the above, the key difference between the banking sector and other sectors of the financial system (as well as other sectors of the economy), which renders imperative the adoption of measures on micro- and macro-prudential regulation of bank operation, lies in the fact that an individual bank's insolvency may, under certain circumstances associated with depositor behaviour, the economic conjuncture, banks' financial structure, and the state's involvement in the banking system:

227 See the report of the **Financial Stability Board (2010)** *"Implementing OTC Derivatives Market Reforms"*, October, available at: http://www.financialstabilityboard.org/publications/r_101025.pdf.

228 See **Financial Stability Board, International Monetary Fund and Bank for International Settlements (2011)**, p. 9, paragraph 5(iv).

- lead to the default of other banks (through various channels, as mentioned above) and, as a result,
- destabilise the banking system and thus have a serious negative impact on the functioning of the real economy.

In this context, there is also a need for interventionist policies aimed at preventing the erosion of the net worth of a bank that is exposed to insolvency.

(a) This objective is firstly achieved by means of reorganisation measures for failing banks. Supervisory authorities can prevent an unviable bank from becoming insolvent to the detriment of its depositors and public confidence in the financial system, by restructuring it.[229] The means to this end include:

- replacing the bank's management and appointing an administrator,
- arranging mergers with healthy banks, and
- increasing mandatorily the bank's own funds (subject to limitations set by company law with regard to the rights of existing shareholders).[230]

(b) In order to ward off the moral hazard in case of 'too-big-to-fail' or 'systemically important' banks, the failure/closing down of which would endanger the stability of the banking (and, more generally, financial) system, or require a government bailout, the following resolution tools may be put in place by a resolution authority:

(i) sell all or part of a failing bank's business to another bank, and simultaneously withdraw the former's licence and liquidate the failing bank,
(ii) transfer the 'clean' assets and essential functions onto a publicly controlled 'bridge bank', again with a simultaneous licence withdrawal of the failing bank and its liquidation,
(iii) separate clean and toxic assets between good and bad banks in order to carry out restructuring, and/or
(iv) impose losses on bondholders and shareholders, by order of seniority.

The resolution fund, necessary in this case in order to provide funding, may be the deposit guarantee scheme or a separate entity funded, in principle, by the banking sector.

(c) Failing all the above, winding-up procedures are put into place following the withdrawal a bank's operating license. Nevertheless, in this case (as opposed to the case of resolution (see under (b) above), the deposit guarantee system must be activated.[231]

It has been rightfully argued that supervisory or other competent authorities are chronically unable to restructure banks before their net worth has been depleted.

229 See **Guttentag and Herring (1988)**, pp. 15-16, and **Santomero and Hoffman (1998)**.

230 On this issue, see **Claessens, Herring and Schoenmaker (2010)**, as well as the individual contributions to the collective volume **Lastra (2011 ed.)**, both with further references. For the detailed concept and content of 'resolution', see **Huertas and Lastra (2011)**, pp. 258-267.

231 For more details on deposit system guarantees, see below, under 2.6.

Guttentag and Herring (1987b) *identify three reasons for this slow response of authorities:*[232]

(i) Firstly, there is a lag between the time the bank has become unviable and the authorities recognise this (the 'recognition lag').
(ii) There is a second lag (the 'reaction lag'), extending from the time the authorities recognise the non-viability of the bank until they decide to terminate it.
(iii) Finally, the 'implementation lag' is the period between the time the authorities initiate the procedure on closing down an unviable bank and the moment when the bank actually terminates its operations.

2.6 Deposit guarantee

2.6.1 Contributions of deposit guarantee systems

The establishment of a deposit guarantee system is first of all required for the protection of small depositors. The concept of 'small depositor' refers to those categories of savers who, given their limited knowledge, are insufficiently informed in order to be in a position to assess the solvency of the banks entrusted with their savings. This category of savers, usually hold a significant share of their total savings in their bank accounts (inter alia, for conducting payments), and they cannot be expected to discipline the market by behaving as 'investors'.[233]

Deposit guarantee systems, however, also act as buffer mechanisms in the event of a banking crisis, contributing to ensuring the stability of the banking system.

The failure of coordination among depositors under adverse market conditions, leading to runs and panics, can be addressed either by suspending the convertibility of deposits into cash, or by the establishment of deposit guarantee systems. A deposit guarantee system is typically funded exclusively by bank contributions (usually without the contribution of the government and/or the central bank, which are only participating in the system's administration), which guarantees the default-free character of deposits in the event of bank failure. The establishment of deposit guarantee systems is aimed at eliminating the incentive for massive withdrawals from individual banks or, in the worst-case scenario, the entire banking system.

In particular, the system is assigned with the task of compensating depositors in the event of their bank's closure and performs a dual function:

232 See **Guttentag and Herring (1987b)**, pp. 48-50.

233 Small depositors must be able to have access to safe financial instruments for their payments and savings. Taking into account that banks – just like all other enterprises operating in accordance with market rules – are exposed to insolvency risk (resulting in authorisation withdrawal), it is through regulatory intervention, i.e. the establishment of deposit guarantee systems, that bank deposits become a relatively safe financial instrument.

(a) On the one hand, it assures small and unsophisticated depositors that the guarantee fund will compensate them if their bank is unable to convert their deposits into cash.[234] This first contribution lies in eliminating the incentive for hurried cash withdrawals from deposits with banks facing real or alleged liquidity and solvency problems and/or the eventuality of ceasing operations. If a bank cannot meet depositor claims, the incentive for such withdrawals is eliminated by the presence of a body responsible for reimbursing each depositor to an amount equal to his/her deposit (normally up to a certain ceiling, known as the 'coverage level').

Where there is no adequate micro-prudential supervision and a bank is particularly exposed to risks associated with the business it conducts in the banking market, but also money and capital markets, and if its own funds do not suffice to absorb losses, the emergence of such risks might lead to a decline in the present value of the banking book and, in a worst-case scenario, render the bank insolvent. In this case, the dissemination of news, even uncorroborated, regarding a potential, temporary or definitive, termination of such a bank's operations might urge depositors to rush to withdraw their deposits from the given bank.[235] *The existence, therefore, of a deposit guarantee system eliminates the incentive for depositor panic after the spreading of news on the financial condition of individual banks.*

(b) On the other hand, the deposit guarantee system protects the banking system from massive withdrawals by panic-stricken depositors. Thus, deposit guarantee systems alleviate some of the inherent problems leading to runs and panics. The second contribution of deposit guarantee systems to the stability of the banking system is that they act as a buffer against the spreading of panic conditions across the entire banking system through indiscriminate cash withdrawals from most banks that result in the depletion of banks' net worth. This is done by guaranteeing depositor coverage across all banks and preventing healthy banks from turning 'bad' due to their objective inability to meet the widespread demand for deposits' withdrawal.

Depositor panic, which might stem from more than one reason, is, as mentioned above, an occurrence that results in mass depositor withdrawals (from their banks). Under such circumstances of mass withdrawals even the most solvent bank would not be in a position to meet credit obligations, but only if it borrows funds on money and capital markets or from its central bank at particularly high rates, or if it liquidates its assets at unfavourably low prices.

234 See **Carisano (1992)**, p. 17.

235 The lack of coordination of depositor actions is justified by the specificity of bank deposits as financial instruments: given that depositor claims have a stable market value which does not vary in accordance with the fluctuating value of a bank's portfolio, those depositors who withdraw in time receive cash payments to the full nominal value of their deposits, while others receive nothing. If the nominal value of bank deposits was marked to market on a daily basis, reflecting their present value (which is a function of the present value of the bank's portfolio), there would be no uncoordinated hurry on the part of depositors. In this case, the loss from the decline in portfolio value would be equally incurred by each depositor (as is the case with unitholders of Undertakings for Collective Investment in Transferable Securities).

As a component of the bank safety net, the deposit guarantee system seeks to curb incentives for depositor involvement in banking runs and panics by guaranteeing the transformation of illiquid bank assets into cash and maintaining public confidence in the banking system.

Deposit guarantee systems are characterised by five (5) main attributes:[236]

(i) The system assumes an explicit obligation; when a bank fails, it is required to compensate its depositors to the extent that their financial claims are covered.
(ii) The guarantee provided by the system is non-discretionary; once the operation of the bank has been terminated, depositors have a direct claim for compensation against the deposit guarantee system, no matter why the bank has failed.
(iii) Deposit guarantee is an *ex-ante* 'safe device' for depositors; it makes them certain of compensation, thus curbing the incentives for banking runs and panics.
(iv) The level of protection offered by the system is usually limited; the value of the intervention has a ceiling depending on the amount of covered deposits and the percentage guaranteed.
(v) The cost of bank failure is incurred by the banking system ('no taxpayers' money solution'), which funds the deposit guarantee system either *ex ante* through the contributions of its members, or *ex post* with payment of the amounts required for the compensation of depositors if a bank's license were to be revoked.[237]

2.6.2 Problems arising from the operation of deposit guarantee systems

The obviously positive contribution of a deposit guarantee system in terms of safeguarding public confidence in the banking system may be mitigated, in reality, by the adverse effects of its operation. There are two main negative effects of deposit guarantee systems:

- banks' exposure to moral hazard (see 2.6.2.1 and 2.6.2.2 below), and
- the 'too-big-to-fail' problem (under 2.6.2.3).

2.6.2.1 Exposure to moral hazard in terms of portfolio riskiness

Participation in a deposit guarantee system enables bank managers to finance risky assets with partially insured liabilities. Excessive risk-taking is also made possible by the fact that insured depositors lack the incentive to monitor and control their bank.

236 See **Carisano (1992)**, pp. 22-29.

237 It should be pointed out that the body responsible for the management of a deposit guarantee system may also have supervisory competencies on banks, the deposits of which are guaranteed by it, as in the case of the Federal Deposit Insurance Corporation (FDIC) in the United States. See **Carisano (1994)**, pp. 156-161.

For these reasons it is claimed that the existence of deposit guarantee undermines the safety of banks and creates the need *per se* for enhanced prudential supervision.[238]

Hence, the first adverse effect is that participation in a deposit guarantee system gives banks an incentive to take greater risks than they would otherwise have, if their depositors were uninsured. Such behaviour on the part of banks, also known as exposure to moral hazard, is a rational reaction to the behaviour of uninsured depositors who seek protection from the competent authority rather than the bank. This also applies to uninsured depositors who consider that they must be compensated by the competent authority *ex post*, once the payment procedure is put into effect.

Inadequate market discipline can be explained by the fact that depositors – either explicitly insured or expecting to be compensated ex post after their bank's authorisation is withdrawn, do not have an incentive to monitor the development of their bank's financial condition. Therefore, depositors do not request (as would normally happen in a market without deposit guarantees) higher interest rates from a bank with relatively lower solvency. Banks' tendency to take greater risks if they participate (precisely because they participate) in deposit guarantee systems is even stronger in the absence of correlation between paid premia and the riskiness of investment decisions (if applicable). The lack of variable premia means that investment proposals can easily be presented to the market as equally safe and increases bank exposure to insolvency as a result of greater exposure to credit risk (and other risks as well).

2.6.2.2 Exposure to moral hazard in terms of capital adequacy

The second adverse effect of deposit guarantee systems regards exposure to moral hazard of participating banks in terms of the level of their own funds. Since insured depositors do not have an incentive to control their bank, the latter tends to reduce its capital adequacy ratio (which supposedly contributes to increasing its solvency and, hence, the level of public confidence), whilst reducing its 'antibodies' for absorbing losses in the event of risk emergence.

In this case, a spillover mechanism may be set in motion. The smaller a bank's capital base, the greater its tendency to take extensive risks, as the profits from higher returns stay with shareholders, whereas losses are rolled over to the deposit guarantee system.

238 Alternative means for encouraging proper portfolio management in the presence of deposit guarantees are market-value accounting, risk-based deposit insurance premiums and radical structural solutions. For a more detailed overview of these alternatives, see **Carisano (1992)**, pp. 128-151.

2.6.2.3 Differential treatment of banks deemed 'too big (to be left) to fail'

The *ex post* treatment of small and large banks participating in a deposit guarantee system can be unequal under given circumstances. Governments may feel urged to bailout depositors of large failing banks, if these are considered 'too-big-to-fail' (or, more accurately, 'too-big-to-be-left-to-fail'), due to the extent of the losses they would cause to their creditors. Hence, depositors in large banks may be covered *ex post* more comprehensively than those of other banks.[239] By contrast, small banks fully assume the losses incurred as a result of an insolvency decision on the part of supervisory or judicial authorities. Such behaviour by the competent supervisory authority can be explained by the fact that if a big bank's authorisation were to be withdrawn, the risk of spillover effects in the banking market would be severe.

2.7 Last-resort lending

Last-resort lending is the provision of liquidity assistance by monetary authorities to one or more banks experiencing difficulties with converting deposits into cash because of an unexpected increase in cash needs.[240] Monetary authorities may intervene in their capacity as 'lenders of last resort' in order to address a solvent bank's extraordinary liquidity needs, so as to avoid its insolvency in the event of a potentially extensive, albeit temporary, exposure to liquidity risk.[241]

This form of intervention is at the bottom of the list of circuit breakers which make up the 'bank safety net', but was historically the first to be introduced by monetary authorities in their effort to manage financial crises.[242] Lending of last resort (or emergency liquidity assistance) performs a dual function:

- on the one hand, it enables solvent banks to control losses resulting from an abrupt exposure to liquidity risk and prevents the development of illiquidity-caused solvency problems, and
- on the other hand, it prevents the closure of banks suddenly exposed to liquidity risk[243] in order to control the negative impact of their failure on the economy.

239 For instance, this was the case of depositors with two big failed US banking institutions, Continental Illinois Bank (defunct in 1984) and the Bank of New England (closed in 1991), who received compensation for the entirety of their claims.

240 See **Guttentag and Herring (1983)**, p. 4.

241 This responsibility is assigned to the central bank due to the operational synergies that exist between the conduct of monetary policy and the oversight of payment systems.

242 This circuit breaker is closely linked to the conduct of monetary policy and provides a good manifestation of the close links existing between the monetary and the financial system.

243 See **Guttentag and Herring (1987a)**, pp. 163-165.

The solvency of a bank is theoretically a precondition for recourse to last-resort lending.[244] However, even though last-resort lending is meant to be confined to solvent banks experiencing a liquidity crisis, the provision of loans (always under 'adequate' collateral) can also be extended to undercapitalised banks, depending on central bank assessment of general market conditions. In fact, during a generalised crisis the latter may be tempted to support even a bank whose solvency is known to be doubtful in order to avoid contagious effects.[245]

The power of central banks to assume the function of lender of last resort can only be substantiated interpretatively. This is due to the fact that, in accordance with the 'principle of constructive ambiguity',[246] no state has explicit legislative provisions granting such competence to the central bank, given that such provisions would:

- alone put the stability of the banking system at greater risk due to banks' greater exposure to moral hazard, and thus insolvency,[247] and as a result,
- render stricter – than generally required – micro-prudential regulations necessary for the prevention of banks' exposure to risks undertaken in the conduct of their business.[248]

When comparing the last-resort lending function to deposit insurance systems, the following differences manifest themselves:[249]

(i) Since the liquidity provided by the central bank to a failing bank is not contingent, this function is discretionary; it depends, in principle at least, on the central bank's assessment of the solvency of the bank experiencing liquidity strains.
(ii) The position of depositors is ambiguous, since they are not certain *a priori* whether the central bank will intervene or not.
(iii) The liquidity provided by the central bank in its function as lender of last resort has no constraints; *in extremis*, it can be limitless.

244 See **Guttentag and Herring (1987a)**, pp. 163-165. Under European law, the provision of liquidity to insolvent banks also goes against provision on the prohibition (in principle) of state aids. For a more detailed discussion, see **Smits (1997)**, pp. 270-271, and **Lastra (2000)**, pp. 207-208.

245 **Guttentag and Herring (1987a**, p. 164) list numerous examples on this situation. The current eurozone fiscal crisis provides another striking example.

246 According to **Herring and Litan (1995)**, pp. 126-131, the 'constructive ambiguity' policy has signfiicant adverse effects, as it leads in reality to unequal treatment between big (systemically important) and small banks. For a detailed overview of this subject, and more particularly on the need for constuctive ambiguity ('explicit last-resort lending function'), see **Guttentag and Herring (1987a)**, pp. 167-172.

247 This debate has been discussed by **Bagehot** already since 1873.

248 In the euro area, there is an emergency liquidity assistance, which (in accordance with what was mentioned above) is not based on specific provisions of european or member state law, but is at the European Central Bank's/National Central Banks' complete discretion. See **European Central Bank (2007)**.

249 See **Carisano (1992)**, pp. 22-29.

It should be pointed out that at times of crisis, there are three (3) alternatives to the 'central bank money solution', i.e. central banks acting as lender of last resort, which are the following:

- provision of liquidity to failing banks through coordinated actions of the private banking sector ('private money solution'),[250]
- government bailouts of banks, the authorisation withdrawal of which is expected to have a serious systemic impact ('taxpayers money solution'),[251] and
- one-off, non-standard monetary policy measures by central banks.[252]

Table 4: Institutional aspects with regard to the preservation of the stability of the banking sector

Policy instruments	Competent institution	Attributes of the institution
Bank authorisation	Supervisory authority	Central bank or other administrative authority
Micro-prudential and macro-prudential regulation of banks	• Parliament • Supervisory authority	• General regulator • upon delegation
Micro-prudential supervision of banks	Supervisory authority	Central bank or other administrative authority
Macro-prudential oversight of the financial system (including the banking sector)	Central bank or monetary authority/agency (in most cases)	
Reorganisation, resolution and winding-up of banks	• Supervisory or judicial authority • Resolution authority and fund	On a case-by-case basis
Deposit guarantee	Deposit guarantee scheme	Entity of private or public law
Last-resort lending	Central bank or monetary authority/agency	
Provision of state subsidies to failing banks (government bailout)	National Ministry of Finance	

250 See **Padoa-Schioppa (2000)**, pp. 24-26.
251 Ibid.
252 See **Borio and Disyatat (2009)**, and **Lenza, Pill and Reichlin (2010)**.

CHAPTER TWO

THE MAKING OF PUBLIC INTERNATIONAL FINANCIAL LAW

SECTION THREE DEFINITION, HISTORICAL EVOLUTION AND LEVELS OF MAKING AND ENFORCEMENT OF PUBLIC INTERNATIONAL FINANCIAL LAW

A. Definition, delimitation and branches of public international financial law

1. Definition

Public international financial law (hereinafter also referred to as 'international financial law'), together with public international monetary law, constitute one of the three (3) branches of international economic law, the other two being international trade law and international law of foreign investments.[253] According to the functional approach adopted in this study, public international financial law[254] is defined as the sum of rules of international economic law aimed at:

(i) the liberalisation of international trade in financial services,[255] and
(ii) the achievement, by resorting to international cooperation, of specific policy objectives justifying regulatory intervention in the financial system.

In this respect, attention should be drawn to the following initial remarks:

(a) Public international financial law, as 'public international law', does not contain any rules of private law.[256]

(b) Public international financial law, as 'international law', is adopted at multilateral level. Hence, it does not include:

- the rules of administrative financial law adopted on a bilateral basis,
- or the rules of financial law adopted on a regional basis, such the rules of the European financial law

253 For the definition and content of international economic law, see **Lowenfeld (2003)**, pp. 1-8, **Carreau et Juillard (2005)**, pp. 1-6, and **Herdegen (2008)**, pp. 1-6.
254 **Norton (2001)**, pp. 11-13, talks about 'global public financial law'.
255 The liberalisation of international trade in financial services is an integral part but still a distinct subset of the liberalisation of international trade in services, which refers to the abolition of measures adopted unilaterally by states, in the form of laws, regulations, procedures, decisions, or administrative actions, and restrictively affecting trade in services. Hence it is also reasonable to argue that the relevant provisions are part of international trade law. This is really a marginal case.
256 On the delimitation of public international financial law vis-à-vis the law of international financial transactions, see just below under 2.2 of this subsection.

(c) Public international financial law, as 'financial law', uses as a point of reference the two functions of the financial system, its infrastructures and the services provided in it (as mentioned above in Section One), as well as the objectives of regulatory intervention in the financial system (under Section Two).

(d) Finally, public international financial law, as 'law', refers to institutions and to rules, which no matter whether legally binding or not,[257] have an impact on the legal order of individual states.

The formation of public international financial law requires resort to specific principles of international law of which:

- some pertain only to the liberalisation of international trade in financial services,
- others pertain only to regulatory intervention in the financial system, and
- some pertain to both.

These principles will be further discussed below in Section Six, which provides detailed examples of the Basel Committee's work.

2. Delimitation

2.1 Delimitation vis-à-vis public international monetary law

Public international financial law must, first of all, be distinguished from public international monetary law. The latter is defined as the set of rules of international law governing the monetary and foreign exchange relations between independent states, hence the operation of the international monetary system.[258] In this context, the following should be pointed out:

(a) Monetary is the system (based on national legislation) which contains the unit of account of a state (by reference to its name and any applicable subdivisions of it), and comprises, at an institutional level, a central bank (or similar 'monetary authority') which enjoys the exclusive privilege of issuing national banknotes (on the liability side of central bank balance sheets).[259]

(b) The financial system (also based on national legislation) is closely connected to the monetary system. The close link between the two systems is mainly attributable to the fact that deposits, out of the main sources of bank financing, are, concurrently, the core component of money in the framework of the monetary system's operation.[260]

257 See below under C 3.1.3 of this Section.

258 From the extensive literature on this issue, see **Lastra (2006)**, pp. 345-370 (on the historical evolution of international monetary law) and pp. 371-445 (on the law of the International Monetary Fund), **Lowenfeld (2003)**, pp. 499-564, **Proctor (2005)**, pp. 499-618, **Bordo and James (2010)** (on the role of the IMF), and **Hagan (2010a)** and **(2010b)** (on the future role of the IMF).

259 See **Proctor (2005)**, p. 57. On the current discussion with regard to the extent of central bank balance sheets, see **Caruana (2011)**.

260 On the different concepts of money, see **Proctor (2005)**, p. 5-44, and **Vicuña (2010)**.

In this sense, the term 'financial system' is frequently used (albeit not in the present study) in a way which also covers the monetary system.

(c) In most cases, the main objective of regulatory intervention in the monetary system is controlling the quantity of money which is produced and circulated, with a view to achieving specific 'macro-economic goals' – *par excellence* – maintaining price stability.[261] Traditionally, the agency which is usually entrusted with the 'management of the monetary system' (that is, the definition and implementation of monetary policy) is the central bank.[262]

This is the reason why the central bank is usually termed 'monetary authority', irrespective of whether it has also been assigned other tasks (such as safeguarding the stability of the financial system), as already discussed under C in Section Two above.[263]

(d) In monetary systems, the interdependence of states arises from the fact that the national currency of one state is exchanged with the currency of other states in order to fulfil the payment leg of international transactions (commercial and/or financial),[264] on the basis of a price which is termed 'foreign exchange' (the level of which is determined initially on the basis of the demand for and the supply of any pair of currencies).

Accordingly, public international monetary law determines the framework governing inter-state foreign exchange relations. In this context, states have a choice mainly between five (5) options:[265]

- a regime of purely floating exchange rates ('free floating'),
- a regime of controlled floating exchange rates in which interventions of central banks are permitted in order to influence the foreign exchange of national currencies ('managed floating'),[266]
- a regime of floating exchange rates within a specific fluctuation range ('target zones'),[267]

261 In some states (such as the United States and Canada), the main objective of monetary intervention does not only consist in maintaining price stability, but also achieving other macroeconomic goals, such as contributing to economic development. For a comparative study of various central bank objectives, see **Central Bank Governance Group (2009)**, pp. 21-25 (summarised in Table 1 of that study).

262 In some states this function has been assigned to 'Currency Boards'. See **Proctor (2005)**, pp. 801-805.

263 **Central Bank Governance Group (2009)**, pp. 25-49 (in particular Table 2), and in more detail **Central Bank Governance Group (2011)**.

264 From a strictly legal point of view, financial transactions are themselves commercial, since financial service providers are usually commercial companies and their operations are commercial.

265 See **Eichengreen (1994)**, pp. 9-28.

266 Such is the current international monetary regime.

267 Such a regime is the current European Exchange Rate Mechanism ('ERM II') linking the single European currency to the currencies of certain member states of the European Union that have opted out of the euro.

- a regime of fixed exchange rates in which, however, adjustment of the foreign exchange through devaluation is permitted,[268] and
- a regime of irrevocably fixed exchange rates, which leads to monetary unification.[269]

It is useful in this context to make also a distinction between international and regional monetary regimes.[270]

Public international monetary law also contains rules with regard to:

- the adequacy of reserve assets, acceptable to the international community, to financially support international economic transactions (the 'question of liquidity'),
- the make-up of the portfolio of assets that may be requested and supplied as international (foreign) reserves (the 'question of credibility'),
- the suitability of the procedures by means of which states can neutralise the imbalances in international payments by having recourse to the use of international reserves (the 'question of adjustment'),
- the transparency in the conduct of monetary policy (as well as public finance policy, which directly and indirectly affects the operation of the monetary and financial system), and ensuring the correctness and accuracy of the economic data published by states in connection with such policies,
- the safeguarding of conditions of normality in the international movement of capital, and
- the adequacy of procedures for the analysis of the sensitivity of economies to crises and the planning of national economic policies.[271]

2.2 Other delimitations

Public international financial law, as defined above, is also to be clearly distinguished from the following branches of law:

(a) The first is the international law of international (or 'cross-border') financial transactions,[272] a subcategory of the international law of business transactions, which contains rules adopted at international level with regard to the contractual content of such

268 Such a regime was the 'Bretton Woods system' governed by the IMF, which was in force from 1945 to 1971. On this see below under B 1.1 of this Section.

269 On the legal aspects of monetary unions and their distinction from other international monetary regimes, see **Proctor (2005)**, pp. 623-633, and 806-816, and **Diatta (2007)**, pp. 53-86.

270 The most typical example of a regional monetary regime nowadays, which also operates in the form of a monetary union, is the monetary union of the European Union in operation since 1 January 1999. For a general overview of existing monetary unions, see **Diatta (2007)**, pp. 3-4. More specifically on the European monetary union, see indicatively **Smits (1997)**, **Hadjiemmanuil (2006a)**, **Lastra (2006)**, **Louis (2009)**, and **Snyder (2011)**.

271 See **Genberg and Swoboda (1991)**.

272 For a definition and the subcategories of these transactions, see **Bizzozero and Robinson (2010)**, pp. 25-35.

transactions. Such rules are adopted by inter-governmental organisations and trade associations, such as:

- the International Chamber of Commerce (ICC),[273]
- the United Nations Commission on International Trade Law (UNCITRAL),[274]
- the International Institute for the Unification of Private Law (UNIDROIT),[275] and
- the International Swaps and Derivatives Association (ISDA).[276]

(b) The second branch is private international financial law, which governs international financial transactions as regards:

- the determination of the law applicable to each individual international financial transaction, which may be the *lex fori* or the *lex causae*, depending on the particulars of each case ('conflicts of law'),
- the public order (or mandatory) rules, and
- the substantial rules of private international law, which directly govern international financial transactions.[277]

The relevant provisions may be adopted either at national level or by means of international treaties and through *lex mercatoria* rules. In the latter case they resemble to the provisions of the law of international financial transactions.

(c) Finally, the third branch is the law pertaining to inter-state financial transactions, which is usually covered by bilateral agreements.

3. Branches of public international financial law

3.1 Introduction

Taking into account the considerations developed above (in Section Two) with regard to the policy objectives justifying regulatory intervention in the financial system, it is the author's view that public international financial law contains seven (separate but closely linked) individual branches:

- public international banking law (see under 3.2 below),
- public international capital markets law (under 3.3),
- public international insurance law (under 3.4),
- public international financial conglomerates law (under 3.5),

273 For more information see http://www.iccwbo.org.

274 For more information see http://www.uncitral.org, as well as **Gross (2007)**, **Berger (2010)**, and **UNCITRAL (2007)**.

275 See http://www.unidroit.org, and also **Oser (2008)** and **Berger (2010)**.

276 See http://www.isda.org, and also **McKnight (2008)**, pp. 611-615, and **Zerey (2010)**, pp. 143-180.

277 On this see **McKnight (2008)**, pp. 167-257, and **Proctor (2010)**, pp. 646-650 (from the perspective of UK law).

- public international payment and settlement systems law (under 3.6),
- public international financial services consumer law (under 3.7), and
- public international law on combating the use of the financial system for the commitment of economic crimes (under 3.8).

The approach adopted for the definition of the individual branches of public international financial law is the 'functional approach' for two reasons:

(a) In the author's view, this approach is not only suitable, but also necessary given that, if the definition is based on an 'institutional approach' (focusing on the categories of financial firms falling within the personal field of application of relevant provisions), there would be extensive overlapping between individual branches.

Indicatively, it can be mentioned that the provisions of a significant subset of the rules contained in the legal acts constituting the sources of all branches of international financial law, as defined above, are applied to banks. If the institutional approach were to be adopted, these provisions would need to be concurrently included:

- *in public international banking law, alternatively defined in this case as the 'law of banks', and*
- *in public international capital markets law, if they also apply to investment firms.*[278]

(b) Taking into account that banks (and all other categories of financial firms) are also subject to the provisions of other branches of international economic law not included in public international financial law (e.g. international competition law),[279] these provisions should also be included, for reasons of consistency, in international banking law, if the functional approach is not adopted, which would lead, in the author's view, to inappropriate results.

3.2 Public international banking law

Public international banking law is defined as the set of rules of international financial law, which apply exclusively to banks, whereby the following two objectives are sought:

- the first is to ensure the liberalisation of trade in banking services,[280] and
- the second consists in ensuring the stability of the banking system, which could be disrupted as a result of the occurrence of contagious bank failures.

278 In the remaining subsections (under 3.2-3.8), specific reference will be made (in *italics*) to the extent to which the rules of other branches of international financial law (apart from international banking law) also apply to banks.

279 On this branch of international law, see **Fox (2003)**.

280 To the extent that payment services are mainly provided by banks (which is the case in several states), it is legitimate to include the rules on the liberalisation of these services in international banking law as well.

For the achievement of the latter objective and in full consistency with the analysis in Section Two above (under B), public international banking law contains rules on:

- the authorisation of banks,
- the micro-prudential and macro-prudential regulation of banks,
- the micro-prudential supervision of banks,
- the macro-prudential oversight of the banking (and, more generally. the financial) system,
- the reorganisation, resolution and winding-up of banks, and
- deposit guarantee.

On the contrary, in principle, there are no rules on the functioning of central banks as lenders of last resort, since this function is exercised in an environment of 'constructive ambiguity'.[281]

3.3 Public international capital markets law

Public international capital markets law is the branch of international financial law containing provisions aimed at complying with four (4) rationales:

- to ensure the liberalisation of trade in investment services,
- to ensure the stability of capital markets,
- to ensure investor protection as well as capital markets' integrity, efficiency and transparency, and
- to ensure the compensation of investors in case of suspension of operations of a firm providing investment services (bank or investment firm), if such firm is not in a position to return funds or financial instruments belonging to the investors.

It is worth mentioning that public international capital markets law does not include the provisions pertaining to regulatory intervention in securities clearing and settlement systems, which constitute the infrastructure for the functioning of capital markets. It is appropriate, in the author's view, for these provisions to be included in the international payment and settlement systems law (see under 3.6 below), since, according to the internationally prevalent practice and terminology, the meaning of the term 'securities clearing and settlement systems' falls within the meaning of the more generic term 'payment and settlement systems'.[282]

A considerable amount of the provisions of public international capital markets law may also apply to banks for two reasons:

281 See under B 2.6 in Section Two above.

282 As mentioned in Section One (under B), the term 'payment and settlement systems' includes both:
- the 'pure' payment systems, including payment clearing and settlement systems, and
- the securities clearing and settlement systems, used in the clearing and settlement of both securities and payments related to the purchase and sale of securities.

- as already mentioned, in several states around the world, banks are entitled to provide the entire range of investment services and activities on an individual basis, according to the 'universal banking model',[283] and
- in addition, a large number of banks are listed in regulated markets and, therefore, the provisions on the obligations pertaining to listed companies also apply to them.

In this sense, the delimitation of the provisions of public international financial law applicable to banks and falling under public international capital markets law, vis-à-vis the provisions applied thereto and coming under public international banking law, usually requires considerable attention.

3.4 Public international insurance law

Public international insurance law is the branch of international financial law containing provisions seeking:

- to ensure the liberalisation of trade in insurance and re-insurance services, and
- to safeguard the stability of the insurance sector of the financial system.

Notwithstanding very few exceptions, the provisions of public international insurance law usually do not apply to banks. This is due to the fact that, in the majority of states, the provision of insurance and reinsurance services is only permitted for undertakings specifically authorised for this purpose (namely insurance and reinsurance companies), and in any event, not banks.

3.5 Public international financial conglomerates law

Public international financial conglomerates law is the branch of international financial law that contains provisions with regard to the supplementary supervision of financial conglomerates (groups combining banks, insurance companies and investment firms), in order to safeguard the stability of the financial system as a whole as regards their activity.[284]

The provisions of this branch apply to banks only to the extent of their participation in financial conglomerates, and over and above the provisions of public international banking law on the supervision of banks, on an individual (solo) and consolidated basis.[285]

283 See under C 2.2.3 in Section One above.

284 With regard to the definition, characteristics and corporate structures of these financial groups, see **Dierick (2004)**, pp. 10-19.

285 Ibid., pp. 20-22.

3.6 Public international payment and settlement systems law

Public international payment and settlement systems law is the branch of international financial law containing provisions seeking to meet two (2) policy objectives:

- safeguarding the stability of payment and settlement systems, and
- safeguarding the efficiency of such systems.

The majority of the provisions of public international payment and settlement systems law apply to banks either as payment services providers, or because of their participation in payment and settlement systems, as members and/or shareholders.

3.7 Public international financial services consumer law

Public international financial services consumer law is the branch of international financial law that contains provisions seeking to ensure the protection of the economic interests of consumers dealing with financial firms, with a view to:

- correcting the information asymmetry usually existing between consumers and financial firms,
- addressing the problem of consumers' reduced negotiating capacity *vis-à-vis* financial services providers, and
- combating consumer over-indebtedness.

Apart from the above 'specific' provisions of public international financial services consumer law, certain provisions of horizontal nature regarding all or certain product or service supplier categories may also apply. Therefore, from a systematic viewpoint, the provisions of international consumer law that apply to the field of financial services would come under three categories:

- provisions applicable exclusively to banks and other categories of undertakings entitled to pursue the business of granting credit in the context of their commercial, business or professional activity,
- provisions applicable to all categories of financial firms, including banks, but not to other categories of services providers, and
- 'horizontal' provisions applicable to all services providers, including financial firms (including banks).

This branch of public international financial law also contains rules pertaining to 'financial literacy'.

3.8 Public international law on combating the use of the financial system for the commitment of economic crimes

The public international law on combating the use of the financial system for the commitment of economic crimes is the branch of international financial law that contains provisions seeking to prevent the use of the financial system for the conduct of economic crimes (such as 'money laundering', terrorist financing and payment instruments fraud), and to contain such crimes.

The relevant provisions apply fully to banks, and it can be reasonably argued that the main reason for their adoption was to combat economic crime committed through the banking sector of the financial system. However, it is not only banks that may come under the scope of these provisions, but also the vast majority of the other categories of financial firms. Moreover, several provisions of this branch of international financial law (especially the ones relating to 'money laundering') apply not only to financial firms, but also to undertakings and professionals outside the financial system (such as casinos, notaries and lawyers), with a view to addressing regulatory arbitrage.[286]

B. The historical evolution of the institutions of public international financial law

1. Introductory remarks

1.1 The environment until 1971

Until 1971, there was no single international institution to discuss issues of international financial law. This was due to the fact that the banking systems, the capital markets, the insurance markets as well as the payment and settlement systems of economically developed and less developed states operated in conditions of intense protectionism and marked restrictive regulatory intervention, since they served as levers for the conduct of national economic policy (with very few exceptions). Consequently, given that the international interconnectedness of systems and markets was limited and the international movement of capital (and therefore most cross-border financial transactions) was very limited throughout this period, the need did not arise:

- either for the setting up of an international organisation or an international forum to deal with matters relating to the operation of financial markets and payment

286 In this sense, it can be argued, *in extremis*, that a new branch of international economic law has emerged outside of international financial law, but fully applicable to financial firms, referred to as the 'international law on combating the use of the economic system for the commitment of economic crimes'.

and settlement systems as well as to the regulation and supervision of financial firms providing services within them, or
- for the adoption of harmonised rules with regard to these aspects.

It should be noted that, despite being set up in during this period, the Organisation for Economic Development and Cooperation (the 'OECD') was not yet given competences on matters relating to the financial system (as currently held).[287] The same is true for the General Agreement on Trade and Tariffs ('GATT'), which had not dealt with the issue of liberalisation of trade in services, including financial services.[288]

On the contrary, from 1945 to 1971, the international architecture of the monetary system was structured, since the international monetary system was governed by the operation of a mechanism of fixed (but adjustable) foreign exchange rates, known as the IMF-governed Bretton Woods system of fixed exchange rates (hereinafter the 'Bretton Woods system').[289] The management and supervision of this system was entrusted to the International Monetary Fund (hereinafter the 'IMF'), which at the same time had (and still has) the statutory purpose of providing financing to its member states faced with balance of payments problems.[290]

In the same field, another international economic organisation, the Bank for International Settlements (hereinafter the 'BIS') was also operating during this period. Founded in 1930, it had as a principal statutory aim to promote cooperation between its central bank members and facilitate the decision-making process on their part in light of the international impact of their operations.[291]

1.2 The three periods for the formation of public international financial law

The two main characteristics of the evolution of public international financial law are that it was:

- gradual, occurring in relatively modest steps since 1971, and
- the international community's response to the onset of crises, in particular those with international dimensions which occurred after the abolition of the Bretton Woods system.

By way of indication, the following examples can be cited:

- *the Basel Committee on Banking Supervision was set up as a reaction of the G10 Central Bank Governors to the bankruptcy of Herstatt Bank;*[292]

287 See below under 3.2.3 of this subsection.
288 See below under 3.2.2 of this subsection.
289 For more details, see below under 2.1 of this subsection.
290 See below under 2.2 of this subsection.
291 See below under 3.2.4 of this subsection.
292 For more details on the Basel Committee, see under B in Section Four below.

- *the Financial Stability Forum and G20 were set up as a G7 reaction to the 'Asian crisis';*[293]
- *the standards contained in many of the reports which are adopted by international organisations and (mainly) fora and constitute the sources of public international financial law were also adopted in order to deal with the problems that ensued from specific crises.*[294]

Accordingly, public international financial law was shaped, in terms of both institutions and rules, during the last four decades. In the author's view, its formation can be divided in three (3) historical periods:

- the period from the abolition of Bretton Woods system until the 'Asian crisis' (1997-1998) (see under 2 below),
- the period from the 'Asian crisis' until the recent (2007-2009) international financial crisis (under 3), and
- the current period after the recent international financial crisis (under 4).

2. The period from the abolition of the Bretton Woods system until the 'Asian crisis' (1997-1998)

2.1 The new environment

2.1.1 The change in the terms of operation of the post-war system

The conditions of operation of national monetary and financial systems began to change significantly in economically developed states from the beginning of the 1970s onwards. Three (3) main catalysts triggered the amendments:[295]

(a) The first was the development of 'Euromarkets', which made it clear for the first time to national authorities responsible for managing national monetary and financial systems that financial firms could be engaged in financial transactions which went beyond the scope of their regulatory range.[296]

293 For a more detailed analysis on the Financial Stability Forum, see below under 4.1 of this subsection.
294 For more details on the sources of public international financial law, see Section Five below.
295 See **Steil (1994)**, pp. 2-5, and **Herring and Litan (1995)**, pp. 13-48.
296 These were national markets for the trading of securities and the acceptance of deposits denominated in a currency different from the official currency of the state where trading took place (e.g. acceptance of deposits in US dollars in banks established in the United Kingdom). This restricted the capacity of national monetary authorities to impose controls on assets denominated in their currency but held by institutions in other states. See **Robinson (1972)**, pp. 155-275, and **Kim (1993)**, pp. 179-200.

(b) The second catalyst was an institutional change which consisted in the abolition of the Bretton Woods system of internationally fixed exchange rates and the transition, in 1971, to a free-floating regime.[297]

It is worth mentioning in this context that despite the abolition of the international system of fixed exchange rates, there were (and still are) many states which chose:

- *either to peg the foreign exchange rate of their national currency to a 'strong' currency (e.g. the US dollar and, most recently, the single European currency), retained as an international reserve (a policy known as 'pegging'),*[298]
- *or to accede to regional regimes of controlled floating foreign exchange rates (e.g. the member states of the EU as early as 1973).*[299]

(c) Finally, a decisive contribution was made by the rapid progress achieved in the fields of information technology (IT) and telecommunications, as this enabled the conduct of large-value cross-border financial transactions in a very short time.

As a result of the concurrence of these factors, significant developments ensued. In particular:

(a) To begin with, a constantly increasing number of states proceeded with the abolition of both the restrictions imposed on cross-border movement of capital and direct administrative interventions which they had imposed on the operation of national financial systems.

This process is known in academic literature as the 'deregulation process'.[300]

(b) In view of the above, it was justified that three important amendments were introduced in the operational conditions of financial systems:

- an increase in the variety of products offered by financial intermediaries and other financial firms both to enterprises and to private consumers,
- an increase in the volume of the international movement of capital for the conduct of cross-border commercial and financial transactions, and, above all,
- the intense internationalisation of banking systems, capital markets, insurance markets and payment and settlement systems, which was gradually reinforced, both in depth and in extent, through the integration of economically developed states into the internationalised financial system.[301]

These developments did not occur simultaneously in all economies, nor were they equally intensive. It is, however, a fact that 35 years after the abolition of the Bretton

297 The 'Bretton Woods system' was *de facto* abolished in December 1971 following the signing of the 'Smithsonian Agreement' by the Group of Ten (G10). *De jure*, the system was abolished in 1978 by the second amendment of the Articles of Agreement of the IMF. For a brief review of this system and the conditions for its abolishment, see **Kapstein (1994)**, **Lowenfeld (2003)**, pp. 524-534, and **Lastra (2006)**, pp. 355-369.

298 See **Proctor (2005)**, pp.801-805.

299 See **Smits (1997)**, pp. 17-26, and **Padoa-Schioppa (2004)**, pp. 68-85.

300 See in more details under A 2 in the Section 'An Overall Assessment' below.

301 See **Brakman, Garretsen, van Marrenwijk and Van Witteloostuijn (2006)**, pp. 196-202.

Woods system in the overwhelming majority of the world's economies, the financial system is governed (to a greater or lesser extent) by the conditions described above and no comparison can be made with the conditions prevailing in the early 1970s.

2.1.2 The increased importance of risk exposure in the financial system

The increase in the volume of international capital movements, the liberalisation of national financial systems from the restrictive regulatory framework in which they had operated, and the internationalisation of financial activity (as described above) have undoubtedly made a particularly positive contribution to the growth rates achieved in recent decades in the world economy. At the same time however, these developments led to the appearance of risks which either did not exist or were not of the same significance in the post-war system up to 1972. More specifically, the following remarks deserve attention:

(a) First of all, as a result of the transition to an international system of floating exchange rates, there was increased exposure of economic agents conducting international (commercial and financial) transactions to exchange rate risk – a risk which is intensified in periods of significant fluctuation of exchange rates. At the same time, the development of capital markets has also increased the exposure of investors (private and institutional) to other market risks arising from price volatility in equities, bonds and derivative financial instruments.

(b) The increased lending activity of banks (due to the higher volume of domestic business credit and international trade financing, as well as the rapid development of housing and consumer credit) has resulted in greater potential exposure to credit risk and country risk.

It is, however, essential to point out in this context that during the last two decades the development of markets has also enabled financial intermediaries and other financial undertakings to:

- *make use of various techniques for hedging the risks to which they are exposed by the use of derivative financial instruments, and*
- *develop internal risk management systems which, in some cases, have proven more effective in forestalling risk exposure than the rules of prudential supervision which the supervisory authorities impose.*[302]

(c) The increase in the volume of commercial and financial transactions (domestic and cross-border) has highlighted the importance of the settlement risk which is inherent

302 This is the reason why the Basel Committee on Banking Supervision included banks' internal risk management systems in the elaboration of the capital adequacy rules it adopted in 2004, by means of which banking supervisory authorities exercise prudential supervision (see in more detail under B in Section Six below).

in payment and settlement systems in financial instruments and foreign exchange transactions.

2.1.3 The emergence of 'systemic crises' with international dimensions

In addition to the above-mentioned financial risks to which financial firms and systems may be exposed, it became evident that in an internationalized environment, given certain spillover effects, a national banking (or more generally, financial) crisis may have negative implications also abroad. As a matter of fact, the period after 1973 saw several banking crises with international ramifications, such as:

- the *Herstatt Bank* crisis (1974),[303]
- the *Banco Ambrosiano* crisis (1980),[304]
- the *Continental Illinois Bank* crisis (1984),[305]
- the *BCCI* crisis (1993),[306] and
- the *Barings Bank* crisis (1996).[307]

During this period remarkable was also the debt crisis in Latin America, which had severe adverse effects on the banking system of the United States, due to the heavy exposure of US banks to credit risk from positions in sovereign debt and loans in states of this region.[308]

2.1.4 National initiatives to redesign financial systems

The amendments in the operation of the financial system, in conjunction with the crises described above, have made it clear that in a liberalised financial system there is increased risk exposure and interconnectedness of economic agents, including financial firms, and that as regards banks in particular, exposure to these risks may activate negative chain reactions with an immediate impact on the stability of the financial system and the economy at large.

In view of the above, several (but unfortunately not the majority) of the states which proceeded to the liberalisation of their financial systems have also undertaken initiatives aimed at safeguarding the stability of their monetary and financial systems, whilst identifying the deficiencies existing in their national institutional infrastructures. This

303 See under B 2.2.1 in Section Four below.
304 See under A 1.1.2 in Section Six below.
305 On this crisis, see **Dewatripont and Tirole (1994)**, pp. 16, 21 and 70.
306 On this crisis, see **Kapstein (1994)**, pp. 155-166.
307 On this crisis, see **Dale (1996)**, pp. 189-195, and **Walker (2001)**, pp. 275-282.
308 On this crisis, which was the main trigger for the adoption by the Basel Committee on Banking Supervision of the 'Basel Capital Accord', see **Kapstein (1994)**, pp. 81-102 (see also under B 1.1 in Section Six below).

was achieved in principle with the adoption of rules on micro-prudential regulation with a view to reducing the exposure of financial firms to the risks they undertake through their operations.

Concurrently, measures have been taken with the objective to reinforce the coordination of monetary policy and transparency of its conduct (as well as the conduct of economic policy in general), the effectiveness of capital markets as well as payment and settlement systems, the combating of the use of the financial system for the conduct of economic crimes, and the strengthening of market infrastructures.

2.2 Institutional developments in the field of public international financial law

The new conditions for the internationalised financial system's operation rendered necessary the establishment of new international institutions. While financial internationalisation began to take on significant dimensions, international cooperation on addressing the problems which arose as a result did not immediately follow the same course. As correctly argued: *"The regulation of financial activities and the institutions that conduct them continues to be carried out mostly by national (...) governments".*[309]

Amidst these conditions, several international fora were gradually established with a view to enhancing cooperation among national authorities (mainly central banks and financial supervisory/regulatory authorities) and adopting rules, in the form of international standards contained in reports which constitute the sources of public international financial law. These fora, still operating, in certain cases considerably modified with regard to their tasks and composition, are the by-product of the historical period under review (with one exception).[310] They were established within the framework of the 'New International Financial Architecture' (the 'NIFA')[311] and are presented systematically in subsection C below. A more detailed analysis can be found in Section Four.

It is also worth mentioning that in 1976 the Group of Seven (G7) was created, the second inter-governmental international forum that played a significant role in the shaping of institutions of public international financial law.[312] Finally, by the end of the period under review the World Trade Organisation was established, the second pillar of which – the General Agreement on Trade in Services – laid down the basis for the liberalisation of trade in financial services.[313]

309 **Herring and Litan (1995)**, p. 1, and **Giovanoli (2000)**, p. 6.

310 The only international forum established during this period was the International Association of Deposit Insurers.

311 This term was used for the first time by **Crocket (2002)**, p. 7. See on this **Norton (2001)**, pp. 45-46, who challenges the accuracy of this term with regard to all its components.

312 See below under C 2.3 of this Section.

313 See below under C 3.2.2 of this Section.

3. The period from the 'Asian crisis' until the recent (2007) international financial crisis

3.1 General overview

The speed at which international capital movements began to take place (following their liberalisation) highlighted the systemic risk that might result from the sudden liquidation of financial investments, mainly as a result of amendments in national macroeconomic policies (or altered expectations – well-founded or speculative – for such a change), resulting, in its turn, in increased exposure of financial firms and markets to potential market and liquidity risks. The occurrence of such risks was the principal underlying factor (but not the cause) of the generalised financial crises which took place in:

- Russia (1996-1999),
- several states of south-eastern Asia (1997-1998), and
- Argentina (2000-2007).[314]

Consequently, partly as a result of imperfect understanding of such risks (owing to a lack of experience) and hence an inability to effectively manage risks which are inherent in liberalised and strongly internationalised financial systems, and also partly due to a lack of adequate institutional and regulatory mechanisms for protecting financial firms and systems against exposure to such risks, the positive effects of the internationalisation of the financial system on economic growth were offset (and in some cases to a great extent) by the occurrence of repeated crises, including the recent international financial crisis.

BOX: Representative example of how a generalised financial crisis unfolds in economically developing states

The standard sequence of events that might lead to the unfolding of generalised financial crises, such as those of the 1990s in economically developing states in central and Latin America as well as south-east Asia, are (in broader and – necessarily – simplified terms) as follows:

314 For a detailed analysis of the crises in question, which were crucial for the evolution of international regulatory interventions in contemporary financial systems, see, *inter alia*, **Caprio and Klingebiel (1996)** and **(1999)**, **Eichengreen and Bordo (2002)**, **Yokoi-Arai (2002)**, pp. 5-52, and **Park and Wyplosz (2010)**, pp. 3-34. For a historic overview of the recent 'systemically important' banking crises all over the world, see **Leaven and Valencia (2008)**, **Lowenfeld (2010)**, pp. 589-595, **Reinhart and Rogoff (2008)**, and **Leaven and Valencia (2012)**.

(a) If a national government has proceeded with the liberalisation of the economy and implements a substantial, restrictive fiscal policy, whilst, at the same time, its central bank conducts an anti-inflationary monetary policy, conditions are created for, *inter alia*, foreign investor confidence in the sustainability of its economic growth coupled with expectations of a boost in corporate profitability.

(b) As a result, there is an inflow of foreign capital in the form of direct investments and also investments (by institutional investors, i.e. mutual funds and large financial institutions) in financial instruments (mainly government bonds, but also corporate bonds and shares of companies listed in regulated markets).

(c) The resulting higher rates of economic growth have multiple effects, given (*inter alia*):

- the increase in the number of companies listed in regulated markets,
- the increase in the supply of bank financing to the economy,
- the rise in real estate prices (often used as collateral for commercial or residential mortgage loans), and
- the potential (depending on each given economy's structure and economic policy mix) to lead to a deterioration of the given state's balance of payments account and, most of all, an appreciation of the national currency.

(d) If, in view of the above, a given state's government and central bank identify the need for an – albeit small – depreciation of its currency, investor confidence in the state's ability to ensure the long-term sustainability of its economic policies and economic growth might be lost (particularly in the case of institutional investors and, all the more so, if they have gained high profits in a relatively short period of time), resulting in capital outflows from this given economy.

(e) In this case, the onset of a crisis in the financial system (and mainly its extent) depend on the following:

- the available room for manoeuvre of the government and central bank in terms of taking corrective measures,
- the extent of problems accumulated in banks due to their significant credit expansion,
- the ability of listed companies to shift towards domestic investors in order to preserve the value of their shares and, most importantly,
- the ability of the banking system and capital markets to address these two abovementioned parameters, and hence the adequacy of both the framework for the micro- prudential regulation and supervision of banks and investment firms, and the auditing rules for listed companies.

3.2 Institutional developments in the field of public international financial law

The above-mentioned crises, and in particular that in south-eastern Asia (the 'Asian crisis') worked as a catalyst for two institutional developments of major importance in the field of public international financial law:

(a) The first was the creation in September 1999, upon a G7 initiative, of a third intergovernmental international forum, the G20. This forum was set up with the intention to bolster cooperation between economically developed and economically 'dynamic' developing states on economic and financial issues, and therewith take initiatives for the preservation of international financial stability to the benefit of sustainable global economic growth.[315]

(b) The second, equally important, institutional development was the creation of the Financial Stability Forum. The objective of the FSF was the coordination of the actions of its members, including the majority of the above-mentioned international fora, with a view to safeguarding the international financial system's stability, improving the conditions for market operation, and limiting the exposure of the financial system to systemic risks.[316]

4. The current period

4.1 The recent (2007-2009) international financial crisis

Despite the existence of an extensive international financial framework, which was established gradually in the course of the last three decades as mentioned above (under 2 and 3), a major international financial crisis erupted recently (2007-2009). This crisis:

- was triggered by events in the financial system of the United States,
- spilled over to the world economy seriously affecting the stability of the financial system in several other states around the globe,
- had a serious negative impact on the real economy worldwide,[317] and
- negatively affected confidence in the financial system at a large scale.[318]

The author uses the term 'recent' (and not 'current') to denote that this crisis lasted from 2007 to 2009 and came to an ending. This is without prejudice either to the fact that the financial systems of certain states remain vulnerable as a result of this crisis, or that in certain cases (especially in the 'eurozone periphery') the current malfunc-

315 See below under C 2.4 of this Section.
316 See below under C 4.1 of this Section.
317 On this see various relevant reports of the International Monetary Fund, available at: http://www.imf.org. For a detailed overview of the crisis' impact in particular on European economy and the European financial system, see **European Central Bank (2008b)**, pp. 17-60 and 61-117, respectively.
318 See **Swoboda (2008)**.

tioning of the European banking system is a corollary of the current 'eurozone fiscal crisis' which occurred, at least to some extent, as a result of the recent international financial crisis.

The analysis of the causes of this crisis is beyond the scope of the present study. Very briefly, it can be pointed out that the crisis mainly relates to the following aspects:[319]

(a) The implementation of inadequate monetary and fiscal policies in several states.[320]

(b) Failures by financial firms, in particular[321] with regard to:

- excesses in the asset securitisation processes according to the 'generate and distribute' banking model,[322] and excessive complexity of transactions,
- poor lending practices (especially in the United States with regard to the household sector),
- excessive leverage,
- inefficient management of liquidity risk by banks, and
- imprudent (*ex post* at least) remuneration policies adopted by several institutions.

(c) Inefficiencies and failures in the regulatory framework of the financial system, such as:

- lack of macro-prudential policies (both in terms of regulation and oversight),
- lack of a regulatory framework for the operation of the 'shadow banking system' (especially in the United States), credit rating agencies and alternative investment vehicles (such as hedge funds),
- other failures in the micro-prudential regulation of financial firms,
- lack of transparency in trading of certain categories of financial instruments (namely bonds and financial derivatives),
- inadequacy of certain valuation methods for financial instruments in accordance with international accounting standards, and
- inadequacy of corporate governance rules for listed companies.

(d) The subsequent extensive scope for regulatory arbitrage among financial products, markets and states.

319 On the causes of this crisis see, by means of indication (out of the vast existing literature) **Kiff and Mills (2007)**, **Borio (2008)**, **Calomiris (2008)**, **Eichengreen (2008b)**, **Goodhart (2009)**, pp. 2-29, **Norberg (2009)**, **Rajan (2010)**, **Posner (2010)**, pp. 13-245, **Lastra and Wood (2010)**, pp. 537-545, **Tirole (2010)**, pp. 11-47, the report of **The Financial Crisis Inquiry Commission (2011)**, as well as the reports of the Committee on the Global Financial System (as regards the latter, see also Section Four below, under A.7.2).
On the actions taken by the US Federal Reserve System in order to contain the crisis, see **Baxter and Gross (2010)**.
For a comparison of the recent crisis with the international financial crisis of 1931 (both in terms of causes and in terms of regulatory reaction), see **Moessner and Allen (2010)**.

320 The primacy of this aspect is illustrated in the studies of **Norberg (2009)** and **Rajan (2010)**.

321 **Lastra and Woods (2010)** correctly point out also the 'usual suspects', i.e. greed and euphoria in periods of rapid growth and extensive credit provision.

322 On this model, see analytically **European Central Bank (2008a)**.

(e) Last but not least, major failures in the conduct of micro-prudential supervision of financial firms in several states.[323]

The consequence of this crisis, especially after the failure of the US investment bank *Lehman Brothers Inc.*,[324] was that several banks and other financial institutions around the world (small or big, even 'systemically important' institutions)[325] were not able to absorb the losses from their risk exposure.[326] This resulted, *inter alia*, in negative effects on the real economy, and obliged several governments (especially in the United States and the EU) to adopt rescue packages and recovery plans[327] in order to support or even bail out individual banks (and, in some cases, the entire banking system).[328] Such governmental interventions weighed on state budgets and, in some cases, created serious fiscal imbalances, some of which evolved to fiscal crises,[329] which, in turn, spread to become new financial crises.[330]

The study of the CGFS identifies four (4) main channels of transmission:

> *(i) the impact of negative sovereign ratings on (individual) bank ratings,*
> *(ii) losses incurred by banks from their sovereign debt holdings,*
> *(iii) the 'collateral/liquidity channel', and*
> *(iv) losses from state guarantees granted to banks (explicit and implicit).*

Adding to these channels is the negative impact on the performance of bank loans (in the event of recession).

Currently, a 'eurozone fiscal crisis' is under way. This crisis was triggered by the severe fiscal imbalances in Greece, which were then spread to other EU member states of the 'eurozone periphery'.[331] This crisis is the main cause of the current instability in the European banking sector, which cannot be fully assessed yet, neither as to the severity of its implications nor as to its potential spillover effects on a global scale.[332]

323 See on this, especially with regard to the EU financial system, the **Larosiére Report (2009)**, Chapter I, paragraphs 6-37 (pp. 7-12), and **Smits (2010)**.

324 See on this **Claessens, Herring, and Schoenmaker (2010)**, pp. 42-46.

325 There is an extensive literature on systemically important financial institutions. For more details see, by means of indication, **Claessens, Herring, and Schoenmaker (2010)**, and the various contributions to **Lastra (2011, editor).**

326 On the case of the Swiss bank *UBS*, see **Thévenoz (2010)**. On the cases of the US-based insurance company *AIG*, the Belgium-based bank *Fortis* and the *Dexia Bank* (whose holding company was also seated in Belgium), see **Claessens, Herring, and Schoenmaker (2010)**, pp. 46-51.

327 For an assessment of these measures in the EU, see **Panetta et. al. (2009)**, **Gortsos (2009b)**, **Petrovic and Tutsh (2009)**, and **De Meester (2010)**.

328 The most striking example in this case is Iceland. See **Claessens, Herring, and Schoenmaker (2010)**, pp. 51-53.

329 The most striking example is that of Ireland. With a sole exception, all Irish credit institutions were exposed to insolvency after the financial crisis and needed to be recapitalised.

330 For more details, see **Committee on the Global Financial System (2011)**.

331 See **Eichengreen, Feldmann, Liebman, von Hagen and Wyplosz (2011)**, pp. 47-64.

332 The only conclusion drawn at present is that the gravest impact was suffered by banks with sovereign debt holdings from states severely affected by this crisis (namely Greece, Ireland and Portugal, and also, more recently Spain and Cyprus).

Amidst this crisis, apart from the initiatives undertaken at the European level in order to enhance the existing institutional and regulatory framework governing the operation of the 'economic pillar' of the European Economic and Monetary Union ('EMU'),[333] *governments and central banks in several eurozone member states resorted to institutional, supervisory and regulatory measures in order to preserve the stability of their domestic banking sectors (and, more generally, financial systems).*[334]

4.2 Institutional developments in the field of public international financial law

Expectedly, this crisis has become a catalyst for 're-adjusting' the rules of public international financial law that applied before the crisis broke out,[335] as is the case with every crisis, no matter if it is a banking crisis (like the recent one), a foreign exchange crisis or a 'twin' crisis.[336] On the contrary, institutional developments were quite restricted and less spectacular. In particular:

(a) Since November 2008, the G20 started holding summits at the level of Heads of State or Government.[337]

(b) At the G20 London Summit, held in April 2009, the decision was taken to re-establish the Financial Stability Forum as 'Financial Stability Board', to expand its membership and enhance its tasks.[338]

(c) Finally, at the same Summit, the decision was taken to expand the membership of several international fora participated in by all of the G20 member states in order to enhance their representativeness.[339]

The current 'eurozone fiscal crisis' has not yet triggered the adoption of measures at international level, even though the issue was intensely discussed at the G20 Cannes Summit.[340]

333 For a thorough discussion of this aspect, see **Stephanou (2012)**.

334 On the Greek case, see **Gortsos (2012a)**.

335 The author uses the term 'readjustment' with a triple meaning, i.e.:
- the adjustment of the existing regulatory framework, aimed at addressing its weaknesses that were identified during the recent financial crisis,
- a 'new' adjustment, as was repeatedly the case in the reasonably dynamic process followed for the elaboration of the currently applicable law (by fortunate coincidence, previous adjustments had been made under normal circumstances and not amidst a crisis – more specifically, by means of the enactment of the Single European Act and the Maastricht Treaty, as well as the start of stage three of the Economic and Monetary Union), and
- not a 'radical amendment' of the current regulatory framework.

336 On this distinction, see **Brakman, Garretsen, van Marrenwijk and Van Witteloostuijn (2006)**, pp. 217-263.
On the substance of this readjustment process, see under B and C in Section Five below.

337 See below under C 2.4 of this Section.

338 See below under C 4.2 of this Section.

339 See in detail Section Four below.

340 For more information on this Summit, see under B 4 in Section Five below.

5. An assessment

It can be strongly argued that the new international architecture of the financial system had taken on historically unprecedented dimensions, even before the recent (2007-2009) international financial crisis. The main constituents of this architecture, which, as mentioned above, was shaped gradually and has been marked by ongoing readjustments to new conditions, can be summarised as follows:

(a) In contrast with the traditional postwar architecture, in the new international architecture there is symmetry between its two pillars (monetary and financial).

(b) The governance of the new international architecture is carried out on a decentralised basis, since there is no international organisation or forum entrusted with the management even of a single aspect of the internationally linked national monetary and financial systems. National authorities remain competent for the conduct of national monetary policy and various aspects of national financial policy.

(c) Governance is also characterised by institutional fragmentation, given that almost twenty (20) inter-governmental fora/international organisations/international fora with the participation of national authorities or other international fora, and private professional associations are active within the framework of this new architecture, and these differ significantly both in their make-up and in the way international cooperation is carried out. However, cooperation between them has been significantly bolstered since 1999 within the framework of the Financial Stability Board, which plays a significant role at the level of coordination.

(d) International organisations and fora, over and above the remainder of their activities, play an important role as fora for cooperation and information exchange between their members.

(e) Finally, an important aspect with regard to the making and enforcement of international financial law is that it takes place at four (4) levels. It is to this latter aspect that the author will now turn his attention, in subsection C below.

C. The four levels of the making and enforcement of public international financial law

1. Introduction

In subsection B we examined the gradual evolution of public international financial law in the course of the last four decades. We identified the existence of several international fora, which along with certain inter-governmental fora and a limited number of international organisations are the main actors in the process of making and enforcing the rules of public international financial law.

In the present subsection we undertake a more in-depth analysis of this process. The starting point is that the making and enforcement of the rules of public international financial law takes place at four levels:

- the level of political decision-making (see under 2 below),
- the level of the adoption of the rules of international financial law (under 3),
- the coordination level (under 4), and
- the level of the indirect enforcement of the rules of international financial law (under 5).[341]

2. The level of political decision-making

2.1 Introductory remarks

The dominant political role within the framework of the international architecture of the financial system has been entrusted to three (3) inter-governmental fora (presented in chronological order of establishment):

- the Group of Ten (or G10, see under 2.2 below),
- the Group of Seven (or G7, under 2.3), and
- the Group of Twenty (or G20), which currently plays the most important role (under 2.4).

Distinct from these fora is the G30. The G30 was set up in 1978 as a not-for-profit international body of private law, with the participation not only of the public, but also of the private sector, as well as the academic community. Its work consists in deepening the understanding of international economic and financial issues, investigating the effects of the decisions made by the public and private sector, and examining feasible alternative solutions. It periodically issues reports with recommendations on matters related to the operation of the international monetary and financial system.[342]

2.2 The G10

The G10 was set up in 1962 with the participation of Belgium, Canada, France, Germany, Italy, Japan, the Netherlands, the United Kingdom, the United States, and Sweden. Switzerland also participates in this forum since 1984 (hence, the members of the G10 are eleven).[343] The justification for setting up the G10 was the creation of a financing mechanism, the so-called General Arrangements to Borrow ('GAB'), for the provision of funds to the IMF when its existing funds proved to be insufficient for the

341 The following analysis is based – albeit differentiated with regard to certain aspects – on **Giovanoli (2000b)**.
342 For more information on the work of this Group, see: http://www.group30.org.
343 The IMF, the BIS, the OECD and the European Commission have observer status.

fulfilment of one of its main statutory tasks, which consists in the financial assistance of its members when facing problems in their balance of payments.[344]

The meetings of the G10 take place either at the level of Finance Ministers and Central Bank Governors (twice a year), or only at the level of Central Bank Governors (six times a year).[345] Without prejudice to the initiatives of the G7 (see under 2.3 below), for more than 30 years, the G10 has been the main inter-governmental forum responsible for matters relating to the governance of the international monetary and financial system. Since 1999 though, these issues are mainly discussed at the G20 (under 2.4).

2.3 The G7

The G7 was set up in 1976, a few years after the abolition of the international system of fixed exchange rates of the IMF, and the first oil crisis, with a view to dealing at a political level with the problems that had arisen accordingly. Its original and current members are the seven economically most developed states in the world (at the time of its creation), notably: the United States, Germany, France, Canada, Japan, the United Kingdom, and Italy (i.e., the members of the G10, with the exception of Belgium, the Netherlands, Sweden and Switzerland).[346]

The meetings of this forum take place at the level of Finance Ministers and Central Bank Governors, where issues concerning the international economic and financial system are discussed. The findings of the discussions in question are published in the form of 'final communiqués'.

Certain indicative initiatives of the G7's important work on the international architecture of the financial system concern the creation of:

- other international inter-governmental fora, such as the G22 and the G20,
- international fora adopting international standards pertaining to the achievement of specific policy objectives relating to regulatory intervention in the financial system, such as the Financial Action Task Force (see under A 6 in Section Four below), and
- the Financial Stability Forum (see below under 4.1 of this subsection).

344 The central bank of Switzerland also takes part in the GAB since April 1984, while an equivalent agreement has been signed with the government of Saudi Arabia as well. On this mechanism, as well as the mechanism of the New Arrangements to Borrow ('NAB'), see **Lowenfeld (2003)**, pp. 556-561.

345 This Forum does not have its own internet address. Its work figures on the website of the BIS: http://www.bis.org/publ/g10.htm.

346 This Forum does not have an internet address either. G7 is to be distinguished from G8, with the participation of the members of G7 plus Russia. The G8 holds meetings on an annual basis at the level of Heads of State or Government to discuss broader political and economic issues of international interest.

2.4 The G20

As already mentioned, the G20 was set up in 1999 on the initiative of the G7, as a successor to G22 which had been set up a year earlier.[347] The purpose of its creation, in the aftermath of the above-mentioned international financial crises of the 1990s, was the need for a forum to enhance the cooperation between economically developed and economically 'dynamic' developing states. Its main task consists in seeking compromise solutions between the (sometimes contradictory) positions of these two groups of states on international monetary and financial matters, so as to ensure the achievement of all the related policy objectives.[348]

Members of the G20, which meets twice a year, are the following:

(a) The member states of the G7 (and not of the G10), represented at the level of Finance Ministers and Central Bank Governors.

(b) Twelve (12) economically developing states (Argentina, Australia,, Brazil, China, India, Indonesia, Mexico, Russia, South Africa, Saudi Arabia, the Republic of Korea (South Korea) and Turkey), also represented at the level of Finance Ministers and Central Bank Governors, considered to be 'systemically important', in the sense that the occurrence of a crisis in their financial system might have an international impact.

(c) The EU, represented by the Presidents of the European Council and the ECB.

Ex officio, the Managing Director of the IMF, the President of the World Bank, and the heads of the International Monetary and Financial Committee and the Development Committee - the two committees which function, respectively, under the auspices of the two international organisations in question.

It is worth mentioning that Switzerland is not a member of the G20, even though Basel is the seat for the BIS and for most of the international fora, including the Financial Stability Board, adopting international financial standards, which are included in the reports constituting the sources of public international financial law.[349]

Due to the severity of the recent (2007-2009) international financial crisis, since November 2008 G20 Summits have been held at the level of Heads of State or Gov-

347 The G20 is also defined as a group of economically developing states (currently 23), which was set up in 2003 in the framework of the World Trade Organisation, and whose main task consists in the further liberalisation of international trade in goods. See on this: http://en.wikipedia.org/wiki/G20_developing_nations.

348 With regard to this forum's work see: http://www.g20.org.
Bremmer and Roubini (2011) criticise heavily the efficiency of the G20's work (talking about a 'G-zero world'). A more general criticism of the efficiency of the G20 to deal with issues pertaining to the financial system is based on three (legitimate) arguments:
- its member states are usually not at the same point of the economic cycle,
- the exposure to fragility of its member states' financial systems is usually significantly different, and
- several of its member states (obviously the less economically developed) do not have deep financial markets and systemically important financial institutions.

349 See under 3.2.4 of this subsection.

ernment. In these Summits, the Chairs invited formally also the Netherlands and Spain to participate under observer status.

The decisions taken at the four (4) most important (in the author's view) G20 Summits (those in London (2009), Pittsburgh (2009), Seoul (2010) and Cannes (2011)) will be discussed in detail below in Section Five (under B), because they constitute the 'political lever' for the readjustment of public international financial law in the aftermath of the crisis.

Table 5: G20 Members

States represented by their Ministers of Finance and Central Bank Governors		**Ex officio**
G7 member states	**Other states**	
Canada France Germany Italy Japan United Kingdom United States	Argentina Australia Brazil China India Indonesia Mexico Republic of Korea Russia Saudi Arabia South Africa Turkey ------------------------------ The Netherlands and Spain (observer status)	• Managing Director of the IMF • President of the World Bank • President of the International Monetary and Financial Committee of the IMF, and • President of the Development Committee of the IMF and the World Bank
The EU is represented by the Presidents of the European Council and the ECB		

3. The level of adoption of the rules of public international financial law

3.1 International fora

3.1.1 Legal characteristics

The vast majority of the rules of public international financial law, in the form of international financial standards, which are aimed at the achievement, with resort to international cooperation, of the majority of the above-mentioned (in Section Two) policy objectives relating to regulatory intervention in the financial system, is being adopted by international fora which do not have the capacity of an international organisation. These fora:

(i) have not been established by virtue of an international treaty,
(ii) do not usually have a charter or articles of association,
(iii) are not administered by formal organs,
(iv) are usually set up, as already mentioned, *ad hoc* and in several cases as a response of the international community to major financial crises with international dimensions, and
(v) are referred to as 'standard-setting bodies', or 'standard-setters', because their main objective (with the exception of the Committee on the Global Financial System) consists in the adoption of international financial standards (see below, under 3.1.3).[350]

Boyle and Chinkin (2007) *characterise these fora as 'transnational networks', making a distinction between:*

- *'sub-state networks with the participation of administrative agencies' - with reference to* ***Slaughter (2000)****, and*
- *'professional networks' - with reference to* ***Baldwin (1997)****.*[351]

3.1.2 Criteria of classification

The international fora under review can be classified in different categories according to several criteria:

(a) Based on their composition, these international fora can be systematically classified in the following five categories:[352]

(i) The first category consists of four (4) international fora with the participation of representatives from national supervisory and regulatory authorities from the three main sectors of the financial system (public administrative authorities and, in certain cases, central banks, mainly for the banking sector).[353] These fora are also usually referred to as 'sector-specific groupings of supervisors and regulators' and include:

- the Basel Committee on Banking Supervision, acting in the subject-areas of micro- and macro-prudential banking regulation and micro-prudential banking supervision,
- the International Organisation of Securities Commissions, acting in the subject-areas of micro- and macro-prudential regulation and micro-prudential supervision of investment firms,

350 On this term, see **Giovanoli (2000b)**, p. 8, and **Norton (2001)**, p. 14.
351 See **Boyle and Chinkin (2007)**, pp. 50-52.
352 See **Giovanoli (2000b)**, pp. 20-29.
353 Hence, at the international level the 'sectoral approach' (as mentioned under B 2.3.2.2 in Section Two above) prevails.

- the International Association of Insurance Supervisors, acting in the subject-area of micro- and macro-prudential regulation and micro-prudential supervision of insurance and re-insurance undertakings, and
- the Joint Forum, acting in the subject-area of micro-prudential regulation and supervision of financial conglomerates.

(ii) The second category consists of the following two international fora with the participation of representatives from national central banks (also called 'committees of central bank experts'):

- the Committee on Payment and Settlement Systems, active in the issue area of payment and settlement systems' oversight, and
- the Committee on the Global Financial System, which is the only international forum which is not a standard-setter.

(iii) The third category comprises only one international forum, the Financial Action Task Force on Money Laundering, with a (mainly) inter-governmental composition, which is active in the subject-area of combating money laundering and terrorist financing.

(iv) The fourth category also comprises only one international forum, the International Association of Deposit Insurers, with the participation of representatives from national deposit insurance organisations.

(v) Finally, the fifth category comprises two private professional associations, and more specifically:

- the International Accounting Standards Board, which adopts international accounting standards, and
- the International Federation of Accountants, which adopts international auditing standards.

(b) Other criteria that can be taken into account for the classification of these international fora are:

- the period during the evolution of international law in which they were established,
- their 'global representativeness,[354] and
- their headquarters, especially taking into account that the majority is based in Basel at the BIS seat.[355]

(c) This study prefers to use as a classification criterion the branch of public international financial law under which their main activity can be categorised (according to the analysis in this Section, under A 3 above). They will be presented in detail in Section Four, under A, with specific reference at the end (under A 7) to the Committee on the Global Financial System, which (as already mentioned) is not a standard-setter. The Basel Committee on Banking Supervision, which is the main forum for the adoption

354 See **Giovanoli (2000b)**, pp. 30-32, and **Lastra (2006)**, pp. 464-465.
355 See below under 3.2.4 of this subsection.

of rules of public international banking law will be presented in even more detail in Section Four, under B.

3.1.3 The legal nature of international financial standards

With the sole exception of the General Agreement on Trade in Services (the 'GATS'),[356] the rules of public international financial law are not included in the traditional sources of international law under Article 38, paragraph 1, of the Statute of the International Court of Justice.[357] Sources of international financial law include the reports issued by the above-mentioned international fora, as well as by international organisations (such as the IMF, the World Bank and the Organisation for Economic Cooperation and Development).[358]

The rules contained in these reports take up the form of 'standards'.[359] In its simplest form, a standard is a 'model rule' which often needs to be further specified due to its inherent vagueness. The specification of their content is made *ad hoc* when there is resort to them. Due to their widespread acceptance, standards are a common point of reference amongst their recipients, which means that a minimum level of international harmonisation is achieved on the regulation of a given issue.[360]

It is commonly accepted that these standards constitute international 'soft law', namely rules whose key feature is that they lack any legally binding character.[361] Soft law, created usually by non-state actors, is not included in the traditional sources of international law: *"The traditional statement of the sources of international law, the Statute of the International Court of Justice (...) assumes states to be the primary actors in international law-making and gives no indication of the ways in which non-state actors impact upon its function"*.[362]

Nevertheless, the importance of these international standards is significant, taking into account the following considerations:[363]

356 For a more detailed presentation of the GATS, see below under 3.2.2 of this subsection.
357 See **Stein-von Buttlar (2009)**, pp. 9-76.
358 See under A in Section Five below.
359 This is the reason why these fora are designated as 'standard-setting bodies'. Note that many international organisations and international fora do not name the standards they issue as such, but they use terms such as: recommendations, core principles, best practices, guidelines, codes of conduct, or codes of best practice. See **Schreiber (2005)** (p.p 10, with further references, and 230), who correctly points out that all these concepts should be considered as synonymous to the concept of standards.
360 Ibid., pp. 44-52.
361 On the concept of 'soft law', see **Giovanoli (2000b)**, pp. 33-44, **Lastra (2006)**, pp. 453-456, **Boyle and Chinkin (2007)**, pp. 211-229, and **Stein-von Buttlar (2009)**, p. 150.
362 See **Boyle and Chinkin (2007)**, p. 41.
363 See on this **Giovanoli (2000b)**, pp. 39-44, **Norton (2001)**, pp. 20-21, **Schreiber (2005)**, pp. 189-229, **Lastra (2006)**, pp. 463-464, **Brummer (2010)**, and **Giovanoli (2010)**, pp. 34-37.

(a) They constitute a benchmark which all states are expected to comply with.

(b) They affect the national law of the states that implement them:

- either on a voluntary basis, or
- by means of peer pressure, or finally
- in the context of the IMF's supervisory competences, based on its statutory task to oversee the economic policies of its member states – currently also including issues related to the safeguarding of the financial system's stability.[364]

(c) They lead *de facto* to the harmonisation of international financial law.

3.2 International organisations

3.2.1 Introductory remarks

The only international economic organisations involved in the making of public international financial law are:

- the World Trade Organisation with regard to the liberalisation of international trade in financial services (see under 3.2.2 below), and
- the Organisation for Economic Co-operation and Development with regard to the adoption of international financial standards on corporate governance (under 3.2.3).[365]

In this context, specific reference must also be made to the BIS, even though this international organisation neither participates *per se* in the adoption of international financial standards nor adopts any rules related to public international financial law (under 3.2.4).

3.2.2 The World Trade Organisation

The World Trade Organisation (hereinafter the 'WTO') was set up in 1994, within the framework of the 'Uruguay Round' of international trade negotiations. The Uruguay Round was the first round of multilateral negotiations, where the issue of the liberalisation of international trade in services was discussed. Part of the Final Act with which

364 See below under 5.1 of this subsection.

365 It is worth mentioning that international standards are also adopted by the IMF on issues of macroeconomic policy and relevant data transparency, as well as by the World Bank on issues concerning, on a horizontal level, the insolvency of businesses. See on this under A 2.2 and 2.3.1, respectively, in Section Five below.

the Uruguay Round was completed was the *"General Agreement on Trade in Services"* (known by the acronym 'GATS').[366]

As of May 2012, the WTO had 153 member states, while 31 states were given observer status.[367]

The GATS was the first multilateral framework of rules and principles by which the member states of the WTO, headquartered in Geneva, undertook general obligations and specific commitments with regard to the liberalisation of international trade in services, in a way which corresponded to the regime governing international trade in goods.[368] However, negotiations on financial services were not completed when the Uruguay Round came to a close, even though the specific provisions which govern trade in financial services were finalised at that time with the signing of the *"First Annex on Financial Services"*,[369] and the *"Understanding on Commitments in Financial Services"*.[370] Since the range of specific commitments which most member states had undertaken with regard to financial services was not broad, while many member states made extensive use of the exemptions from the obligations of Article II (including the United States), the prolongation of the negotiations until 30 June 1995 was decided upon, in accordance with the *"Second Annex on Financial Services"*.[371]

However, the completion of the negotiations in 1995 did not prove possible either, since the progress which was made by the members as to the undertaking of specific commitments and the abolition of exemptions from the obligations of Article II continued to be unsatisfactory. The *"Second Protocol to the General Agreement on Trade in Services"* contains the product of a so-called *"Interim Agreement"* of 24 July 1995,[372] by which:

- some of its members undertook additional specific commitments in the field of financial services entering into force on 1 September 1996, and
- the next deadline for the completion of the negotiations was set on 12 December 1997.

This new deadline was abided by. The outcome of the negotiations is included in the *"Fifth Protocol to the General Agreement on Trade in Services"*,[373] which had to be approved by all WTO members that submitted a Table of specific commitments by 29 January 1999, and came into force on 1 March of that year. Annexed to this Protocol were:

366 The Treaty establishing the WTO was signed in Marrakech (Morocco) on 15 April 1994 and its provisions came into force on 1 January 1995.

367 The list of WTO members and observers can be found at: http://wto.org/english/the wto_e/whatis_e/tif_e/org6_e.htm.

368 See **Lowenfeld (2003)**, pp. 68-109, and **Van den Bossche (2008)**.

369 See **von Bogdandy and Windsor (2008)**, pp. 618-639.

370 Ibid., pp. 647-666.

371 Ibid., p. 640.

372 Ibid., pp. 641-642.

373 Ibid., pp. 643-646.

- sixteen (16) lists of exemptions from the obligations of Article II,
- fifty-six (56) Tables of specific commitments (which involved 70 members, since the member states of the EU were represented by the European Commission and submitted a single Table).

3.2.3 The Organisation for Economic Co-operation and Development

The Organisation for Economic Co-operation and Development (the 'OECD') was set up in 1961 by virtue of the Paris Convention.[374] In May 2012, the OECD, which is based in Paris, was participated in by thirty four (34) economically developed and developing states from across the world.[375] Its statutory tasks consist in the following:

(i) achieving the highest sustainable economic growth and development and a rising standard of living among its members, while maintaining financial stability, in order to contribute to the development of the world economy,
(ii) contributing to sound economic expansion in its member states, as well as in its non-member states in the process of economic development, and
(iii) the contribution to the expansion of world trade on a multilateral, non- discriminatory basis in accordance with international obligations.[376]

The inclusion of the OECD in the group of international economic organisations taking part in the governance of the international financial architecture can be attributed to two factors:

(a) Firstly, it elaborates international standards with regard to the corporate governance of companies which are listed in regulated markets.[377]

(b) Furthermore, the Financial Action Task Force operates under the auspices of the OECD.[378]

3.2.4 The Bank for International Settlements

The BIS is an international organisation established in 1930 by the Hague Convention and signed among six (6) states and Switzerland,[379] and its seat is located in Basel. In May 2012, shareholders of the BIS, which is a private company limited by shares (a

374 The text of this Convention is available at: http://www.oecd.org.
375 The list of OECD members is available at: http://www.oecd.org/document/25.
376 **Paris Convention (1960)**, article 1.
377 See under A 2.3.2 in Section Five below.
378 See under A 6 in Section Four below.
379 The text of this Convention is available at: http://www.bis.org/about/convention-en.pdf. The initial Statutes of the BIS are available at: http://www.bis.org/about/charter-en.pdf.

'société anonyme'[380] under Swiss law),[381] were fifty-nine (59) national central banks and monetary authorities/agencies, as well as the ECB.[382]

The statutory tasks of the BIS consist in the following:

(i) the promotion of cooperation between its member central banks,
(ii) the provision of additional facilities to central banks for international financial transactions (in this sense, it is also a bank, since it has the power to accept deposits from central banks and international organisations and provide short-term credit to other central banks), and
(iii) acting as a trustee or agent with regard to international financial settlements entrusted to it under agreements with the parties concerned.[383]

In fulfilling its first task as above, the BIS plays an additional important role in the context of the international financial architecture. This is due to the close links existing between the monetary and the financial system and the fact that in several states the central bank is the supervisory and regulatory authority of one or more main sectors of the financial system.[384] In this framework it provides secretarial support:

- to six (6) of the above-mentioned international fora (namely, the Basel Committee, the International Association of Insurance Supervisors, the Joint Forum, the Committee on Payment and Settlement Systems, the Committee on the Global Financial System, and the International Association of Deposit Insurers (see Section Four below), and
- to the Financial Stability Board (see below under 4.2 of this subsection).

For all these fora, the BIS secretariat prepares meetings, draws up background papers and reports and publishes their work.

The following international fora were also operating under the auspices of the BIS in May 2012:

(a) *The 'Markets Committee' (formerly known as the 'Committee on Gold and Foreign Exchange'), dealing with structural developments that can have an impact on short-term market dynamics. Members of this committee are senior officials responsible for market operations in the G10 central banks and the ECB.*[385]

380 **Statutes (2005)**, Article 1. The Statutes of the BIS, as in force in May 2012, are available at: http://www.bis.org/about/statutes-en.pdf.

381 The operation of the BIS in Switzerland is governed by the provisions of the *"Headquarters Agreement"* of 1987 (as currently in force). This agreement is available at: http://www.bis.org/about/headquart-en.pdf.

382 The ECB has become a shareholder of the BIS in 2000, by amendment of Article 15 of its Statutes, according to which members of the BIS are central banks in general, and not only national central banks (as initially provided for).

383 **Statutes (2005)**, Article 3, as further specified in Articles 19-25. For an analytical study on the work of the BIS in the 1930-1973 period, see **Toniolo (2005)**.

384 See under C in Section Two above.

385 On the work of this Committee see: http://www.bis.org/about/factmktc.htm.

***(b)** The 'Irving Fisher Committee on Central Bank Statistics'. Members of this Committee are senior officials responsible for statistics in the G10 central banks and the ECB.*[386]

***(c)** The 'Central Bank Governance Forum' serving as a venue for the exchange of views on matters of interest relating to the design and operation of central banks. Members of this forum are central bankers in personam.*[387] *This Forum consists of:*

- *the 'Central Bank Governance Network', which connects individuals with central banks, and*
- *the 'Central Bank Governance Group', which provides a discussion forum for central bank governors and also acts as a steering committee for the Forum.*

***(d)** The 'Financial Stability Institute', set up in 1999 by the BIS and the Basel Committee on Banking Supervision, whose work consists in assisting financial sector national supervisory authorities around the world in improving and strengthening their financial systems.*[388]

4. The level of coordination: the Financial Stability Board

4.1 The Financial Stability Forum as a 'forerunner'

4.1.1 Establishment and membership

The significant number of international fora set up in the context of the international architecture of the financial system with regard to the adoption of international financial standards, according to the above analysis (under 3), and subsequently the fragmented nature of the system, is a direct corollary of the fact that the achievement of policy objectives relating to regulatory intervention in the financial system, as well as instruments for their achievement are up to various national authorities and systems. Accordingly, the representation of all these authorities and systems in one single international forum would render its operation ineffective.

In view of this institutional fragmentation, the coordination of the work of all these fora is deemed of primary importance. This role was entrusted, in 1999, to the Financial Stability Forum (the 'FSF'). Its constitution was the result of the proposals included in the 'Tietmeyer Report' (entitled "*International Cooperation and Coordination in the Area of Financial Market Supervision and Surveillance*"), which had been sub-

386 On the work of this Committee see: http://www.bis.org/ifc/index.htm.
387 On the work of this Forum see: http://www.bis.org/hub/cbgf.htm.
388 On the work of this Institute see: http://www.bis.org/fsi/aboutfsi.htm.

mitted to the G7 Bonn meeting of Finance Ministers and Central Bank Governors, in 1999.[389]

The FSF numbered forty-three (43) members. With the exception of its President, who participated *in personam*, members were states and international bodies responsible, directly or indirectly, for the supervision, regulation and oversight of of financial firms and the financial system. More specifically, the following were represented in the FSF:

(i) the G7 member states, all represented by three (3) members from the Ministry of Finance, the central bank and the relevant supervisory authority (in total, twenty-one (21) members),
(ii) five (5) states which are considered international financial centers (Australia, Hong Kong, the Netherlands, Singapore, and Switzerland, represented by one (1) member (in total, five (5) members),[390]
(iii) the international economic organisations participating in the governance of the international financial system, i.e.:
    - the IMF and the World Bank, both represented by two (2) members,
    - the BIS and the OECD, both represented by one (1) member (in total, six (6) members),
(iv) three (3) of the above-mentioned international fora with the participation of national supervisory authorities in the three main sectors of the financial system, i.e. the Basel Committee on Banking Supervision, the International Organisation of Securities Commissions and the International Association of Insurance Supervisors, each represented by two (2) members (in total, six (6) members),
(v) the International Accounting Standards Board, represented by one (1) member,
(vi) the above-mentioned international fora with the participation of central banks, i.e. the Committee on Payment and Settlement Systems and the Committee on the Global Financial System, each one represented by one (1) member (in total, two (2) members), and
(vii) the ECB, represented by one (1) member.

4.1.2 Tasks

The objective of the FSF, which was located in Basel and received secretarial support from the BIS, was to coordinate the actions of its members with a view to safeguarding the international financial system's stability, improving the conditions for market op-

389 This report was the result of the mandate, given in October 2008 in Washington, to the then Governor of the Central Bank of Germany ('Deutsche Bundesbank'), Hans Tietmeyer, by the G7 Finance Ministers and Central Bank Governors for the submission of proposals on setting up new institutions necessary for bolstering cooperation between national supervisory authorities and international organisations and fora, in order to enhance the stability of the financial system.

390 Out of these states, only Australia belongs to the sub-group of the twelve (12) economically developing states of the G20, which initially became a member of the FSF.

eration, and limiting the exposure of the financial system to systemic risks. As Tietmeyer mentions in his report: *"Although there are various international fora which monitor developments in the international financial system and have taken important initiatives to ensure its stability, the need to set up the Forum stems from the fact that these fora have their attention focused on the three sectors of the financial system (banking, capital markets, insurance) and consequently are not in a position to study and deal effectively with the problems which arise in financial conglomerates and complex structures."*

There are three (3) fields of activity in which initiatives were required immediately, which constituted the tasks of the FSF:

- the identification and assessment of the causes of systemic risks in the financial system and the submission of proposals for dealing with these risks in a timely manner,
- the adoption and implementation of standards of good practice to be implemented in a uniform manner by all categories of financial firms, and
- the strengthening of cross-border cooperation and information exchange among all sectoral supervisory and regulatory authorities of the financial system.

Among other initiatives, the FSF also issued a 'Compendium of Standards and Codes', which will be discussed in detail in Section Five below (under A 2).

4.2 The Financial Stability Board

4.2.1 Seat and membership

At the G20 London Summit in April 2009 the decision was taken to re-establish the Financial Stability Forum by renaming it 'Financial Stability Board' (FSB).[391] In this way, the G20 signalled the enhancement of this body's institutional role with regard to safeguarding the stability of the international financial system.

It is worth mentioning that in September 2009, the FSB became the first international forum on the financial system to have a formal Charter,[392] *which constitutes a major institutional development.*[393] *This Charter contains provisions on the criteria for ad-*

391 See **G20 (2009a)** "*Declaration on Strengthening the Financial System*", available at: http://www.g20.org/Documents/Fin_Deps_Fin_Reg_Annex_020409_-_1615_final.pdf, and **G20 (2009b)** "*The Global Plan for Recovery and Reform*", paragraph 15, second sentence, first point. See also **Financial Stability Forum (2009a)** *"Press release: Financial Stability Forum re-established as the Financial Stability Board"*, 2 April, available at: http://www.fsforum.org/press/pr_090402b.pdf, paragraph 1.

392 The Charter of the FSB (hereinafter the 'FSB Charter') is available at: http://www.financialstabilityboard.org/publications/r_090925d.pdf.

393 According to Article 16 of the FSB Charter: *"This Charter is not intended to create any legal rights or obligations".*

mission as member, as well as the internal organisation of the FSB, according to the decisions taken at the G20 London Summit.[394]

Members of the FSB, which is based in Basel and receives secretarial support by the BIS (apart from its own secretariat),[395][396] include:

- several states (mainly the members and the observers of the G20),
- international organisations,
- international fora adopting financial standards, and
- EU institutions.[397]

The eligibility of members will be reviewed periodically by the FSB Plenary in light of the FSB's objectives.[398]

The current members of the FSB are listed in Annex A of its Charter[399] *(see* ***Table 6*** *below). The participation of the EU and its member states in the FSB is significant, as it is represented by:*

- *four (4) member states (France, Germany, Italy and the United Kingdom) which are members of the G20,*
- *the Netherlands and Spain (the two observers of the G20), and also*
- *the European Central Bank and the European Commission.*

The FSB members have undertaken the following commitments:[400]

(i) pursue the maintenance of financial stability,
(ii) maintain the openness and transparency of the financial sector,
(iii) implement international financial standards, and
(iv) undergo periodic peer reviews, using, among other evidence of the Financial Sector Assessment Program, reports of the IMF and the World Bank.[401]

The FSB has to report on these commitments and the evaluation process.[402]

394 **FSB Charter (2009)**, Article 4, paragraph 1.
395 See below under 4.2.3.1 of this subsection.
396 **FSB Charter (2009)**, Article 15, paragraph 7.
397 Ibid., Article 4, paragraph 1.
398 Ibid., Article 4, paragraph 1, last sentence.
399 Ibid., Article 4, paragraph 2.
400 Ibid., Article 5, paragraph 1.
401 For more information on this program, see below under 5.2 of this subsection.
402 **FSB Charter (2009)**, Article 5, paragraph 1, last sentence.

Table 6: Members of the Financial Stability Board

G20 member states	**Other states**	• **International organisations** • **International fora** • **EU institutions**
Australia	Hong Kong	World Bank
Canada	Singapore	IMF
France	Switzerland	BIS
Germany		OECD
Italy		--
Japan		Basel Committee on Banking Supervision
United Kingdom		International Organisation of Securities Commissions
United States		International Association of Insurance Supervisors
The Netherlands (*)		International Accounting Standards Board
------------------------		Committee on Payment and Settlement Systems
Argentina		Committee on the Global Financial System
Brazil		--
China		ECB
India		*European Commission*
Indonesia		
Mexico		
Rebuplic of Korea		
Russia		
Saudi Arabia		
South Africa		
Turkey		
Spain (*)		
In personam: President		
Italics indicate new members of the FSB since 2009 (*) Both these states have an observer status		

4.2.2 Objectives and tasks

The statutory objective of the FSB consists in coordinating, at international level, the work of national financial authorities and international standard-setting bodies in order to develop and promote the implementation of effective regulatory, supervisory and other financial sector policies. In association with international financial institutions, the FSB also has to address vulnerabilities affecting financial systems in the interest of international financial stability.[403] In order to meet these objectives, the tasks of the FSB have been defined as follows:

403 Ibid., Article 1.

(a) The main tasks of the FSB consist in the following:[404]

(i) advising on and monitoring best practice in meeting regulatory standards,
(ii) assessing vulnerabilities affecting the international financial system and identifying and reviewing on a timely and ongoing basis the regulatory, supervisory and related actions needed to address them, as well as their outcomes,
(iii) promoting coordination and information exchange among national authorities responsible for financial stability,
(iv) monitoring and advising on market developments and their implications for regulatory policy,
(v) undertaking joint strategic reviews of the policy development work of the international standard-setting bodies to ensure their work is timely, coordinated, focused on priorities and addressing gaps,
(vi) setting guidelines for and supporting the establishment of 'supervisory colleges',[405]
(vii) supporting contingency planning for cross-border crisis management, particularly with respect to systemically important firms,
(viii) collaborating with the IMF to conduct Early Warning Exercises, and
(ix) undertaking any other tasks agreed by its members in the course of its activities and within the framework of its Charter.

(b) Additional tasks of the FSB are:

- the promotion of the coordination of the alignment of the activities of standard-setting bodies to address any overlaps or gaps, and
- the clarification of demarcations in light of amendments in national and regional regulatory structures relating to prudential and systemic risk, market integrity and investor and consumer protection, infrastructures, as well as accounting and auditing.[406]

In order to meet the above-mentioned tasks, the Plenary of the FSB[407] may establish Standing Committees and Working Groups as necessary and mandate them,[408] while the chairs of these Standing Committees and Working Groups can extend *ad-hoc* invitations to non-members to attend the whole or part of their meetings.[409] The current Standing Committees and Working Groups of the FSB are listed in Annex B of the Charter[410] (see **Table 7** just below).

404 Ibid., Article 2, paragraph 1.
405 A 'supervisroy college' (or 'college of supervisory authorities') is a group of national supervisors from different states in which an international bank is established and has foreign presence through subsidiaries and branches. Hence, each international bank has a different college of supervisory authorities ('variable geometry').
406 **FSB Charter (2009)**, Article 2, paragraph 2.
407 Ibid., Article 11, paragraph 1.
408 On this decision-making body of the FSB, see under 4.2.3.2 below.
409 **FSB Charter (2009)**, Article 11, paragraph 5.
410 Ibid., Article 11, paragraph 7.

Table 7: Standing Committees and Working Groups of the Financial Stability Board

Standing Committees	Working Groups
Standing Committee on Assessment of Vulnerabilities	Cross-border Crisis Management Working Group
Standing Committee on Supervisory and Regulatory Cooperation	Expert Group on Non-cooperative States
Standing Committee on Standards Implementation	Working Group on Compensation

4.2.3 Governance

4.2.3.1 Introductory remarks

According to the decisions taken at the London Summit, the governance of the FSB has been structured to consist of the following:[411]

(a) A Plenary (see under 4.2.3.2 below).

(b) A Steering Committee (under 4.2.3.3).

(c) A Chairperson, who is appointed by the Plenary for a term of three years, renewable once. The Chairperson, who must have a recognised expertise and standing in the field of international financial policy, will convene and chair the meetings of the Plenary and of the Steering Committee, oversee the Secretariat, be the principal spokesperson for the FSB, and represent it externally.[412]

(d) A full-time Secretary General and an enlarged Secretariat based in Basel.[413]

In May 2012, Chairman of the FSB was Mark Carney, Governor of the Bank of Canada, and Secretary General Dr. Svein Andersen.

4.2.3.2 The Plenary

The Plenary is the decision-making body of the FSB[414] and it is participated in by the following:[415]

(i) national central bank governors or immediate deputies,
(ii) heads or immediate deputies of the main national supervisory/regulatory agencies;
(iii) national deputy finance ministers or deputy heads of finance ministries,

411 Ibid., Article 6.
412 Ibid., Article 14.
413 Ibid., Article 15.
414 Ibid., Article 7, paragraph 1.
415 Ibid., Article 8, paragraph 1.

(iv) the chairs of the above-mentioned six (6) international fora which adopt international financial standards, and
(v) high-level representatives of the IMF, the World Bank, the BIS and the OECD.

The Chair can extend, after consultation with Members, ad-hoc invitations to representatives of non-FSB members to attend the whole or part of the Plenary Meetings. In the context of specific sessions of the Plenary, the Chair can also invite, after consultation with members, representatives of the private sector.[416]

The regular meetings of the Plenary, whose duties are enumerated in Article 7, paragraph 3, of the FSB Charter, are bi-annual (normally in March and September).[417] Decisions of the Plenary are taken by consensus.[418]

4.2.3.3 The Steering Committee

The responsibility of the Steering Committee is to provide operational guidance between the Plenary meetings to carry forward the directions of the FSB.[419] The composition of the Steering Committee, whose duties are enumerated in Article 13, paragraph 4, of the FSB Charter:

- is decided by the Plenary at the proposal of the Chair in a manner that ensures maximum effectiveness in taking forward the FSB's work while having regard to balanced representation in terms of geographic regions and institutional functions,[420] and
- shall be reviewed periodically.[421]

5. The level of the indirect enforcement of the rules of public international financial law

5.1 Tasks and powers of the IMF

The power for the indirect enforcement of the rules of public international financial law, in the form of international financial standards adopted by the above-mentioned international fora, which as soft law have no legally binding nature, is the competence of the IMF.

416 Ibid., Article 8, paragraph 3.
417 Ibid., Article 9, paragraph 1.
418 Ibid., Article 7, paragraph 2.
419 Ibid., Article 13, paragraph 1.
420 Ibid., Article 12, paragraph 1.
421 Ibid., Article 12, paragraph 2.

The IMF is an international economic organisation of one hundred eighty-eight (188) states which belongs to the group of specialised organisations of the United Nations.[422] It was set up by virtue of an international treaty concluded at the United Nations Monetary and Financial Conference in Bretton Woods (New Hampshire, United States, widely known as the 'Bretton Woods Agreement'), which was signed in 1944 and entered into force on 27 December 1945.

The initial principal tasks of the IMF consisted of:

- monitoring the international system of fixed (but adjustable) exchange rates, already mentioned in Section Three above as the Bretton Woods system,[423] and
- providing financial assistance to its member states when faced with problems in their balance of payments, upon conditionality.[424]

Hence, the IMF was established as both an international monetary organisation and as a lender of last resort for sovereign states.

By the second amendment of its Articles of Agreement, which entered into force on 1 April 1978, following the abolition of the international system of fixed exchange rates, the IMF was assigned the task to *"oversee the international monetary system in order to ensure its effective operation and (...) the compliance of each member with its obligations under Chapter 1 of this Article"*.[425] In order to fulfil this function, the IMF has the right to *"exercise firm surveillance over the exchange rate policies of (its) members, and (...) adopt specific principles for the guidance of all members with respect to those policies"*.[426]

Within this framework, the member states must provide the IMF with any information deemed necessary for the effective exercise of its supervisory competence. They must also take part in consultations with executives of the IMF (known as 'Article IV consultations')[427] in order to render possible an assessment of the compatibility of national economic policy measures with the general obligations that they have undertaken towards the IMF.[428]

422 This category includes fifteen (15) international organisations which are linked to the United Nations by special agreements and whose activity covers a wide range of issues (monetary relations, economic development, agricultural policy, education, health, telecommunications, meteorology).

423 **Articles of Agreement (1945)**, Article IV.

424 **Articles of Agreement (1990)**, Article V (Operations and Transactions of the Fund). On this see also **Lowenfeld (2003)**, pp. 549-556, and **Lastra (2006)**, pp. 406-412.

425 **Articles of Agreement (1990)**, Article IV (Obligations Regarding Exchange Arrangements), Chapter 3, paragraph (a).

426 Ibid., Article IV, Chapter 3, paragraph (b), first sentence.

427 See **Lastra (2006)**, pp. 399-406, and **Lowenfeld (2003)**, pp. 538-545.

428 **Articles of Agreement (1990)**, Article IV, Chapter 3, paragraph (b), second sentence.

5.2 The Financial Sector Assessment Program

5.2.1 Introductory remarks

In order to fulfil this supervisory task (widely referred to as 'surveillance'), the IMF formulates specific guidelines addressed to its member states determining the framework within which their foreign exchange policy must be exercised. In 1995, the Executive Council laid down the main principles pertaining to the strategy of the IMF in connection with its supervisory task. Two points of this strategy are of particular importance in the current context:

(a) The first is imposing the obligation on member states to provide to the IMF promptly reliable and immediately available statistics of economic and financial nature, in accordance with the general data dissemination and specific data dissemination standards.

(b) The second is the IMF's interest in the stability of the financial system of its member states, in view of the frequency and the critical nature of systemic problems that have manifested themselves in recent years affecting the stability of the international financial system.

Within this context, the IMF, in cooperation with the World Bank, adopted the Financial Sector Assessment Program (the 'FSAP' or the 'Programme) in May 1999. The aim of this initiative was to facilitate the assessment of the resilience of the member state financial sectors and their compliance with the international standards and codes contained in the Compendium of the FSB, in order to:

- identify weaknesses and sources of instability in the international financial system, and
- ensure that member states will undertake efforts to correct macroeconomic policies and strengthen their financial system and their economy as a whole.

Also related to this are the 'Reports on the Observance of Standards and Codes' (the 'ROSCs').[429]

The FSAP was first launched as a one-year pilot project, including twelve (12) member states respresenting the entire range of economic development levels. One year later, upon review of the progress made, the IMF and the World Bank decided to continue the program in the following year and included another twenty-four (24) states, with the prospect of including all member states of the IMF within five (5) years.

429 On both the FSAP and the ROSCs, see **Bergsten (2000a)**, **Reddy (2001)**, **Conthe and Ingves (2001)**, and **Lastra (2006)**, pp. 404-406.
It is worth mentioning in this context that the IMF also has the power of indirectly imposing on member states resorting to it for financial assistance the implementation of the international financial standards contained in the Compendium on the basis of the 'conditionality principle' (**Articles of Agreement (1990)**, Article V, Chapter 3, paragraph (a)). On this principle, see **Lowenfeld (2003)**, pp. 545-549, and **Lastra (2006)**, pp. 412-427.

In the context of the FSAP, the reports prepared touch on economic and monetary transparency, banking supervision, securities regulation, insurance supervision, oversight of payment systems, and, more rarely, corporate governance or accounting and auditing standards.[430] Banking supervision as well as economic and monetary transparency are examined in every case, while it is possible for some of the above sectors to be examined individually, under the Technical Assistance Programs, rather than within the framework of the FSAP.

The wide range of subjects usually covered by the FSAP, has also made it necessary to mobilise experts outside the IMF and the World Bank. A large number of central banks, international economic institutes, international organizations, non-governmental organizations (NGOs) and standard-setting fora have agreed to provide experts – members of their scientific staff – to help achieve a positive outcome as part of this endeavour.

5.2.2 Methodological tools

In order to be in a position to play a decisive role in strengthening the financial sector of interested states, the FSAP must constantly provide high-quality assessments, always taking into account the particularities of the economies examined. To this end, expert groups working on the Program use methodology tools specially designed for the purposes of the FSAP. Such tools include macro-prudential analysis, the study and implementation of potential negative scenarios for the economy, and the assessment of the adoption and implementation of international financial standards.

(a) Macro-prudential analysis is aimed at showing the two-way relationship that exists between the economy's macroeconomic robustness and the positive financial sector performance. For the purpose of this analysis, Macro-Prudential Indicators ('MPIs') are used to make an in-depth examination of both the robustness and solvency of commercial banks and of the broader framework of national economic policy choices. Experience has shown that when analysis reveals weaknesses in both aforementioned sectors, then there is increased likelihood of a future economic crisis.

(b) The study and implementation of various scenarios (stress tests, scenario, sensitivity and contagion analysis) are aimed at examining the impact of a potential serious financial crisis would have on market operation and the solvency of banks. These are applied to large commercial banks as well as banking systems as a whole. To properly conduct stress tests, it is imperative that the IMF and the World Bank have all the information deemed necessary.

The problem in this case is that, usually, the competent national authorities hesitate to reveal such information, despite the fact that it is subject to a confidentiality clause. Another problem relates to the different level of economic development between the

430 In the pilot project, each of the twelve (12) FSAPs that were conducted examined on average 3.8 sectors.

states that developed the scenarios (developed states) and the ones applying them (mostly developing ones). Many claim that such scenarios presume the existence of a well-organised banking system, a functioning robust capital market, and a large number of well-informed actors. Such prerequisites are rarely encountered in many developing states participating in the Program.

(c) Assessment of the progress achieved by a member state in adopting and implementing international financial standards, aims at revealing the positive aspects of the economy in question regarding its adaptability to new situations, on the one hand, and at identifying any institutional gaps and the weaknesses of its financial sector, on the other. The interest here is mainly focused on the sectors of banking supervision, economic and monetary transparency, payment systems, securities and insurance.

5.3 The evaluation procedure

Initially, the assessment procedure is launched upon request of the interested state. After the recent international financial crisis the following qualification was adopted:

- for those states whose financial system is considered by the IMF to be 'significant', the assessment under the FSAP is necessarily an integral part of 'Article IV consultations' and will be conducted on a five-year basis, and
- for other states, access to the procedure remains voluntary.[431]

Within the framework of the assessment, which may include one or more standards and codes, three reports are drawn up:[432]

(a) In the first report ('Main Report') there is an overall evaluation of the financial sector of the member state. This report identifies the economy's weaknesses and vulnerabilities, while underscoring its strengths. It also includes assessments made by the experts in connection with the short-term and medium-term risks that the economy faces, and in the end makes recommendations/proposals for specific measures. This report is confidential and delivered to the competent national authorities. Its Appendix includes a summary presentation of the progress that the state has made with regard to the adoption and implementation of international financial standards.

(b) The second report ('Selected Financial Sector Issues') includes a detailed analysis using tables and statistics to support the first report. It is also confidential, and is delivered to the national authorities, only if requested. The first and second reports are usually not published by the IMF, the World Bank or the state that requested the assessment.

(c) The third report ('Assessment of Observance of International Standards and Codes') contains a detailed analysis of the progress made by the member state with

431 More information on the FSAP can be found at: http://www.imf.org/external/np/fsap/ fsap.asp, and http://www.worldbank.org/finance/html/fsap.html.

432 On the need to upgrade the FSAP, see **Hagan (2010a)**, pp. 961-962.

regard to the adoption and implementation of international financial standards. Therefore, it is the basis for the preparation of the ROSCs. The group of experts of the IMF and the World Bank, the group of specialised international organisations and the competent national authorities jointly share responsibility for assessing each standard. However, it is the IMF and the World Bank who are solely accountable.

The member state may publish the third report but only with the consent of the IMF and the World Bank (if the member state is not a World Bank client, then the IMF's consent suffices).

5.4 The reports of the IMF and the World Bank

Based on the findings of the FSAP experts, the staff of the two organisations prepare separate reports to their respective boards, according to each organisation's area of interest:

- the IMF experts' report then serve as the basis for the Financial Stability Assessment (the 'FSA'), while
- the report of the World Bank's experts is the basis for the Financial Development Assessment (the 'FDA').

(a) The FSA focuses on the long-term weaknesses and vulnerabilities of the economy. In other words, it is a broader and more comprehensive examination of the state of the economy, and the potential risks it might face in the long run. The FSA is submitted to the IMF's Board of Directors along with the rest of the material to be used in 'Article IV consultations', i.e. the annual talks between the IMF and its member states on macroeconomic policy issues.

Consequently, the FSA reports are the connecting link between the FSAP Program and the IMF's surveillance policy, which results from Article IV consultations, offering all the necessary information/material to conduct the policy. The difference is that:

- while the FSAP is conducted on behalf of the requesting state, the
- FSA is drawn up only in order to serve the IMF's supervision needs.

The FSA report may be published by the IMF, with the member state's consent and is usually accompanied by the report resulting from Article IV consultations.[433]

(b) On the World Bank's part, the FDA is used as a diagnostic tool offering a complete picture of the economies of the Bank's members, thus enabling the Bank to better assess

433 During the Program's pilot phase, none of the participants was allowed to publish the FSAP results. Later on, however, it was decided that since this practice was against the IMF's and the World Bank's transparency policy, publication of the Program's findings were permitted, provided that all the interested parties agree thereto. Nevertheless, the established practice is that only the third FSAP report (*Assessment of Observance of International Standards and Codes*) is published.

their needs in terms of economic and technical assessment. The FDA findings are used in various World Bank programs, such as:

- the Country Assistance Strategies ('CAS'),
- the Social and Structural Reviews ('SSR'), and
- the Poverty Reduction Strategy Papers.

In the above programs, emphasis is placed on institution-building to allow the state to develop a sound and robust financial sector in the long run.

5.5 Recent developments

The recent (2007-2009) international financial crisis highlighted many of the FSAP's strengths, but also revealed its weaknesses (including its voluntary nature). This led to the following developments:

(a) In September 2009, the IMF and the World Bank 'revamped' the FSAP to include four (4) new features:

- more systematic, candid and transparent assessments,
- new assessment methodologies (improved analytical toolkit),
- more flexible modular assessments, tailored to country needs, and
- better targeting of standards assessments.

In particular:

(i) The IMF has introduced a 'Risk Assessment Matrix', designed to render the analysis of stability assessments in the context of the FSAP more systematic, candid and transparent.
(ii) The IMF has developed new assessment methodologies to better identify linkages between the broader economy and the financial sector and cover a greater variety of risk sources. In addition, more emphasis has been put on cross-country links, spillover effects and coordination arrangements.
(iii) Flexibility has been introduced with regard to the conduct by the IMF or the World Bank, respectively, of financial stability or development assessments in separate modules (instead of 'one-size-fits-all' assessments).
(iv) Finally, risk-based assessments of the standards that apply to the regulation and supervision of banks, securities markets, and insurance have been introduced to better target the assessments of these standards.

(b) In April 2010, the IMF's Executive Board agreed on making stability assessments under the FSAP a mandatory part of its surveillance policy. In September 2010, this agreement was concretised, when the IMF made it mandatory for twenty-five (25) states with systemically important financial systems to undergo financial stability assessments under the FSAP every five (5) years. The list of states falling under these mandatory assessments:

- is based on the size and interconnectedness of their financial systems, and
- will be reviewed periodically in order to ensure that it reflects developments in the international financial system.[434]

Table 8: Institutions of public international financial law

<table>
<tr><td colspan="5">G7, G10, G20: Political decisions</td></tr>
<tr><td colspan="5">• G20 members (19 states, plus 2 observers)
• 3 other states (significant financial centres: Hong Kong, Singapore, Switzerland))
• European Central Bank – European Commission</td></tr>
<tr><td>International fora
(subject-area of objective)</td><td colspan="4"></td></tr>
<tr><td>BCBS
(banking regulation)</td><td colspan="2" rowspan="6">Financial Stability Board (FSB)
• no financial supervisory authority
• in principle, no standard-setting body
• forum for international coordination of financial standards
• early warning system monitoring body (in cooperation with IMF)</td><td colspan="2" rowspan="6">IMF
• no financial supervisory authority
• standard-setting body (on macroeconomic issues)
• monitoring body for implementation of financial standards (FSAP – conditionality)
• early warning system monitoring body (in cooperation with FSB)</td></tr>
<tr><td>IOSCO
(capital markets' regulation)</td></tr>
<tr><td>IAIS
(insurance regulation)</td></tr>
<tr><td>CPSS
(payment systems oversight)</td></tr>
<tr><td>CGFS
(market functioning)</td></tr>
<tr><td>IASB
(accounting standards)</td></tr>
<tr><td rowspan="2"></td><td colspan="4">International organisations</td></tr>
<tr><td>BIS
(international monetary cooperation)</td><td colspan="2">World Bank
(economic development, standard-setter)</td><td>OECD
(corporate governance)</td></tr>
<tr><td>Joint Forum (supervision of financial conglomerates)</td><td colspan="4" rowspan="4"></td></tr>
<tr><td>IFAC (auditing standards)</td></tr>
<tr><td>FATF (money laundering and terrorist financing)</td></tr>
<tr><td>IADI (deposit guarantee)</td></tr>
<tr><td colspan="5">Italics indicate states, international organisations and international fora represented in the Financial Stability Board.</td></tr>
</table>

434 See on this: http://www.imf.org/external/np/exr/facts/fsap.htm.

Table 9: States' participation in the institutional structure of the international architecture of the financial system following the G20 Summit in London

G7 member states	. Canada, France, Germany, Italy, Japan, United Kingdom, United States
G10 member states (11)	• G7 member states • Belgium, The Netherlands, Sweden, Switzerland
G20 member states (19+2) (*)	• G7 member states • Argentina, Australia, Brazil, China, India, Indonesia, Mexico, Russia, Saudi Arabia, South Africa, Republic of Korea, Turkey (12) • Spain – The Netherlands (observers)
States represented in the Financial Stability Board (FSB) (24)	• G20 member states (19) • Netherlands, Hong Kong, Singapore, Spain, Switzerland
States represented in the Basel Committee on Banking Supervision (BCBS) (27)	• G20 member states (19) • G10 member states not represented in the G20: Belgium, Netherlands, Sweden, Switzerland • Hong Kong, Luxemburg, Singapore, Spain
(*) The EU is also a member of the G20.	

State	G7	G10	G20	FSB	BCBS
Canada, France, Germany, Italy, Japan, United Kingdom, United States (7)	√	√	√	√	√
The Netherlands		√	observer	√	√
Switzerland		√		√	√
Spain			observer	√	√
Argentina, Australia, Brazil, China, India, Indonesia, Mexico, Russia, Saudi Arabia, South Africa, Republic of Korea, Turkey (12)			√	√	√
Belgium, Sweden (2)		√			√
Hong Kong, Singapore (2)				√	√
Luxemburg					√

Table 10: The four levels of the making and enforcement of public international and European financial law (*): a comparative view

Levels	International financial law (multi-national law)	European financial law (supranational law)
Level of political decision-making	G7, G10, G20	European Council
Level of adoption of rules	Standard-setting bodies (international financial standards – soft law) *No authority to issue legal acts of hard law and create binding rules*	• European Parliament and EcoFin Council (legal acts according to the ordinary legislative procedure – hard law) • European Commission (delegated and implementing acts in the form of technical standards - hard law) • EBA – ESMA – EIOPA (guidelines - soft law) **(**)**
Level of coordination	Financial Stability Board	Joint Committee (common organ of EBA – ESMA – EIOPA)
Level of enforcement	IMF (indirectly)	• European Commission (for hard law) • EBA – ESMA – EIOPA (for soft law)

(*) For a detailed analysis of the legal acts of European financial law, see **Gortsos (2012b)**, Chapters 2 and 3.

(**) Mainly for European banking law, capital markets law and insurance law.

SECTION FOUR IN DETAIL: THE INTERNATIONAL FORA

A. The international fora adopting international financial standards and the Committee on the Global Financial System

1. Public international banking law

1.1 The Basel Committee on Banking Supervision

The Basel Committee on Banking Supervision is the main forum for the adoption of rules of public international banking law, in the form of international financial standards. This Committee will be presented in detail in subsection B below.

1.2 The International Association of Deposit Insurers

1.2.1 Establishment, seat and membership

The International Association of Deposit Insurers (hereinafter the 'IADI') was set up in May 2002 as a non-profit organisation under Swiss law, upon an initiative of the Financial Stability Forum.[435] In May 2012, the IADI, which is seated in Basel, had sixty-four (64) full members from across the world (among which only eleven 11) EU member states) that represent national deposit guarantee[436] organisations responsible for the management of national deposit guarantee systems.[437] In accordance with its Statutes,[438] it also has:

- seven (7) associate members representing other 'bank safety-net organisations' (i.e. central banks, supervisors and regulators) from states that have established or are considering the establishment of a deposit insurance system,
- three (3) professional firms having observer status, and

435 The Financial Stability Forum (FSF) set up a 'Study Group on Deposit Insurance' in 1999. Drawing from the latter's findings, the FSF constituted a 'Working Group on Deposit Insurance' in 2000, which led to the establishment of the IADI two years later.

436 The IADI makes consistent use of the term 'deposit insurance' (also in its name) rather than the term 'deposit guarantee', which prevails in European banking law. Without undermining the significance of the underlying differences, in the author's view the two terms can be used alternatively.

437 Unlike other international fora, membership of the IADI is open in the sense that any deposit guarantee organisation may become a member.

438 The Statutes and By-laws of the IADI are available at: http://www.iadi.org/aboutIADI.aspx?id=71.

- twelve (12) partners, i.e. entities that entered into a cooperative arrangement with IADI in the pursuit and furtherance of its objects, including the International Monetary Fund (IMF), the World Bank, the European Bank for Reconstruction and Development (EBRD), the Inter-American Development Bank and the European Forum of Deposit Insurers (see **Box** below).[439]

> **Box: EU law**
>
> At the European level, national deposit insurance organisations cooperate within the European Forum of Deposit Insurers (hereinafter 'EFDI'), which was also set up in 2002. In May 2012, the EFDI, which is seated in Brussels and formally became an international non-profit association in June 2007, was participated in by fifty-seven (57) deposit guarantee organisations from forty-four (44) European states, including all of the EU member states.[440]
>
> The objective of the EFDI consists mainly in investigating, analysing and exploring cross-border issues, burden-sharing and the efficiency of the national deposit guarantee systems of its members. It also plays an important role, upon explicit request of the European Commission, in the ongoing review and amendment of Directive 94/19/EC of the European Parliament and of the Council on deposit guarantee systems,[441] which is expected to be completed in 2012.[442]

1.2.2 Objective

The objective of the IADI, which is based at the Bank for International Settlements (BIS) in Basel, is to enhance the effectiveness of deposit insurance systems by promoting guidance and international cooperation through the following:

(a) Conducting research and setting out guidance to the benefit of states seeking either to establish deposit insurance systems or improve existing ones, leading, *inter alia*, in 2009, to the joint adoption by the IADI and the Basel Committee on Banking Supervision, of the *"Core Principles for Effective Deposit Insurance Systems"*, which are included in the Compendium of the FSB.[443]

(b) Sharing knowledge and expertise through participation in international conferences (including the Annual IADI Conference) and other fora.

(c) Providing training and educational programs.[444]

439 For more detail see: http://www.iadi.org/aboutIADI.aspx?id=48.
440 For more information on the work of the EFDI, see http://www.efdi.net.
441 OJ L 135, 31.5.1994, pp. 1-4, as amended by Directive 2009/14/EC of the European Parliament and of the Council (OJ L 68, 13.3.2009, pp. 3-7).
442 See the proposal for a Directive of the European Parliament and of the Council on Deposit Guarantee Schemes (recast), COM(2010), 368 final.
443 See under A 2.3.7 in Section Five below.
444 See also http://www.iadi.org.

1.2.3 Governance

According to its Statutes and By-laws, the IADI is governed by the General Meeting of Members and the Executive Council composed of individuals elected by the Members. The Chair of the Executive Council also acts in the capacity of President of the IADI.[445] The Executive Council is assisted in its work by:

- six (6) Standing Committees (Governance, Audit, Finance and Planning, Membership and Communications, Research and Guidance,[446] Training and Conference) participated in by members of the Executive Council, and
- a permanent Secretariat.

In view of reflecting regional interests and common issues through the sharing and exchange of information, eight (8) Regional Committees have also been created for Africa, Asia-Pacific, the Caribbean, Eurasia, Europe, Latin America, the Middle East and North Africa, and North America.

2. Public international capital markets law

2.1 The International Organisation of Securities Commissions

2.1.1 Establishment, seat and membership

The International Organisation of Securities Commissions (hereinafter 'IOSCO') was set up in 1983 as an international association of securities regulators. In May 2012, IOSCO, which is seated in Madrid, numbered:

- one hundred and fifteen (115) full members, which are the national public administrative authorities responsible for the micro-prudential supervision of financial firms providing investment services (either on an individual or collective basis), as well as the micro- and macro-prudential regulation of these firms and of capital markets,
- eleven (11) associate members, and
- seventy-seven (77) affiliate members.[447]

445 In May 2012, the President of IADI was Martin Gruenberg, Chairman (acting) of the Federal Deposit Insurance Corporation (FDIC) of the United States.
446 This Committee is responsible for issuing research and guidance papers.
447 Compared to the Basel Committee and other international fora, IOSCO has a definitively broader global representativeness in terms of its membership.

2.1.2 Objectives

The objectives of IOSCO are the following:[448]

(a) The promotion of cooperation between its members' supervisory (and regulatory) authorities.

(b) The provision of mutual assistance among them for the enhancement of market integrity.

(c) The elaboration and adoption of international financial standards relating to:

- the stability of capital markets,
- the protection of investors, and
- capital markets' integrity, efficiency and transparency.[449]

Box: EU law

In the EU, cooperation between member states' capital markets' supervisory (and regulatory) authorities takes place within the European Securities and Markets Authority (ESMA). ESMA began its operations on 1 January 2011 as successor to the Committee of European Securities Regulators (CESR), which had been operating since 7 June 2001.[450]

Compared to CESR, ESMA has been endowed with enhanced tasks and powers according to the provisions of Articles 8 and 9 of Regulation 1095/2010 of the European Parliament and of the Council establishing ESMA.[451]

2.1.3 Governance

IOSCO has two (2) main governing committees:

(a) The first is the Presidents' Committee, which meets once a year during the Annual Conference of the Organisation, and is composed of all the Presidents of its members (regular and associate). Its competence consists in pursuing the achievement of the purpose of IOSCO.

448 To find out more about the work of this forum, see http://www.iosco.org. It should be pointed out that recommendations relating to the disclosure of information by banks and investment firms are adopted jointly with the Basel Committee through the 'BCBS Transparency Group and IOSCO TC Working Party on the Regulation of Financial Intermediaries'.

449 IOSCO's main report (*'Objectives and Principles of Securities Regulation'*) is included in the Compendium of the FSB (see under A 2.4.2 in Section Five below).

450 Article 8 of Decision 2001/527/EC of 6 June 2001 establishing the Committee of European Securities Regulators, OJ L 191, 13.7.2001, pp. 43-44.

451 Regulation (EU) No 1095/2010 of the European Parliament and of the Council of 24 November 2010 establishing a European Supervisory Authority (European Securities and Markets Authority), amending Decision No 716/2009/EC and repealing Commission Decision 2009/77/EC, OJ L 331, 15.12.2010, pp. 84-119.

(b) The second is the Executive Committee, which is composed of the following nineteen (19) members:

- the Chairmen of the Technical and the Emerging Markets Committees,
- the Chairmen of each Regional Committee,
- four (4) ordinary members elected by each Regional Committee among their ordinary members, and
- nine (9) ordinary members elected by the Presidents' Committee.

The Executive Committee meets periodically in the course of the year and, subject to the By-Laws of IOSCO, takes all the decisions necessary for the achievement of its objectives.[452]

IOSCO also has four (4) Regional Standing Committees dealing with specific regional problems of its members: one for Africa and the Middle-East, one for Asia-Pacific, the European Regional Committee, and the Inter-American Regional Committee.

2.2 The International Accounting Standards Board

2.2.1 Establishment, seat and membership

The International Accounting Standards Board (hereinafter 'IASB') was set up in 1973 and is seated in London. It is the independent standard-setting body of the 'International Financial Reporting Standards' (the 'IFRS') foundation, a not-for-profit private organisation. Its fifteen (15) members, specialists in the field of corporate accounting, are appointed by the International Accounting Standards Committee Foundation, which is administered by twenty-one (21) trustees.[453]

2.2.2 Objective

The IASB's objective consists in the elaboration and adoption and promotion of 'international accounting' (or 'financial reporting') standards (as from 2000), used for drawing up the financial statements of companies, particularly those listed in regulated markets.[454] Interpretations of these standards, issued by the fourteen-member Standing Interpretations Committee, also fall within the competence of the Board.[455]

452 In May 2012, Chairperson of the Executive Committee was Maria Helena Santana, Chairperson of the Comissão de Valores Mobiliários of Brazil.

453 In January 2009, the trustees voted to expand the IASB members to sixteen (16) as of July 2012.

454 The international accounting standards are included in the Compendium of the FSB (see under A 2.3.3 in Section Five below).

455 For more details on the work of the IASB see http://www.ifrs.org.

From 1973 to 2000, the standards in question were issued by the International Accounting Standards Committee, founded by agreement of the professional accounting agencies in ten (10) economically developed states. Its present composition is a result of amendments adopted in 1999 and approved in 2000.

2.3 The International Federation of Accountants

2.3.1 Establishment, seat and membership

The International Federation of Accountants (hereinafter 'IFAC') was set up in 1977 as the international organisation for the accountancy profession and is seated in New York. In May 2012, its members (regular and associate) included one hundred and sixty-seven (167) national professional accounting associations, from both the private and the public sector, representing 127 states.[456]

2.3.2 Objectives

The objectives of the IFAC consist in strengthening the accountancy profession, close cooperation with the IASB, as well as the adoption and promotion of international professional standards. In regard to the latter, it adopts 'international auditing standards'[457] for companies listed in regulated markets through a technical committee, the International Auditing and Assurance Standards Board.

3. Public international insurance law: the International Association of Insurance Supervisors

3.1 Establishment, seat and membership

The International Association of Insurance Supervisors (hereinafter 'IAIS'), which is based in Basel at the BIS, was set up in 1994. It is an international non-profit organisation representing insurance regulators and supervisors. In May 2012, it numbered one hundred and forty-six (146) members from 190 states. These are national supervisory (and regulatory) authorities responsible for the micro-prudential supervision of insurance and reinsurance companies. There are also more than one hundred and twenty (120) observers representing industry associations, professional associations,

456 For a more detailed presentation of the work of this association, see http://www.ifac.org.
457 The international auditing standards are also included in the Compendium of the FSB (see under A 2.3.4 in Section Five below).

insurance and reinsurance companies, consultants and international financial institutions.

3.2 Objectives

The main objectives of the IAIS consist in:

(i) the promotion of cooperation between its members,
(ii) the provision of mutual assistance among them,
(iii) the elaboration and adoption of international financial standards relating to the micro-prudential supervision, as well as the micro- and macro-prudential regulation of insurance and co-insurance companies,[458] and
(iv) the provision of training services and support on issues related to insurance regulation and supervision, as well as the organisation of meetings and seminars for insurance supervisors.

Box: EU law

In the EU, cooperation between member states' insurance and reinsurance supervisory authorities takes place within the European Insurance and Occupational Pensions Authority ('EIOPA'). EIOPA began its operations in January 2011 as a successor to the Committee of European Insurance and Occupational Pensions Supervisors ('CEIOPS'),[459] which had been in operation since 24 November 2003.

Compared to CEIOPS, EIOPA has been endowed with enhanced tasks and powers according to the provisions of Articles 8 and 9 of Regulation 1094/2010 of the European Parliament and of the Council establishing EIOPA.[460]

3.3 Governance

The main governing body of the IAIS is the Executive Committee, whose members represent different geographical regions. It is supported by four (4) committees: the Financial Stability Committee, the Technical Committee, the Implementation Committee and the Budget Committee.[461]

458 IAIS's main report (*Insurance Core Principles*) is also included in the Compendium of the FSB (see under A 2.4.3 in Section Five below).
459 Commission Decision 2004/6/EC of 5 November 2003 establishing the Committee of European Insurance and Occupational Pensions Supervisors, OJ L 3, 7.1.2004, pp. 30-31.
460 Regulation (EU) No 1094/2010 of the European Parliament and of the Council of 24 November 2010 establishing a European Supervisory Authority (European Insurance and Occupational Pensions Authority), amending Decision No 716/2009/EC and repealing Commission Decision No 2009/79/EC, OJ L 331, 15.12.2010, pp. 48-83.
461 The By-laws of the IAIS are available at: http://www.iaisweb.org/By-laws-45.

4. Public international financial conglomerates law: the Joint Forum

4.1 Establishment, seat and membership

The Joint Forum, initially known as 'Joint Forum on Financial Conglomerates', was set up in 1996 as a successor to the 'Tripartite Group'[462] under the auspices of the Basel Committee, the IOSCO, and the IAIS.

The Forum's name was shortened to 'Joint Forum' in 1999 in view of the fact that its mandate was extended beyond issues relating to financial conglomerates to cover issues of common interest to all three sectors of the financial system, i.e. the banking, capital markets and insurance sectors. Nevertheless, its main objective remains the same; which is why, in the author's view, the Joint Forum should be considered mainly as a standard-setter with regard to international financial conglomerates law.

In May 2012, members of this forum of technical experts, which is also seated in Basel at the BIS, were:

- representatives of the national supervisory (and regulatory) authorities of the three main sectors of the financial system (banking, capital markets, as well as insurance and reinsurance) from the member states of G10 (with the exception of Sweden, while the USA are represented by both the Board of Governors of the Federal Reserve System and the Federal Reserve Bank of New York), Australia and Spain, and
- representatives of the Basel Committee, IOSCO, and IAIS.

The European Commission has observer status.[463]

4.2 Objectives

The objectives of the Joint Forum are the following:[464]

(a) The first consists in dealing with issues relating to the micro-prudential supervision and regulation of financial conglomerates. In this respect, the Joint Forum is requested to:

- enable bank, insurance and securities supervisory and regulatory authorities to share information about issues arising from the implementation of the principles adopted and the techniques developed by the Joint Forum,[465]

462 The Tripartite Group was set up in 1993, at the initiative of the Basel Committee, to address issues relating to the micro-prudential supervision and regulation of financial conglomerates.

463 It is worth noting that the Joint Forum is not participated in by the ECB as observer, but the European Commission.

464 For more details on this mandate, see http://www.bis.org/bcbs/jfmandate.htm.

465 These are pertaining to coordination, supervisory information-sharing, capital adequacy, fit-and-proper tests, intra-group transactions and exposures, as well as risk concentrations.

- study financial conglomerate structures that may impair effective micro-prudential supervision and, if appropriate, develop guidance and principles, as well as identify best practices, and
- assess the appropriateness of group-wide methods of supervision and, if appropriate, develop guidance and principles as well as identify best practices.

(b) The second objective consists in dealing with issues of common interest to its three founding organisations, such as:

- the assessment and management of risks, internal controls, corporate governance and regulatory capital,
- the use of audit and actuarial methods in the micro-prudential supervision of financial conglomerates containing regulated financial firms,
- the outsourcing of functions and activities by regulated financial firms,
- the different definitions of banking, insurance and investment services, which allow for regulatory arbitrage, and
- the identification of the core principles for the three sectors of the financial system.

Box: EU law

In the EU, the coordination of the work conducted by ESMA, EIOPA and EBA takes place within the 'Joint Committee', which has been established pursuant to Articles 54-57 of the Regulations establishing these three Authorities.[466]

4.3 Governance

The Joint Forum does not have a founding charter or by-laws. Its Chairmanship, for a two-year term, rotates between its three founding international fora.[467] The work of the Joint Forum, which meets regularly three times annually, is supported by three Sub-Groups: the Risk Assessment and Capital Sub-Group, the Conglomerate Sub-Group, and the Customer Suitability Sub-Group.

466 See **Gortsos (2011c)**, p. 7.

467 In May 2012, the Joint Forum was chaired by Therese M. Vaughan, National Association of Insurance Commissioners, United States.

5. Public international payment systems law: the Committee on Payment and Settlement Systems

5.1 Establishment, seat and membership

The Committee on Payment and Settlement Systems (hereinafter 'CPSS') was set up in 1990 by the G10 Central Bank Governors. In May 2012, members of CPSS, which is also seated in Basel at the BIS, were high-level officials from central banks or monetary authorities and agencies of:

- seventeen (17) out of nineteen (19) members of the G20 (the Central Bank of Argentina and Indonesia do not participate in the CPSS, while the United States is represented both through the Board of Governors of the Federal Reserve System and the Federal Reserve Bank of New York),
- the three (3) G10 member states that are not members of the G20 (Belgium, Switzerland and Sweden), and
- the Netherlands, Hong Kong and Singapore.

The ECB is also a member.

5.2 Objective

The objective of the CPSS consists in the elaboration and adoption of international financial standards in view of ensuring the stability and efficiency of payment and settlement systems. In this respect, it has issued important reports on:[468]

- large-value payment systems,
- retail payment instruments (including electronic money) and systems,
- securities clearing and settlement systems, as well as clearing and settlement arrangements for derivatives transactions,[469]
- settlement risk in foreign-exchange transactions,
- interdependencies of payment and settlement systems, and
- central bank oversight in payment and settlement systems.

468 For more details on the work of this forum, see http://www.bis.org/cpss. Three main reports of the CPSS ("*Core principles for systemically important payment systems*", "*Recommendations for Securities Settlement Systems*" and "*Recommendations for central counterparties*") are included in the Compendium of the FSB (see under A 2.3.5 in Section Five below).

469 These reports are issued jointly with IOSCO through the 'CPSS-IOSCO Task Force on Securities Settlement Systems'.

5.3 Governance

Similarly to the Joint Forum, the CPSS has neither a founding charter nor by-laws. Its regular meetings are held on the occasion of four (4) of the bimonthly meetings of the Governors of the BIS member central banks. As of January 2010, the Chairman of the CGFS[470] reports on its monitoring discussions and other initiatives to the 'Global Economy Meeting'.[471]

6. Public international law on combating the use of the financial system for the commitment of economic crimes: the Financial Action Task Force

6.1 Establishment, seat and membership

The Financial Action Task Force (hereinafter 'FATF') was founded in 1989, on the initiative of the G7 during its annual summit in Paris, as an inter-governmental body. In May 2012, the FATF, which is headquartered in Paris and receives secretarial support from the OECD, numbered thirty-four (34) member states, including the seven founding-members of the G7, as well as the European Commission, and the Gulf Co-operation Council (GCC) (total thirty-six (36) members).
The associate members of the FATF are:

- the Asia/Pacific Group on Money Laundering (APG),
- the Caribbean Financial Action Task Force (CFATF),
- the Eurasian Group (EAG),
- the Eastern and Southern Africa Anti-Money Laundering Group (ESAAMLG),
- the Council of Europe Committee of Experts on the Evaluation of Anti-Money Laundering Measures and the Financing of Terrorism (MONEYVAL),
- the Financial Action Task Force on Money Laundering in South America (GAFISUD),
- the Inter-Governmental Action Group against Money Laundering in West Africa (GIABA), and
- the Middle East and North Africa Financial Action Task Force (MENAFATF).

The United Nations Office on Drugs and Crime (UNODC), the IMF, the World Bank, the OECD, the ECB, Interpol and Europol, the World Customs Organisation, as well as other international organisations, have observer status.

470 In May 2012, Chairman of the CPSS was Paul Tucker, Deputy Governor of the Bank of England.
471 The Global Economic Meeting (hereinafter 'GEM') comprises a group of thirty-one (31) Governors of the BIS member central banks. In May 2012, the GEM was chaired by Mervyn King, Governor of the Bank of England.

6.2 Objective

The objective of the FATF consists in the adoption of international financial standards to counter (i.e. prevent and contain) the use of the financial system by criminals, and in particular the legitimisation of proceeds from illegal activities (a practice and criminal activity known as 'money laundering') and terrorist financing. Within this framework, the FATF:

- monitors members' progress in implementing the standards on combating money laundering and terrorist financing,
- prepares reports on money laundering and terrorist financing techniques, and
- promotes the adoption and implementation of appropriate measures globally.

Its objectives are achieved by means of the compilation and assessment of annual reports on the results of international cooperation initiatives on combating money laundering and terrorist financing, as well as the examination and adoption of further measures to enhance international cooperation.[472]

6.3 Governance

The FATF does not have a strictly defined constitution or an unlimited life span.[473] Its decision-making body is the FATF Plenary, which meets three times per year.

7. The Committee on the Global Financial System

7.1 Establishment, seat and membership

The Committee on the Global Financial System (hereinafter 'CGFS') was set up in 1971 by the G10 Central Bank Governors as the 'Euro-Currency Standing Committee'. At that time, its mandate was to monitor international banking markets and the monetary implications of the rapid growth of off-shore deposit and lending markets ('Euromarkets').[474] It was given its current name in 1999 in order to reflect that the focus of its work gradually shifted to issues of financial stability and broader issues related with structural amendments in the financial system.

472 For a more detailed overview of the work of this forum, see http://fatf-gafi.org. Its main report (*"Forty Recommendations on Money Laundering/Nine Special Recommendations on Terrorist Financing"*) is included in the Compendium of the FSB (see under A 2.3.6 in Section Five below).

473 In May 2012 (and until 30 June 2012), FATF was chaired by Giancarlo Del Bufalo (Italy).

474 See under B 2.1.1 in Section Three above.

The initial members of the CGFS, which has been seated in Basel at the BIS, were Deputy-Governors and high-level officials from the G10 central banks (the United States are represented in this forum, as in the Joint Forum, by the Board of Governors of the Federal Reserve System and the Federal Reserve Bank of New York) and Luxembourg. The Economic Adviser of the BIS is also a member. Gradually, membership increased with the participation of representatives from the central banks of Spain, Hong Kong and Singapore, as well as the ECB. In 2009, membership was extended to another six (6) central banks of G20 member states (Australia, Brazil, China, India, Korea and Mexico). In May 2012, its members totalled twenty-three (23).

7.2 Objectives

As already mentioned, unlike all other international fora mentioned above, the CGFS is not a standard-setting body. Its current objectives were set out in a statement of the G10 Central Bank Governors of 8 February 1999[475] and consist in the following:

(a) The first objective is to seek to identify and assess potential sources of stress in the international financial environment. The target set in order to achieve this objective is regular and systematic monitoring of developments in financial markets and systems, including through an evaluation of macroeconomic developments.[476]

(b) The second objective is to further the understanding of the functioning and underpinnings of financial markets and systems. In order to achieve it, the CGFS is:

- monitoring the evolution of financial markets and systems, and
- conducting in-depth analyses, with particular reference to the implications for central bank operations and broader responsibilities for monetary and financial stability.

(c) The third objective is to promote the development of well-functioning and stable financial markets and systems. The targets set in order to achieve this objective are examining alternative policy responses and drawing up corresponding policy recommendations.

In this respect, the CGBS has issued since 2008 several reports, which constitute excellent sources for the analysis of the causes and impact of the recent international financial crisis, as well as the necessary regulatory intervention:[477]

- *Private equity and leveraged finance markets (July 2008),*
- *Central bank operations in response to the financial turmoil (July 2008),*
- *Ratings in structured finance: what went wrong and what can be done to address shortcomings? (July 2008),*

475 See also http://www.bis.org/cgfs/mandate.htm.
476 According to its mandate, this forum was responsible for the macro-prudential oversight of the international (or global) financial system, a task which it has obviously not fully discharged.
477 These reports are available at: http://www.bis.org/list/cgfs/index.htm.

- *Capital flows and emerging market economies (January 2009),*
- *The role of valuation and leverage in procyclicality (April 2009),*
- *Credit risk transfer statistics (September 2009),*
- *The role of margin requirements and haircuts (March 2010),*
- *The functioning and resilience of cross-border funding markets (March 2010),*
- *Macro-prudential instruments and frameworks: a stocktaking of issues and experiences (May 2010),*
- *Funding patterns and liquidity management of internationally active banks (May 2010),*
- *Research on global financial stability: the use of BIS international financial statistics (June 2010),*
- *Long-term issues in international banking (June 2010),*
- *Interactions of sovereign debt management with monetary conditions and Financial stability (May 2011),*
- *The impact of sovereign credit risk on bank funding conditions (July 2011),*
- *Fixed income strategies of insurance companies and pension funds (July 2011),*
- *Global liquidity - concept, measurement and policy implications (November 2011), and*
- *The macrofinancial implications of alternative configurations for access to central counterparties in OTC derivatives markets (November 2011).*

The CGFS also oversees the collection of international banking and financial statistics compiled by the BIS.

7.3 Governance

Similarly to the CPSS, the CGFS does not have a founding charter or by-laws, and its regular meetings are held on the occasion of four (4) of the bimonthly meetings of Governors of the BIS member central banks. In addition, since January 2010, the Chairman of the CGFS[478] reports to the 'Global Economy Meeting' with regard to its monitoring discussions and other initiatives.

478 In May 2012, Chairman of the CGFS was William C. Dudley, President and Chief Executive Officer of the Federal Reserve Bank of New York.

Table 11: International fora (in chronological order of establishment)

Forum	Year of establishment	Seat	Regular membership	Objective
Committee on the Global Financial System (CGFS)	1971	Basel	Central banks	Study of financial systems
International Accounting Standards Board (IASB)	1973	London	Accountancy	International accounting standards
Basel Committee on Banking Supervision (BCBS)	1974	Basel	Banking supervisory authorities	Banking regulation and supervision
International Federation of Accountants (IFAC)	1977	New York	Professional accounting associations	International auditing standards
International Organisation of Securities Commissions (IOSCO)	1983	Madrid	Capital markets' supervisory authorities	Capital markets' regulation and supervision
Financial Action Task Force on Money Laundering (FATF)	1989	Paris	G7 States, the European Commission, and the Gulf Cooperation Council	Com bating money laundering and terrorist financing
Committee on Payment and Settlement Systems (CPSS)	1990	Basel	Central banks	Oversight of payment and settlement systems
International Association of Insurance Supervisors (IAIS)	1994	Basel	Supervisory authorities for the insurance sector	Insurance sector regulation and supervision
Joint Forum	1996	Basel	BCBS, IOSCO, IAIS and national supervisory authorities	Regulation and supervision of financial conglomerates
International Association of Deposit Insurers (IADI)	2002	Basel	Deposit guarantee organisations	Operation of deposit guarantee systems

B. In detail: the Basel Committee on Banking Supervision[479]

1. Establishment, seat, membership and legal nature

1.1 Establishment and seat

The Basel Committee on Banking Supervision (hereinafter 'Basel Committee') is probably the most widely known among the international fora founded after 1971, the year when the Bretton Woods system of fixed exchange rates was *de facto* abolished,[480] with a view to safeguarding the stability of the international financial system and, in particular, the international banking system.[481] It was set up on 8 October 1974 by an informal decision of the Governors of G10 member states' central banks and the Governor of the Swiss National Bank as a reaction of the international community to the systemic impact caused, at the international level, by the revocation of Herstatt Bank's operating licence.[482]

Indicative of the very informal character of the Committee, at the time, is the fact that the original mandate assigned to the Committee by the Governors was included in a press release issued by the BIS on 12 February 1975.[483]

From the beginning of its operations until 1988, the Committee's name was 'Standing Committee on Banking Regulations and Supervisory Practices'. In its early years, it was also known as the 'Blunden Committee' or 'Cooke Committee', after the names of its first two chairmen.[484]

The Basel Committee is seated in Basel. It operates under the administrative auspices of the BIS, which provides it with standing secretarial support.[485]

479 The literature on the Basel Committee is very extensive. See indicatively **Kapstein (1994)**, pp. 44-57 and 103-128, **Herring and Litan (1995)**, pp. 95-113, **Norton (1995)**, pp. 171-243, **Walker (2001)**, pp. 17-162, and **Giovanoli (2010)**, pp. 25-26. For a brief historical outline of the Committee (and its current membership), see also the Committee's paper *"History of the Basel Committee and its Membership"* (August 2009), available at: http://www.bis.org/bcbs/history.htm.

480 See under B 2.1.1 in Section Three above.

481 See **Norton (2001)**, pp. 20-21, and **Giovanoli (2000)**, pp. 11-12 and 20-27.

482 See also below under 2.2.1 of this subsection.

483 See **Norton (1995)**, p. 177.

484 See **Walker (2001)**, p. 41. For a list of all former chairmen of the Basel Committee, see the above-mentioned paper *"History of the Basel Committee and its Membership (August 2009)"*, p. 1.

485 Although several other international fora also receive secretarial support by the BIS, as already mentioned, one cannot overlook the fact that this Committee is the only one seated in Basel to be named after this city (despite the fact that it was not the first to be established there).

1.2 Membership

1.2.1 Initial membership

The initial members of the Committee, from its establishment in 1974 until March 2009, were:

- on the one hand, the central banks of the G10 member states, Switzerland and Spain (since 2001),[486] and
- on the other hand, banking (or, more generally, financial) supervisory (and regulatory) authorities in these states, to the extent that their central bank is not exclusively responsible for the conduct of micro-prudential banking supervision,[487] as well as the financial authority of Luxembourg.[488]

The inclusion of both monetary and (other) supervisory authorities in the composition of the Basel Committee was deciced on the consideration that central banks are competent for safeguarding the stability of the banking system (which is the main policy objective of the Committee), even in states which have adopted the "principle of separation of the monetary and supervisory functions of central banks".[489]

Since 1999, the ECB has observer status at the meetings of the Committee and also participates in several of its sub-committees.

1.2.2 Expansion of membership in 2009

In its meeting of 10 and 11 March 2009, the Basel Committee decided to broaden its membership[490] upon an invitation by the G20 to all international fora to review their composition; the expansion was completed in June.[491] The new members of the Basel

486 These central banks are also the most important shareholders of the BIS.

487 Unlike all other supervisory authorities represented on the Basel Committee, the French Banking Commission is responsible for micro-prudential banking supervision, rather than the authorisation of banks, which falls under the competence of another administrative authority, the *Comité des Etablissements de Crédit et des Entreprises d' Investissement.*

488 Luxembourg, albeit not a G10 member state, was included mainly because of its great importance as an international financial centre and also partly as a result of its monetary union with Belgium (on this argument, see **Walker (2001)**, pp. 42-43). Until 1998, it participated only through its 'Monetary Institute', which was not a central bank. Even today the Central Bank of Luxembourg, whose establishment in 1998 was deemed necessary following Luxembourg's EMU accession, is not a member of the Basel Committee. Luxembourg is only represented through its single financial supervisory authority ('Surveillance Commission for the Financial Sector').

489 See under C in Section Two above.

490 **Basel Committee on Banking Supervision (2009a)** *"Expansion of membership announced by the Basel Committee"*, Press release, 13 March, available at: http://www.bis.org/press/p090313.htm.

491 **Basel Committee on Banking Supervision (2009b)**: "Basel Committee broadens its membership", Press release, 10 June, available at: http://www.bis.org/press/p090610.htm.

Committee are the central banks and (as appropriate) the banking (or, more generally, financial) supervisory authorities from the twelve (12) member states of the G20 that were not represented in it.

Accordingly, in May 2012, the Basel Committee was participated in by representatives from the central banks and, as appropriate, other banking (or, more generally, financial) supervisory authorities of the following twenty-seven (27) states:

- all nineteen (19) states, which are members of the G20,
- the two members of the G20 with observer status (the Netherlands and Spain),
- the three (3) members of G10 which are not members of the G20 (Belgium, Sweden and Switzerland), and
- Hong Kong SAR, Singapore and Luxembourg (see **Table 12** below).

In May 2012, Chairman of the Basel Committee was Stefan Ingves, Governor of the Sveriges Riksbank (central bank of Sweden).

Box: EC law

In the EU, cooperation between member states' banking or financial (as appropriate) supervisory authorities takes place within the European Banking Authority (hereinafter 'EBA'). The EBA began its operations in January 2011 as a successor to the Committee of European Banking Supervisors (CEBS), which had been in operation since 1 January 2004.[492] The national central banks of the member states, including those with no formal micro-prudential banking supervisory powers, were full members of CEBS,[493] as they are also of the Basel Committee, but not members of the EBA. As compared to CEBS, the EBA has been endowed with enhanced tasks and powers according to Articles 8 and 9 of Regulation 1093/2010 of the European Parliament and of the Council establishing it.[494]

EBA, ESMA EIOPA and the European Systemic Risk Board, which is responsible for the macro-prudential oversight of the EU financial system,[495] constitute the European System of Financial Supervision (the 'ESFS').[496]

492 Commission Decision 2004/5/EC of 5 November 2003 establishing the Committee of European Banking Supervisors (OJ L 3, 7.1.2004, pp. 28-29, Article 8). In January 2009, this decision was replaced by Commission Decision 2009/78/EC (OJ L 25, 29.1 2009, pp. 23-27). Moreover, cooperation between member state banking supervisory authorities is also effected, since 1998, within the 'Banking Supervision Committee of the ESCB. On the composition and tasks of this Committee, see **European Commission (2000)**, pp. 11-13.

493 Decision 2009/78/EC, Article 7.

494 Regulation (EU) No 1093/2010 of the European Parliament and of the Council of 24 November 2010 establishing a European Supervisory Authority (European Banking Authority), amending Decision No 716/2009/EC and repealing Commission Decision 2009/78/EC (OJ L 331, 15.12.2010, pp. 12-47).

495 Regulation (EU) No 1092/2010 of the European Parliament and of the Council of 24 November 2010 on European Union macro-prudential oversight of the financial system and establishing a European Systemic Risk Board (OJ L 331, 15.12.2010, pp. 1-11).

496 On the composition of EBA, as well as its tasks and powers, see **Gortsos (2011c)**, pp. 21-37.

1.2.3 The two categories of members: central banks and national banking supervisory authorities

As already indicated above, the members of the Basel Committee can be divided in two broad categories:

- national central banks (see under a below), and
- national (administrative) authorities responsible for micro-prudential banking supervision (under b).

(a) National central banks

The first category comprises the national central banks of all member states represented (with the mere exception, as already mentioned, of Luxembourg. According to the relevant national administrative law currently in force, twelve (12) of these central banks are formally competent for conducting micro-prudential banking supervision.[497]

(b) National administrative (supervisory and regulatory) authorities

The second category comprises the national administrative (supervisory and regulatory) authorities of some of its members which have been empowered, pursuant to applicable national administrative law, to conduct micro-prudential banking supervision according to the 'principle of separation of the monetary and supervisory functions of central banks.[498] These supervisory authorities can be classified in three (3) groups depending on the range of their supervisory powers over the financial system. In particular:

(i) The first group is comprised of four (4) supervisory authorities (those in China, France, Turkey and the United States)[499] which are solely responsible for banking micro-prudential supervision in accordance with the 'sectoral approach' to financial supervision.[500]

497 As already mentioned in Section Two, central banks are also usually the institutions entrusted with the task of exercising macro-prudential oversight not only over banks but over the entire financial system.
498 On this principle, see under B 2.3.2.2 in Section Two above.
499 The United States is the only state participating in the Basel Committee with three (3) federal banking supervisory authorities, in addition to its dual participation in the field of central banking (see **Table 12** below).
500 On this approach, see under B 2.3.2.2 (a) in Section Two above.

(ii) The second group comprises the supervisory authorities of Luxembourg and Mexico, which are responsible for micro-prudential supervision both in banking and capital markets, in accordance with the 'modified sectoral approach'.[501]
(iii) The third (and bigger) group contains the remaining nine (9) supervisory authorities which are responsible for the micro-prudential supervision of the entire financial system. Accordingly, these are single financial supervisory authorities in accordance with the 'full integration approach' to financial supervision.[502]

For a summary account of the different approaches adopted by the various states, see **Table 13** *below. Nevertheless, it is worth mentioning that, when this study was being finalised (May 2012), the modification of financial supervisory structures was under way in several states, and these developments could not be covered in it.*

Table 12: Members of the Basel Committee

States	National central banks	National administrative authorities
Argentina	Central Bank of Argentina	
Australia	Reserve Bank of Australia	Australian Prudential Regulation Authority
Belgium	National Bank of Belgium	Banking, Finance and Insurance Commission
Brasil	Central Bank of Brasil	
Canada	Bank of Canada	Office of the Superintendent of Financial Institutions
China	People's Bank of China	China Banking Regulatory Commission
France	Banque de France	Banking Commission
Germany	Deutsche Bundesbank	Financial Supervisory Agency (BaFin)
Hong Kong SAR	Hong Kong Monetary Authority	
India	Reserve Bank of India	
Indonesia	Bank of Indonesia	
Italy	Bank of Italy	
Japan	Bank of Japan	Financial Services Agency
Luxembourg		Surveillance Commission for the Financial Sector
Mexico	Bank of Mexico	National Banking and Securities Commission
Netherlands	The Netherlands Bank	
Russia	Central Bank of the Russian Federation	

501 In Luxembourg, this supervisory authority is also responsible for the supervision of pension funds, which in other states usually falls under the competence of insurance supervisors.
502 On this approach, see under B 2.3.2.2 (b) in Section Two above.

States	National central banks	National administrative authorities
Saudi Arabia	Saudi Arabian Monetary Agency (SAMA)	
Singapore	Monetary Authority of Singapore	
South Africa	South African Reserve Bank	
Republic of Korea	Bank of Korea	Financial Supervisory Service
Spain	Bank of Spain	
Sweden	Sveriges Riksbank	The Swedish Financial Supervisory Authority
Switzerland	Swiss National Bank	Swiss Federal Banking Commission (FINMA)
Turkey	Central Bank of the Republic of Turkey	Banking Regulation and Supervision Authority
United Kingdom	Bank of England	Financial Services Authority
USA	Board of Governors of the Federal Reserve Board Federal Reserve Bank of New York	Office of the Comptroller of the Currency Federal Deposit Insurance Corporation

Table 13: Classification of members of the Basel Committee according to their competences in micro-prudential banking (financial) supervision

		Members of Basel Committee (reference to the relevant state)	
		National central banks	**National administrative authorities**
Approaches on micro-prudential financial supervision	**Sectoral approach**	Argentina Brasil Hong Kong SAR India Indonesia Italy Russia Suadi Arabia Singapore South Africa Spain	***Only for banking:*** China France Turkey United States ***Both for banking and capital markets:*** Luxembourg Mexico
	Functional approach	Netherlands	–
	Full integration approach	–	Australia Belgium Canada Germany Japan Rebublic of Korea Sweden Switzerland United Kingdom

1.3 Legal nature

1.3.1 Legal nature of the Basel Committee

As already mentioned, the Basel Committee is an international forum and not an international organisation. Although it is involved in issues pertaining to banking micro-prudential supervision, it is not a supranational supervisory authority itself, since it does not have the formal power to supervise banks legally incorporated in states whose central banks and banking (or, more generally, financial) supervisory authorities are represented in it. Micro-prudential banking supervision continues to be carried out by the competent national supervisory (and regulatory) authorities, either central banks or independent national administrative authorities, as appropriate.

In accordance with the international financial law currently in force, no international organisation has the power to conduct micro-prudential supervision over banks.[503]

1.3.2 Legal nature and impact of the rules of Basel Committee

As already mentioned, the rules contained in the reports issued by the Basel Committee (as well as those of all other international fora) are not legally enforceable and constitute 'international soft law'. The Basel Committee works on the conviction that its members endeavour for the implementation of the rules incorporated in the reports adopted by it, by any appropriate means, in their national law. Prior to their adoption, the reports are submitted to the Group of Governors and Heads of Supervision (hereinafter 'GHOS') for political approval.[504]

Despite the fact that the rules contained in the reports of the Basel Committee are not legally enforceable, the influence of its work is significant both within and outside the ranks of its members. In particular:

(a) Firstly, a significant part of its work has been adopted by the supervisory authorities that constitute its membership.

(b) In addition, the work of the Basel Committee has definitively been exerting an influence on the provisions of European banking law with regard to both the micro- and macro-prudential regulation, and the micro-prudential supervision of European credit institutions.[505]

(c) It is also worth mentioning that some of the Basel Committee's rules are not only adopted by its member states, but also by third states, as they are considered to be regulatory benchmarks. They are adopted:[506]

- on own initiative,
- under pressure exerted by the markets, or
- in the context of the IMF's supervisory powers – by virtue of its statutory object of monitoring the economic policy of its member states – and as far as issues on safeguarding the stability of the financial system are concerned.[507]

503 For a more detailed analysis of the various proposals for the creation of an international financial supervisory (and regulatory) authority, see, by means of indication, **Eatwell and Taylor (2000)**, **Evans (2001)** and **Goldstein (1997)**. See also **Grubel (1979)** on his proposal for the establishment of an international deposit guarantee organisation.

504 See below under 3.1 of this subsection.

505 See **Sousi-Roubi (1995)**, pp. 198-206, **Hadjiemmanuil (2006b)**, pp. 786-829, **Lastra (2006)**, pp. 297-303, and **Fernandez-Bollo et Tabourin (2007)**, pp. 114-128. On the most recent developments in European banking law, as influenced by the work of the Basel Committee, see **Gortsos (2012b)**, pp. 31-39.

506 See **Schreiber (2005)**, p. 229.

507 See under C 5.1 in Section Three above.

Box: EC law

The issue of creating a supranational banking or, more generally, financial, supervisory authority has been examined extensively, especially in the aftermath of the recent (2007-2009) international financial crisis and in the 'de Larosière Report',[508] but no decision to this end has been taken as yet. In this context, it is worth mentioning that even the ECB, the single monetary authority in the eurozone since 1 January 1999, has not been elevated to the status of a single supervisory authority in the EU neither for the entire financial system of the EU nor for any of its individual sectors. According to the provisions of Article 127(5), of the *"Treaty on the Functioning of the European Union"*, which is repeated *verbatim* in Article 3.3 of the Statutes of the ESCB and of the ECB,[509] the role of the ESCB in this field is confined to *"contribut[ing] to the smooth conduct of policies pursued by the competent authorities relating to the prudential supervision of credit institutions and the stability of the financial system"*.[510]

However, according to the provisions of Article 127(6) of the Treaty (repeated *verbatim* in Article 25.2 of the Statute and referred to as the 'sleeping beauty article'), the ECB could, by unanimous decision of the EcoFin Council, become a supranational micro-prudential supervisory authority in the EU for the banking and the capital markets sectors, but not for the insurance and reinsurance sector.[511] The 'de Larosière Report' argued against the enactment of this provision as well, considering that the ECB should be solely responsible for macro-prudential financial oversight in the EU.[512]

2. Objectives

2.1 Introductory remarks

In the author's view, the objectives of the Basel Committee can be broken down into one principal objective and two ancillary ones:

(a) The principal objective is to contribute to safeguarding the stability of the banking system. This issue will be examined in more detail under 2.2 below.

508 Report of the High-Level Group on Financial Supervision in the EU chaired by Jacques de Larosière, Brussels, 25 April 2009, available at: http://ec.europa.eu/commission_barroso/president/pdf/statement20090225_en.pdf.

509 On the historical evolution of these provisions, which do not apply to the member states with a derogation (Statutes of the ESCB and the ECB, Article 42.1), including the United Kingdom (**Protocol No. 15**, paragraphs 5 and 8), see **Smits (1997)**, pp. 334-338.

510 See **Smits (1997)**, pp. 334-350, **Hadjiemmanuil (2006b)**, pp. 822-824, and **Lastra (2006)**, pp. 298-299.

511 On this Article, see **Smits (1997)**, pp. 355-356.

512 See **de Larosière Report**, para. 146 (on this report, see **Gortsos (2010b)**).

(b) The two ancillary objectives (see under 2.3 below) concern:

- ensuring conditions of competitive equality (with regard to the supervisory regime) between international banks established in states which are represented in the Committee,
- ensuring conditions of competitive equality (once again with regard to the supervisory regime) between international banks, on the one hand, and undertakings providing investment services, on the other, and
- formulating positions on various issues concerning the operation of the banking system but do not touch directly on safeguarding its stability.

2.2 The main objective: safeguarding the stability of the banking system

2.2.1 Recourse of banking supervisory authorities to international cooperation

As already mentioned, the start of operations of the Basel Committee dates back to 1971 when the international monetary system of fixed exchange rates was abolished, leading to a remarkable increase in the volatility of nominal foreign exchange and interest rates in developed economies. This resulted, *inter alia*, in making banks particularly vulnerable to these risks.

In 1974, a grave banking crisis of worldwide magnitude occurred, set off by the excessive exposure of the German bank *Bankhaus I.D. Herstatt* (hereinafter 'Herstatt Bank') to exchange-rate risk as a result of major open positions in forward foreign-exchange transactions.[513] Its fallout was not only the revocation on 26 June of the bank's operating licence by its supervisory authority (*Bundesaufsichtsamt*), but also an unprecedented upheaval in the international interbank market, given that:

- in August 2004, the German supervisory authority also revoked the operating license of three other (smaller) German banks (*Bass & Herz Bankhaus, Bankhaus Wolff KG, and Frankfurter Handelsbank AG*), while
- several banks in other states (such as the British *Hill Samuel Group Ltd*, as well as *Morgan Guarantee Trust Company and Seattle First National Bank* in the United States) were severely exposed to foreign-exchange risk as a result of open positions in forward contracts with Herstatt Bank, which could not be settled.[514]

Concurrently with the initiatives of the banking supervisory authorities in several states aimed at dealing with the causes and effects of this occurrence, the bankruptcy of

513 Due to this event, the risk involving the possibility of loss from transactions in foreign currency due to failure of settlement has since been recorded as 'Herstatt risk'. See the 1996 report of the CPSS: *'Settlement risk in foreign transactions'* (known as 'Allsopp Report'), available at http://www.bis.org/cpsspubl.

514 For an in-depth analysis of this banking crisis and its impact, see **Walker (2001)**, pp. 28-30, **Herring and Litan (1995)**, pp. 95-96, and **Kapstein (1994)**, pp. 39-45.

Herstatt Bank and the crisis which ensued from the bankruptcy of American Franklin National Bank of New York in the two-year period between 1973 and 1974,[515] demonstrated the need to strengthen international cooperation in the field of banking supervision. The concern of the G10 central bank governors (including Switzerland) about the solvency of banks operating in their territory in an environment of marked volatility of key macroeconomic indicators, coupled with the expansion of banking activities as a result of their internationalisation:

- made a priority the establishment of international cooperation between the monetary and (for the first time in history) banking supervisory authorities with a view to preventing systemic crises and safeguarding the stability of the international banking system,[516] and
- led to the establishment of the Basel Committee.[517]

2.2.2 The pillars of international cooperation within the Basel Committee

Cooperation within the Basel Committee from 1974 to date for the achievement of its principal objective has revolved around six (6) pillars, as detailed below.

2.2.2.1 Exchange of views among members

The first pillar concerns the exchange of views among its members, in order to better understand the new environment of the international banking system after the abolition of the Bretton Woods system and the ascertainment of various financial risks to which banks are exposed as part of their operations. Indeed, the Basel Committee started to serve as an informal forum for the exchange of views between its members regarding the stability of the international banking system, given the significant amendments in its operating conditions.[518]

515 For more detail, see **Walker (2000)**, pp. 26-28.

516 It is worth mentioning that, whereas the bankruptcy of *Bankhaus Herstatt* brought about problems mainly as regards the operation of payment and settlement systems, these problems were nevertheless dealt with at a global level much later. See the CPSS report entitled *"Report of the Committee on Interbank Netting Schemes of the central banks of the Group of Ten countries"* ('Lamfalussy Report', 1990), available at: http://www.bis.org/cpsspubl.

517 A detailed account of the history of the Basel Committee's creation is given in **Walker (2001)**, pp. 35-39.

518 See **Walker (2001)**, pp. 47 and 51-54, and **Kapstein (1994)**, pp. 45-46.

2.2.2.2 Cross-border supervisory issues

The second pillar concerns:

- the strengthening of (bilateral and multilateral) cooperation between banking supervisory authorities,
- the elaboration of rules on the incorporation of international banks operating in more than one state through branches and/or subsidiaries within the jurisdiction of supervisory authorities (by allocating responsibilities among home and host supervisors), and
- the creation of effective communication channels for the exchange of essential information (and the provision of mutual assistance) between home and host state supervisory authorities, in order to ensure effective oversight of international banks.

Some of the Committee's reports also contain rules on the conditions for the authorisation of international banks (and particularly their foreign subsidiaries and branches).[519]

2.2.2.3 Standard-setting on issues of banking regulation

The third pillar is more ambitious: it refers to the elaboration of international financial standards on banking micro- and macro-prudential regulation, which should:

- be adopted by its members, and
- be appropriate to contribute to the reduction of banks' exposure to insolvency and, in this way, the safeguarding of the stability of the international banking system.

2.2.2.4 Core minimum regulatory and supervisory practices

In the early years of the Basel Committee's operation, its reports dealt exclusively with banks having significant international activity and a statutory registered office (of the parent undertaking) in one of its members. Gradually, however, and in the aftermath of the severe financial crises of the mid-1990s in various emerging markets, it became evident that, because of the globalisation of financial activities, appropriate supervision of only a sub-total of the international economy's banks was not sufficient for achieving the policy objective of ensuring the stability of the international banking system as a whole.[520]

519 See under A in Section Six below.
520 See **Norton (2001)**, pp. 6-13, **Walker (2001)**, pp. 282-302, and **Giovanoli (2000)**, pp. 6-8.

It was therefore deemed necessary for initiatives to be taken in order to enhance the banking supervisory and regulatory framework in developing states as well. This objective has become, since then, the fourth pillar of cooperation within the framework of the Basel Committee. The Committee now also promotes, apart from further improvement of supervisory measures concerning international banks incorporated in economically developed states, the adoption of appropriate minimum banking supervisory and regulatory standards at international level.

2.2.2.5 Reorganisation, resolution and winding-up of international banks

The issue of the reorganisation and winding-up of international banks exposed to insolvency has preoccupied the Committee only to a limited extent until very recently. Its work was confined to a report in December 1992 entitled *"The insolvency liquidation of an international bank"*.[521] This report listed the problems faced by supervisory authorities as regards the reorganisation of banks operating in more than one state through branches and/or subsidiaries without touching upon issues concerning:

- the harmonisation of the rules governing the winding-up, reorganisation and liquidation of insolvent banking undertakings,[522] and
- the allocation of competences among home and host competent authorities (supervisory and/or judicial) regarding the winding-up and reorganisation of international banks with foreign establishments.

However, especially following the outbreak of the recent (2007-2009) international financial crisis, the G20 entrusted the Basel Committee with the task of increasing its focus on this issue by thorough work on comparing national policies and legal frameworks and allocating responsibilities for the resolution of banks with significant cross-border operations.[523]

2.2.2.6 Deposit guarantee systems

The international coordination of the rules governing deposit guarantee systems and the coverage of deposits with foreign branches of international banks has also not been touched upon by the Basel Committee. On this topic, its work was confined to a com-

521 All the reports of the Basel Committee can be found at: http://www.bis.org/publ/bcbs.
522 The following bodies are mainly active in this field at the international level:
• the United Nations Commission on International Trade Law (UNCITRAL), which developed the Model Law on Cross-Border Insolvency (see **Sekolec (1999)**), and
• since the summer of 2000, the Contact Group on the Legal and Institutional Underpinnings of the International Financial System of G-10, participated in by international organisations, the ECB, and national central banks.
523 See under A 1.2.2.2 in Section Five below.

parative study in June 1998 (*"Deposit protection schemes in the member countries of the Basel Committee"*) in connection with the main features of deposit guarantee systems operating in its member states. Recently, however, it has started addressing this issue, in close cooperation with the IADI.[524]

2.2.3 Subject-area outside the reach of the Basel Committee

The Basel Committee has explicitly stated that its work does not touch upon the role of the central banks as lenders of last resort in crisis periods providing financial support to solvent banks which have been exposed to liquidity risk.[525] This position results from a statement of the Governors of its member central banks, according to which they are not willing to extend their relevant competence to the foreign subsidiaries of banks incorporated within their jurisdiction.[526]

2.2.4 Means of achieving the main objective

2.2.4.1 The reports of the Basel Committee

The main instrument for achieving the principal objective of the Basel Committee is the publication of reports containing international banking standards. From a systematic point of view,[527] various reports have been published between 1974 and May 2012, and they can be classified in seven (7) categories containing standards on:

(i) the cross-border cooperation of banking supervisory authorities and the allocation of responsibilities between home and host authorities,
(ii) international harmonisation of methods for exercising micro-prudential banking regulation,
(iii) the supervisory aspects of the management of risks to which banks are exposed,
(iv) the provision of information by banks to supervisory authorities and the dissemination of information by banks to the public,
(v) core principles of banking supervision and regulation,
(vi) the reorganisation, resolution and winding-up of international banks, and
(vii) deposit guarantee systems.

524 See under A 2.3.7 in Section Five below.
525 See under B 2.7 in Section Two above.
526 See the Committee's 1983 report *"Principles for the Supervision of Banks' Foreign Establishments"* (May 1983), Chapter 1, second sub-paragraph.
527 It should be noted, however, that many of the Basel Committee's reports address several issues rather than exclusively one issue, since the degree of affinity of these issues is particularly high, in certain cases at least.

The most important of these reports are presented in Sections 5 and 6 below, regarding the sources of public international banking law.

2.2.4.2 Promotion of the creation of an informal world forum of banking supervisors

With regard to the achievement of the fourth pillar of cooperation as above, which consists in contributing to the establishment of sound banking supervisory standards at world level, the Committee is also promoting (apart from the formulation of rules of soft law) the creation of an informal world forum for the discussion of issues of banking supervision and regulation. This forum operates through the establishment of regular cooperation:

- with banking supervisory authorities from states that are not represented in the Basel Committee (see under (a) below); and
- with regional associations of banking supervisory authorities which operate throughout the world (under (b)).

(a) Since the mid-1980s, the Basel Committee has pursued ongoing cooperation with the banking supervisory authorities of third states, which are not included in its membership.[528] This cooperation is pursued by:

(i) fostering bilateral relations,
(ii) providing technical assistance to such supervisory authorities in order to support their banking and, more generally, financial system through the above-mentioned Financial Stability Institute, which was created, in 1999, jointly with the BIS,[529] and
(iii) holding an 'International Conference of Banking Supervisors' on matters of interest to banking supervisory authorities, with an increasingly broader participation.

(b) The Basel Committee is also in close cooperation with regional associations of banking supervisory authorities worldwide, many of which were assisted by the Committee at their initial phase. This group of associations includes:[530]

- the Offshore Group of Banking Supervisors (founded in 1980),
- the Commission of Latin America and Caribbean Banking Supervisory and Inspection Organisations (1981), transformed in 1999 into the Association of Supervisors of Banks of the Americas (ASBA)
- the Gulf Cooperation Council (GCC) Committee of Banking Supervisors (1981),
- the South East Asia, New Zealand and Australia (SEANZA) Forum of Banking Supervisors (1984),
- the Caribbean Banking Supervisors Group (1990),

528 See **Norton (1995)**, pp. 182.
529 See under C 3.2.4 in Chapter Three above.
530 For more detail on all these associations, see **Walker (2001)**, pp. 60-67.

- the Group of Banking Supervisors from Central and Eastern Europe (1990),
- the Arab Committee on Banking Supervision (1991),
- the East and Southern Africa Banking Supervisors Group (1993),
- the Committee of Bank Supervisors of West and Central Africa (1994), and
- the Regional Group on Banking Supervision of Transcaucasia, Central Asia and the Russian Federation (1995).

2.3 Subsidiary objectives

2.3.1 Competitive equality between international banks

Recourse to international cooperation within the Basel Committee was also deemed necessary in order to achieve conditions of competitive equality between international banks incorporated in states represented in it. The achievement of this objective is also pursued through the rules contained in the Committee's reports, according to the above-mentioned.

In the early 1980s, economically developed states came to the conclusion that existing prudential banking supervision did not suffice to cover the stability needs of the international banking system in view of newly internationalised conditions. None of these states, however, was willing to take a unilateral initiative for the adoption of the necessary measures that would strengthen the regulatory framework on the basis of which prudential supervision was exercised over banks in their territory. Such an initiative would bring national banks in an unfavourable position in the face of ever-increasing global competition. In light of this and given that the problems which ensued in the mid-1980s from the crisis of the less developed, heavily indebted states, it became imperative to further cooperation in the context of the Basel Committee, aimed at international coordination of prudential supervision instruments, notably capital adequacy rules, and ensure not only the international banking system's stability, but also competition equality (as far as the regulatory framework is concerned) among international banks incorporated in states represented in the Basel Committee.

2.3.2 Competitive equality between international banks and international investment firms

The second ancillary objective of the Basel Committee is the adoption of equivalent rules pertaining to the micro- and macro-prudential regulation of international banks and international investment firms, in terms of their exposure to the same risks from similar financial (and, more particularly, investment) services. The objective is met by means of the Committee's reports issued in collaboration with IOSCO.

2.3.3 Positions on other issues

2.3.3.1 Introductory remarks

The Basel Committee's second ancillary objective is the elaboration of positions on various technical issues pertaining to the operation of the banking system, even though not directly associated with safeguarding its stability. This category includes mainly:

- bank accounting (see under 2.3.3.2 below), and
- combating the use of the financial system for the commitment of economic crimes (under 2.3.3.3).

It also worth noting that the role played by the Basel Committee in the drafting of international financial law has been considerably strengthened since the mid-1990s, given that, in addition to pursuing its own objectives,[531] it takes an active part in two (2) other international fora: the Financial Stability Board and the Joint Forum, as already mentioned.[532]

In addition, a high-level 'Coordination Group' was set up, comprising the Chairmen and Secretaries-General of the Basel Committee, IOSCO, IAIS and the Joint Forum. The Coordination Group meets twice annually to exchange views on the priorities and key issues of common interest.

2.3.3.2 Bank accounting

In recent years, the Basel Committee has also begun dealing with bank accounting issues and, in particular:

- accounting for loans extended and the provisions needed for potential losses of banks from 'bad loans', and
- the content of some of the international accounting standards adopted or drawn up by the IASB.

In pursuit of its mandate, the Basel Committee publishes relevant reports and has an ongoing cooperation with the IASB.

531 See under B 2 of this subsection.
532 See under C 4.2 in Section Three above, and under A 4 of this subsection, respectively.

2.3.3.3 Combating the use of the financial system for the commitment of economic crimes

Finally, the Basel Committee also addresses the issue of combating the use of the financial system for the commitment of economic crimes, notably money-laundering and terrorism-financing, by specifying the implementation of the relevant FATF rules in the case of banks.[533] In order to meet its tasks, the Basel Committee publishes relevant reports in close cooperation with the FATF.

3. Internal organisation

3.1 Introductory remarks

The Basel Committee does not have formal bodies given that it is not an international organisation. As already mentioned, the central bank governors and heads of supervision of its member organisations constitute the Committee's governance body, i.e., the 'Group of Governors and Heads of Supervision' ('GHOS'). This is also the Basel Committee's oversight body, which regularly meets four (4) times a year.[534]

Both the extent and diversified nature of the Basel Committee tasks, as above, required technical expert sub-committees to be set up, in order to deal with specific aspects of the Committee's tasks. In May 2012, the Basel Committee had the following four (4) main expert sub-committees:

- the Standards Implementation Group (see under 3.2 below),
- the Policy Development Group (under 3.3),
- the Accounting Task Force (under 3.4), and
- the Basel Consultative Group (under 3.5).

Other sub-committees include:

- the Core Principles Group,
- the Anti Money Laundering Expert Group,
- the Macroprudential Supervision Group, and
- the Group on replacement of IAS 39.[535]

533 The relevant technical work within the Basel Committee has been assigned to the 'Anti-Money Laundering and Countering the Financing of Terrorism Expert Group' of the International Liaison Group.

534 In May 2012, President of the GHOS was Mervyn King, Governor of the Bank of England.

535 The organisational chart of the Basel Committee is available at: http://www.bis.org/bcbs/organigram.pdf.

3.2 The Standards Implementation Group

The initial mandate of the Standards Implementation Group (SIG) was to share information and promote consistency in the implementation of the Basel II Capital Accord.[536] Currently, its mandate consists in the monitoring of the implementation of the rules adopted by the Basel Committee.[537]

In May 2012, four (4) subgroups were reporting to the SIG:

(i) The 'Operational Risk Subgroup', which addresses issues related to banks' implementation of the advanced measurement approaches for operational risk under the Basel II Capital Accord.

(ii) The 'Task Force on Colleges', which promotes the Basel Committee's work on the 'colleges of supervisory authorities',[538] by developing guidelines on enhancing the effectiveness of these colleges and providing assistance to national supervisory authorities with regard to the implementation of these guidelines.

(iii) The 'Task Force on Remuneration', which contributes to promoting the adoption by Basel Committee's members of sound remuneration practices consistent with the FSB 'Principles for Sound Compensation Practices' of July 2009.[539]

(iv) Finally, the 'Standards Monitoring Procedures Task Force' supports the implementation of the Basel Committee standards and guidelines by its members, by developing appropriate tools and procedures.

3.3 The Policy Development Group

The mandate of the Policy Development Group (the 'PDG') is to support the Committee by:

- identifying and reviewing issues relating to the micro-prudential supervision and regulation of banks, and
- submitting proposals for the adoption of international financial standards which can contribute to the stability of the banking sector.[540]

536 See under B 1.2 in Section Six below.

537 In May 2012, this Group was chaired by Ryozo Himono, Deputy Commissioner for International Affairs at the Financial Services Agency, Japan.

538 For a more detailed definition of these colleges, see under C 4.2.2 in Section Three above.

539 This report is available at: http://www.financialstabilityboard.org/publications/r_0904b.pdf.

540 In May 2012, this Group was chaired by Wayne Byres, Secretary General of the Basel Committee.

In May 2012, seven (7) working groups were reporting to the PDG, which can be classified in two categories:

(a) The first category contains three (3) working groups dealing with specific aspects of the Basel II Capital Accord:

(i) The 'Trading Book Group' addresses issues relating to the implementation of the Basel II Capital Accord to certain exposures arising from trading activities, including (currently) the appropriate capital treatment of event risks in trading books. Furthermore, it addresses implementation issues relating to the revisions to the Basel II market risk framework.

(ii) The 'Definition of Capital Subgroup' explores emerging trends in eligible capital instruments in member states, including (currently) reviewing issues relating to the quality, consistency and transparency of capital, with a particular focus on Tier 1 capital under the Basel II Capital Accord.

(iii) The work of the 'Basel II Capital Monitoring Group' consists in sharing national experiences in monitoring capital requirements under the Basel II Capital Accord in order to ensure that banks maintain a solid capital base throughout the economic cycle.

(b) The second category contains four (4) working groups dealing with other areas falling under the remit of the Basel Committee. In particular:

(i) The 'Risk Management and Modelling Group' is the Basel Committee's contact point with banks as far as the measurement and management of risks is concerned (with the exception of liquidity risk) in view of the adoption of relevant international financial standards.

(ii) The 'Working Group on Liquidity' is a forum for the exchange of information on the national approaches to liquidity risk management, regulation and supervision, and the promotion of relevant international financial standards (especially for cross-border banks).

(iii) The 'Research Task Force' serves as a forum for research economists from member institutions to exchange information and engage in research projects on supervisory and financial stability issues, as well as a mechanism for facilitating communication between economists at member institutions and in the *academia*.

(iv) Finally, the 'Cross-border Bank Resolution Group' is responsible for comparing national policies, legal frameworks and allocating responsibilities for the resolution of banks with significant cross-border operations.

3.4 The Accounting Task Force

The mandate of the Accounting Task Force (ATF) is to ensure that international accounting and auditing standards and practices promote sound banking risk management, support market discipline through transparency, and reinforce the safety and soundness of the banking system.[541] To this purpose, the Task Force develops prudential reporting guidance for banks and takes an active role in the development of international accounting and auditing standards, mainly through the 'Audit Subgroup'.

3.5 The Basel Consultative Group

Finally, the 'Basel Consultative Group' (the 'BCG) is a forum for deepening the Basel Committee's cooperation with supervisors from across the world on a broad range of issues (as discussed under 2.2.4.2 above).[542]

541 In May 2012, this Group was chaired by Sylvie Mathérat, Deputy Director General of the Banque de France.

542 In May 2012, this Group was chaired by Karl Cordevener, Deputy Secretary General of the Basel Committee.

CHAPTER THREE

THE SOURCES OF PUBLIC INTERNATIONAL BANKING LAW

SECTION FIVE AN OVERVIEW OF THE SOURCES OF PUBLIC INTERNATIONAL FINANCIAL LAW

A. The main sources of public international financial law

1. Introductory remarks

1.1 General remarks

The international fora mentioned in Section Four above have issued hundreds of reports since their establishment, containing international financial standards and constituting the sources of public international financial law, in its various branches, in accordance with what is mentioned in Section Three (under A.2). The presentation of all these reports is beyond the scope of this study, and their mere enumeration would not serve any academic purpose. The interested reader can consult the relevant internet sites of these fora.

Another source of public international financial law is the General Agreement on Trade in Services (GATS). With regard to international trade in financial services the provisions of the following documents are also relevant in this context (as already mentioned in Section Three above, under C 3.2.2):

- the Second Annex of GATS on Financial Services,
- the Second Protocol to GATS which replaces the schedules of specific commitments and lists of exemptions relating to financial services set out in Article II of the GATS, and
- the Understanding on Commitments in Financial Services.

Further analysis of these provisions is also not deemed appropriate in this study.[543]

On the contrary, we will concentrate on the following aspects with regard to the sources of public international financial law:

(a) First of all, subsection A 1.2 (immediately below) makes a general reference to the main sources of international banking law, four (4) out of five (5) of which are analysed in more detail in subsection A 2 and also in Section Six below.

(b) Subsection A.2 contains a brief presentation of the *"Key Standards for Sound Financial Systems"*, included in the FSB Compendium.

(c) Finally, subsection B focuses on the initiatives of the four (4) more significant G20 Summits held after the recent (2007-2009) international financial crisis, resulting in

543 For a more detailed analysis on this, see **von Bogdandy and Windsor (2008)**.

several reports that have been issued (or will be issued) by the FSB or other international fora and constitute the most recent sources of public international financial law (see **Table 14** below).

1.2 In particular: the sources of international banking law

1.2.1 Comprehensive view

In the author's view, out of dozens of reports constituting the sources of international banking law the main sources are the following:

(i) the Basel Committee's reports on micro-prudential supervision of international banks and cross-border cooperation between supervisory authorities (see under A in Section Six below),
(ii) the Basel Committee's reports on micro- and macro-prudential regulatory intervention in the operation of banks (ibid., under B),
(iii) the "Core Principles for Effective Banking Supervision", issued by the Basel Committee and included in the FSB's Compendium (see below under 2.4.1),
(iv) the "Core Principles for Effective Deposit Insurance Systems", jointly issued by the Basel Committee and the IADI, also included in the FSB's Compendium (under 2.3.7), and
(v) the Basel Committee and FSB reports on the definition of systemically important banks and their resolution in the event of solvency problems (just under 1.2.2).[544]

1.2.2 Reports on the resolution of systemically important banks

1.2.2.1 Global systemically important banks (G-SIBs): Evaluation methodology and loss-absorption requirements

The Basel Committee published a report in November 2011 regarding global systemically important banks ('G-SIBs'), which included the methodology to be used for eligibility under this category, as well as additional loss-absorption requirements that

544 These reports, still under consultation, are presented by way of exception in this subsection rather than subsection B, which looks into the progress made following the recent (2007-2009) international financial crisis, because they will be included in the main body of international banking law. The FSB's relevant involvement is a corollary of:
• the increasingly important role assigned to it at the current juncture, and
• the fact that in this subject-area measures are also taken for other categories of financial firms (in particular investment firms, insurance and reinsurance undertakings), and the FSB coordinates the relevant work of the competent international fora.

need to be fulfilled.[545] As pointed out by the Committee, the recent international financial crisis has brought to the fore significant problems, *inter alia*, relating to the resolution of certain large-scale, internationally active banks given the systemic risk and general risks to financial stability arising from their resolution.

Despite measures and initiatives taken to reinforce the resilience of banks, particularly through the well-known 'Basel III' regulatory framework,[546] these are considered insufficient to address negative externalities associated with banks falling under the category of G-SIBs. As a result, it is deemed necessary to adopt special provisions on G-SIBs, aimed at:

- limiting the possibility of bank failure by bolstering capacity of G-SIBs to absorb losses, on the one hand, and
- mitigating the impact of their failure by improving the international regulatory framework on bank resolution.

Measures adopted with the above-mentioned report are aimed at achieving the first objective, i.e. laying down further requirements on the absorption of losses. The Basel Committee has also developed the methodology to be used in order for a bank to be eligible as a G-SIB, which is based on both quantitative and qualitative parameters. The selected parameters reflect different aspects of the main causes of negative externalities rendering a bank 'critical' to financial stability, i.e.:

- size,
- interconnectedness,
- lack of substitutability,
- international (cross-border) activity, and
- complexity of banking activities.

The report provides a detailed overview of these parameters, their weight (20% equally to each parameter) and specific aspects that need be taken into consideration for each one of them, as well as their exact calculation and assessment. Additional capital requirements regarding loss absorption imposed on such banks, as well as their expected impact, are also analysed in detail.

These additional requirements should be implemented in parallel with the Basel III requirements on the capital conservation and countercyclical buffers from 1 January 2016 until end-2018 and fully enter into force on 1 January 2019.[547]

545 **Basel Committee on Banking Supervision (2011f)**: *"Global systemically important banks: Assessment methodology and the additional loss absorbency requirement – Rules text"*, November, available at: http://www.bis.org/publ/bcbs207.pdf.

546 See under B in Section Six below.

547 See in particular under B 3.1.3.2 in Section Six below.

1.2.2.2 Resolution of systemically important banks

On 19 July 2011, the FSB submitted a consultative document with regard to effective resolution frameworks for systemically important financial institutions (hereinafter referred as 'SIFIs'), including banks par excellence.[548] The document's proposed policy measures aim to improve the capacity of authorities to resolve SIFIs:

- without systemic disruption, and
- without exposing the taxpayer to the risk of having to bear resolution costs.

The consultative document is divided into four (4) sections (see under I-IV below).

(I) *Resolution powers and tools*

(A) *Effective resolution regimes*

This section points out the need to adopt national legislative provisions on the resolution of SIFIs, providing competent authorities with the tools for safe and swift intervention, ensuring a firm's ongoing business and preventing the destabilisation of financial markets. The main reason for establishing such legislation is that the applicable framework on corporate liquidation under bankruptcy law does not take account of the specificities and problems arising from the activities of systemically important financial service providers.

According to the FSB, an effective national framework for the resolution of SIFIs presupposes the assignment of relevant powers to an administrative authority with the statutory objective to promote financial stability in the conduct of its tasks and have the necessary expertise, resources, capacities and operational independence to perform its responsibilities. Resolution tools are classified by the FSB into the following three (3) main categories:

- sale of the entire firm (or at least of all its viable activities) as an ongoing business to a new owner,
- separation and eventual sale of functions that are systemically important or have franchise value as a separate operation while the residual parts of the firm are wound down (or alternatively carving out and transferring the bad assets to a separate asset management vehicle), and
- recapitalisation of the firm by restructuring its liabilities (the 'bail-in' resolution tool).

548 **Financial Stability Board (2011)**: *"Effective Resolution of Systemically Important Financial Institutions-Recommendations and Timelines"*, Consultative Document, July, available at: http://www.financial stabilityboard.org/publications/r_110719.pdf. See also **Financial Stability Board (2011b):** *"Effective Resolution of Systemically Important Financial Institutions-Recommendations and Timelines"*, Consultative Document, July, available at: http://www.financial stabilityboard.org/publications/r_110719.pdf.

(B) *Bail-in powers*

The FSB proposes the adoption of provisions on the absorption of resolution costs by financial institutions' shareholders and unsecured creditors, by enabling resolution authorities to write-down or convert into equity unsecured and uninsured claims ('bail-in within resolution'). The bail-in tool is to be used, according to the FSB, coupled with other resolution tools in most cases, while competent authorities must be given the ability, rather than be obliged, to resort to it.

As a general rule, the bail-in process should be initiated by the home authority of the parent firm in resolution or, if resolution measures are taken at subsidiary level, by the host authorities of the subsidiary's state of establishment. However, taking into account that this initiation could result in a change of the firm's ownership structure, host authorities should consult with the home authorities of the parent undertaking.

(II) *Facilitation of cross-border cooperation*

In the absence of a relevant international multilateral agreement, the conclusion of bilateral and multilateral cross-border agreements is recommended, laying down the manner of cooperation amongst relevant resolution authorities to facilitate resolution of internationally active institutions.

(III) *Resolvability assessment and improvement*

In order to identify the factors preventing a smooth and swift resolution and address them effectively, the FSB recommends the production of evaluation reports on each individual SIFI's resolvability, in accordance with relevant standards laid down in Annex 4. It also suggests drafting Recovery and Resolution Plans ('RRPs'), in association with individual enterprises and competent authorities for each undertaking that is deemed by competent national authorities to be systemically important, mandatory in the case of global SIFIs. The consultative document also proposes detailed recommendations on improving and bolstering the capacity of SIFIs for smooth resolution.

(IV) *Issues for further review*

Finally, the question arises as to whether it is possible to pursue further harmonisation of national provisions on:

- the ranking of creditors' claims,
- depositors' protection, and
- the conditions under which a temporary suspension of contractual early termination rights should apply in the event of a firm's entry into resolution.

2. An overview of the Compendium of the Financial Stability Board

2.1 Overall examination

As already mentioned, in April 2001, the Financial Stability Forum (FSF) published a Compendium entitled *"International Standards and Codes to Strengthen Financial*

Systems". This 'Compendium of Standards and Codes' (hereinafter the 'Compendium') has been gradually expanded by the FSB and in May 2012, it included fourteen (14) of the numerous reports issued by the above-mentioned international organisations and fora assigned with the task of governing both the international monetary and the international financial system. The selection was made on the premise that the rules included therein, in the form of standards and codes,[549] are of fundamental importance to ensuring the stability of the international monetary and financial system, as well as achieving other objectives of regulatory intervention in the monetary and financial system.

The standards and codes of the FSB's Compendium are divided into three (3) categories of reports:

- four (4) reports pertaining to national macroeconomic policies and the transparency of data supplied by the competent authorities (see under 2.2 below),
- seven (7) reports pertaining to institutional and market infrastructure (under 2.3), and
- three (3) reports pertaining to the regulatory intervention in the financial system, and the financial system's supervision (under 2.4).[550]

It is strongly expected that the Compendium will be further expanded from 2012 onwards to include one or more reports containing international standards on financial resolution regimes.

2.2. Codes pertaining to national macroeconomic policies and the transparency of data supplied by competent authorities

2.2.1 Code of Good Practices on Transparency in Monetary and Financial Policies

Issued by the IMF in 1999, this Code identifies desirable transparency practices for:

- central banks in their conduct of monetary policy, and
- central banks and other supervisory authorities in the individual financial system sectors (banking, insurance, capital market) in the performance of their supervisory and regulatory responsibilities.

These transparency practices are desirable according to the IMF for two main reasons:

- the first one is the effectiveness of monetary and financial policies, which can be strengthened if the objectives and the means of achieving them are known to the public, and

549 As already mentioned in Section Three above, the terms 'standard' and 'code' are used as synonyms.

550 For an overview of the content of the reports initially included in the Compendium, see also **Walker (2001a)**, pp. 317-326, and **Norton (2001)**, pp. 16-19.

- the second one is that accountability of central banks and other supervisory authorities may strengthen their governance and ensure policy consistency, especially where these authorities have a high degree of autonomy.

2.2.2 Code of Good Practices on Fiscal Transparency

This code, which was also issued by the IMF a year earlier (1998) and updated in June 2007, identifies the desirable transparency requirements regarding:

- the clarity of the role and the responsibilities between government and commercial activities,
- 'open' budget processes,
- public availability of information with respect to the (past, current and projected) fiscal activity and major fiscal risks, and
- assurances with regard to the integrity of fiscal data and practices.

Taking into account that transparency is a key aspect of good governance, the main objective of the Code is to reassure the public and the capital markets that reliable and sufficient information is available on the government structure and finances, so as to allow the soundness of fiscal policy to be assessed.

2.2.3 Special Data Dissemination Standard and General Data Dissemination System

This framework of standards, also elaborated by the IMF, was issued in 1996 and 1997 and contains two parts:

(a) The first part (SDDS) is addressed to states that have, or that might seek, access to international capital markets with respect to dissemination of economic and financial data to the public.

(b) The second part (GDDS) is addressed to states that do not have or intend to obtain access to international capital markets, taking into account the particularities of each state's economy, as well as the data dissemination systems developed in each state.

States adopting the SDDS or the GDDS commit to abide by good statistical practices with regard to:

- coverage, periodicity and timeliness of disseminated data,
- access by the public,
- correctness of data, and
- the quality of data.

Data dissemination practices under these two codes cover twenty (20) categories of data, referring to the real, fiscal, financial and external sectors of the economy.

2.3 Codes pertaining to institutional and market infrastructure

2.3.1 Principles for Effective Insolvency and Creditor Rights Systems

This report of the World Bank is aimed at the elaboration of specific principles on the legal and institutional aspects of insolvency, as well related creditors' rights in economically developing states. It was issued in 2001 and amended in December 2005. The report contains principles underlying effective:

- systems for formal reorganisation and liquidation/insolvency proceedings,
- organisation and functioning of commercial courts and insolvency professionals,
- out-of-court restructuring practices and procedure,
- credit access and protection mechanisms,
- commercial enforcement, and
- credit risk management frameworks.

2.3.2 Principles of corporate governance

In 1999, the OECD issued a report with specific principles aimed at improving the legal, institutional and regulatory framework on corporate governance in OECD member states and non-OECD states. These principles, which were amended in 2004, concern:

- the rights and equal treatment of shareholders,
- disclosure and transparency obligations in order to ensure timely and accurate disclosure on all material matters regarding the operation of companies, and
- the responsibilities of board members in order to ensure the strategic guidance for companies (pursuing objectives in the interest of the company and its shareholders) and the effective monitoring of the management.

The OECD principles focus mainly on listed companies; their application in companies whose shares are not listed in regulated markets is, however, not excluded.

2.3.3 International Financial Reporting Standards (IFRS)

The International Financial Reporting Standards ('IFRS'), previously known as 'International Accounting Standards', are issued by the International Accounting Standards Board. These standards (thirty-eight (38) in total, in May 2012):

- are constantly being updated,
- are accompanied by specific Interpretations (in total twenty-eight (28)), and

- have been adopted for implementation mainly, but not exclusively, by enterprises listed in regulated markets (always on a consolidated basis, namely at 'group level').

In order for enterprises to be considered as compliant with the IFRS, they must meet all of the individual IFRSs and IFRS Interpretations issued by the IASB.

2.3.4 International Standards on Auditing (ISA)

The International Federation of Accountants, through its International Auditing and Assurance Standards Board, issues international financial standards on the convergence of national rules and standards pertaining to the external audit of the financial statements of enterprises and other data provided to shareholders (and for companies listed in regulated markets, to the public). These International Standards on Auditing ('ISA') concern, *inter alia*:

- the importance of professional scepticism,
- aspects of financial statements that generally have a higher risk of material misstatement (e.g. estimates, fair values and related parties),
- the quality of audit evidence, and
- auditors' communications and reporting.

2.3.5 Principles for financial market infrastructures

These principles, adopted in May 2012 by CPSS and IOSCO, replaced and codified three (3) previous reports of the same fora, issued in 2001-2004, on the principles which should regulate financial market infrastructures, taking into account existing experience, lessons from the recent (2007-2009) international financial crisis and recent policy work by the CPSS and IOSCO.[551] The twenty-four (24) principles apply to:

- systemically important payment systems,
- central securities depositories,
- securities settlements systems,
- central counterparties, and
- trade repositories.

551 **CPSS (2001)**: *"Core principles for systemically important payment systems"*, January, available at: http://www.bis.org/publ/cpss43.htm, **CPSS (2001)**: *"Recommendations for securities settlement systems"*, November, available at: http://www.bis.org/publ/cpss46.htm, and **CPSS - IOSCO (2004)**: *"Recommendations for central counterparties"*, November, available at: http://www.bis.org/publ /cpss64.htm.

The new principles concern mainly the following subject areas:

(i) credit risk and liquidity risk management, including collateral and margin which should be risk-based,
(ii) settlement finality and money settlement,
(iii) governance central securities depositories and securities settlement systems,
(iv) participant default rules and procedures,
(v) general business and operational risk management,
(vi) access and participation requirements to financial market infrastructures,
(vii) efficiency, effectiveness and transparency of financial market infrastructures, and
(viii) responsibilities of authorities to provide for the effective regulation, supervision and oversight of financial market infrastructures.

2.3.6 Forty (40) Recommendations and nine (9) Special Recommendations on Money Laundering and Terrorist Financing

The FATF issued a report in 1990 (updated in 1996 and 2003) laying down forty (40) recommendations which set the framework for combating money laundering. In 2001, just a few months after the terrorist attacks of 11 September 2001, the FATF also issued eight (8) special recommendations on combating terrorist financing, complemented with a ninth recommendation in 2004. Revised comprehensive recommendations were re-issued in February 2012, providing the main framework to detect, prevent and contain such crimes. The FATF Recommendations cover, *inter alia*:

- identification of the risks,
- criminalisation of money-laundering and terrorist financing,
- preventive measures to be adopted by financial institutions and designated non-financial professions,
- institutional measures, such as the creation of a Financial Intelligence Unit,
- transparency measures, and
- international cooperation.

2.3.7 Core Principles for Effective Deposit Insurance Systems

On 18 June 2009, the Basel Committee and IADI jointly issued a report containing eighteen (18) *"Core Principles for Effective Deposit Insurance Systems"*. As mentioned in this report, a deposit guarantee system can be credible and avoid banks' exposure to moral hazard, if it forms an integral part of a well-structured and effective 'safety net' for the banking system and if it does not operate independently of its other components.[552] More specifically, these principles refer to:

552 This is fully consistent with the analysis under B in Section Two above.

- the policy objectives of deposit guarantee systems,
- the powers of these systems,
- the principles on their governance,
- the relationship with other components of the 'bank safety net',
- the obligation for all banks to participate in a deposit guarantee system and the coverage provided to depositors by these systems,
- their funding mechanisms,
- the information provided to depositors,
- specific legal issues,
- the procedures for the resolution of failing banks), and
- the pay-out to depositors.

2.4 Codes on financial micro-prudential regulation and supervision

2.4.1 Core Principles for Effective Banking Supervision

This report is the result of cooperation between the Basel Committee and non-participating banking supervisory authorities. It was issued in 1997, then revised in October 2006, and contains a list of twenty-five (25) principles that serve as a main point of reference for banking supervisory authorities and govern the micro-prudential supervision (and regulation) of banks in every state in order to ensure its effectiveness.
In order to facilitate implementation and evaluation of these principles, the Committee issued a methodology report in 1999 entitled "Core Principles Methodology" (also revised in 2006).[553]
For the most part, these principles are derived from recommendations and guidelines contained in other Basel Committee reports[554] and refer to seven (7) subject-areas:

(i) the macroeconomic and institutional requirements that must be fulfilled so that the supervisory authorities can exercise effective micro-prudential banking supervision,
(ii) the conditions for the provision of operating licenses to banks, as well as the approval of amendments in shareholders' structure,
(iii) the micro-prudential regulatory framework for exercising micro-prudential banking supervision,
(iv) methods to be used by supervisory authorities, in cooperation with internal and external auditors, for the control of supervised banks,

553 In December 2011, the Basel Committee issued a consultative document on the revision of the Core Principles and the consolidation of both the principles and their methodology into a single text, available at: http://www.bis.org/publ/bcbs/bcbs213.htm.
554 Most of these principles will be discussed in detail in Section Six below, as part of the analysis of the 'Basel Concordat' and the 'Basel Capital Accords'.

(v) the range of information to be submitted by banks to their supervisory authorities and disclosed to the public,
(vi) the necessary powers of supervisory authorities, and
(vii) the relevant cross-border cooperation of supervisory authorities.

These principles are currently under review.[555]

2.4.2 Objectives and Principles of Securities Regulation

This report of the International Organisation of Securities Commissions (IOSCO) was issued in 1998 and revised in 2003 and 2010. It sets out 38 principles/standards, accompanied by examples of specific existing practices as regards micro-prudential supervision and regulation of capital markets and investment service providing firms with a view to meeting three policy objectives:

- safeguard the protection of investors,
- ensure the integrity, efficiency and transparency of capital markets, and
- safeguard the stability of capital markets (by reducing systemic risk).

The IOSCO principles are grouped into eight (8) categories depending on their recipient and subject-matter, as follows:

- principles for the regulator,
- principles for self-regulation,
- principles for the enforcement of securities regulation,
- principles for cooperation in regulation,
- principles for issuers,
- principles for collective investment schemes,
- principles for market intermediaries, and
- principles for the secondary market.

2.4.3 Insurance Core Principles

The twenty-six (26) principles of the IAIS included in a 1997 report that was revised in 2000, 2003, and 2011, refer to the conditions that need to be met in order for a national insurance supervisory and regulatory system to be effective. The code:

555 See on this *"Core principles for effective banking supervision – Consultative Document"*, available at: http://www.bis.org/publ/bcbs213.htm.

- sets out the framework for insurance micro-prudential supervision,
- identifies areas of major importance that need to be addressed though national micro-prudential regulations in this sector of the financial system, and
- relevant powers of the competent supervisory authorities.

Table 14: Compendium: Key Standards for Sound Financial Systems

Area	Report	Issuing body
A. Macroeconomic Policy and Data Transparency		
Monetary and financial policy transparency	Code of Good Practices on Transparency in Monetary and Financial Policies	IMF
Fiscal policy transparency	Code of Good Practices on Fiscal Transparency	IMF
Data dissemination	• Special Data Dissemination Standard/ • General Data Dissemination System	IMF
B. Institutional and Market Infrastructure		
Insolvency	Insolvency and Creditor Rights	World Bank
Corporate governance	Principles of Corporate Governance	OECD
Accounting	International Financial Reporting Standards (IFRS)	IASB
Auditing	International Standards on Auditing (ISA)	IFAC
Payment and settlement	Principles for Financial Market Infrastructures	CPSS/IOSCO
Market integrity	Forty Recommendations and Nine Special Recommendations on Money Laundering and Terrorist Financing	FATF
Deposit guarantee	Core Principles for Effective Deposit Insurance Systems	Basel Committee/ IADI
C. Financial Regulation and Supervision		
Banking supervision	Core Principles for Effective Banking Supervision	BCBS
Securities regulation	Objectives and Principles of Securities Regulation	IOSCO
Insurance supervision	Insurance Core Principles	IAIS

B. *International supervisory and regulatory developments after the recent (2007-2009) international financial crisis: the contribution of the G20 and the Financial Stability Board (FSB)*

1. The G20 London Summit (April 2009)

1.1 Introductory remarks

A G20 Summit of major importance took place in London in April 2009, where member states were represented by their Heads of State or Government. Prior to the London Summit, a G20 Summit was held in Washington in November 2008. The latter Summit's Declaration includes an annex entitled "Action Plan to Implement Principles for Reform" (hereinafter 'the Washington Action Plan'),[556] which was broadly based on the FSF Report entitled *"Enhancing Market and Institutional Resilience"*.[557]

More particularly, in October 2007 the G7 assigned the FSF with analysing the causes that led to the recent international financial crisis and submitting a set of proposals on the readjustment of international financial law. The Report was conducted with the close cooperation of all the above-mentioned international organisations and fora participating in the governance of the international architecture of the financial system, as well as the national supervisory and regulatory financial authorities from major financial centres, and was submitted in April 2008. Following the above-mentioned report, FSF submitted new update reports on the implementation of the proposals.[558]

556 See **G20 (2008)**, pp. 6-10.

557 **Financial Stability Forum (2008a)**, April, available at: http://www.fsforum.org/ publications/ FSF_Report_to_G-7_11_April.pdf.

558 See on this the following reports of the **Financial Stability Forum:**

- **(2008b)**: "Follow-up Report on the Implementation of the FSF's April Recommendations", October,
- **(2009b)**: "Report of the Financial Stability Forum on Enhancing Market and Institutional Resilience, Update on Implementation", April,
- **(2009c)**: "Overview of Progress in Implementation – Report by Financial Stability Board to G20 Leaders", September,
- **(2009d)**: "Progress since the Pittsburgh Summit in Implementing the G20 Recommendations for Strengthening the Financial Stability", November,
- **(2010a)**: "Progress since the St. Andrews meeting in Implementing the G20 Recommendations for Strengthening the Financial Stability", April,
- **(2010b)**: "FSB Chair letter to G20 Leaders 24 June 2010", June,
- **(2010c)**: "FSB Report on Progress since the Washington Summit", November,
- **(2011a)**: "Progress in the Implementation of the G20 Recommendations for Strengthening the Financial Stability", February,
- **(2011b)**: "Progress in the Implementation of the G20 Recommendations", April,

At the London Summit, the G20 Leaders committed themselves to the implementation of the just above-mentioned Washington Action Plan. Moreover, they published a *"Declaration on Strengthening the Financial System"*,[559] the context of which, from a systemic point of view, is analysed below. In this context, they agreed to take action on the following fields:

- on certain rules pertaining to financial regulation (see under 1.2.1 below),
- on the micro-prudential supervision of international financial firms and other issues pertaining to international financial cooperation (under 1.2.2),
- on the macro-prudential oversight of the financial system (under 1.2.3),
- on compensation (under 1.2.4), and
- on tax havens and non-cooperative states (under 1.2.5).

1.2 The decisions taken

1.2.1 Micro-prudential financial regulation

1.2.1.1 Extension of regulation and oversight to all systemically important financial institutions, instruments and markets

The G20 Leaders agreed on the need to extend regulation and oversight to all systemically important financial institutions, instruments and markets. This means that systemically important hedge funds will be included for the first time.[560] In this respect, the following decisions were taken:

(a) National regulators will possess the powers for gathering relevant information on all material financial institutions, markets, and instruments in order to assess the potential for their failure or severe stress to contribute to systemic risk. This should be done in close coordination at international level in order to achieve as much consistency as possible across states.

(b) In order to prevent regulatory arbitrage, the IMF and the FSB should produce guidelines for national authorities to assess whether a financial institution, market, or an instrument is systemically important by the next meeting of the G20 Finance Ministers and central bank governors. These guidelines should focus on what institutions do rather than their legal form.

- **(2011d)**: "Framework for Monitoring and Reporting on the Implementation of G20 Financial Reforms", October, and
- **(2011e)**: "FSB Report on the Overview of Progress in the Implementation of the G20 Recommendations for Strengthening the Financial Stability", November.

All these reports are available at: http://www.financialstabilityboard.org/list/fsb_publications/tid_133/index.htm. See also below under C of this Section.

559 See **G20 (2009a)** "*Declaration on Strengthening the Financial System*", available at: http://www.g20.org/Documents/Fin_Deps_Fin_Reg_ Annex_020409_-_1615_final.pdf.

560 **G20 (2009b)** "*The Global Plan for Recovery and Reform*", paragraph 15, fourth indent.

(c) With regard to the regulation and supervision of hedge funds and their managers the decisions made refer to the following principles:

- hedge funds and their managers will be registered and will be required to disclose appropriate information on an ongoing basis to supervisors or regulators, including on their leverage, necessary for assessment of the systemic risks that they pose individually or collectively,
- where appropriate, registration should be subject to a minimum size,
- hedge funds will be subject to oversight to ensure that they have adequate risk management,
- the FSB will develop mechanisms for cooperation and information-sharing between relevant authorities in order to ensure that effective oversight is maintained where a fund is located in a different jurisdiction from the manager, and
- through the FSB, measures will be developed for the implementation of these principles by the end of 2009.

(d) Finally, supervisors should require that institutions which have hedge funds as their counterparties have effective risk management. This should include mechanisms to monitor the funds' leverage and set limits for single counterparty exposures.[561]

1.2.1.2 Improvement of accounting standards

Accounting standard setters have been encouraged to work, as a matter of urgency, with supervisors and regulators to improve standards on valuation and provisioning and achieve a single set of high-quality international accounting standards.[562] In particular, it was agreed that accounting standard setters should take action by the end of 2009 in order to:

(i) reduce the complexity of accounting standards for financial instruments,
(ii) strengthen accounting recognition of loan-loss provisions by incorporating a broader range of credit information,
(iii) improve accounting standards for provisioning, off-balance sheet exposures and valuation uncertainty,
(iv) achieve clarity and consistency in the application of valuation standards internationally, working with supervisors,
(v) make significant progress towards a single set of high quality international accounting standards, and
(vi) within the framework of the independent accounting standard setting process, improve involvement of stakeholders, including prudential regulators and emerging markets, through the IASB's constitutional review.[563]

561 **G20 (2009c)** *"Leaders' Statement"*, Section "The scope of regulation", third to sixth indents.
562 **G20 (2009b)**, paragraph 15, eighth indent.
563 **G20 (2009c)**, Section "Accounting standards".

1.2.1.3 Oversight of credit rating agencies

The G20 Leaders agreed that there is a need to extend regulatory oversight and registration to credit rating agencies in order to ensure that they meet the international code of good practice of IOSCO, particularly to prevent unacceptable conflicts of interest.[564] In particular, the following has been agreed upon:

(i) all credit rating agencies whose ratings are used for regulatory purposes should be subject to a regulatory oversight regime that includes registration,
(ii) the regulatory oversight regime should be established by end-2009, it should be consistent with the IOSCO Code of Conduct Fundamentals, and IOSCO should coordinate full compliance,
(iii) national authorities will cnforce compliance and require amendments to a rating agency's practices and procedures for managing conflicts of interest and assuring the transparency and quality of the rating process,
(iv) credit rating agencies should differentiate ratings for structured products and provide full disclosure of their ratings track record and the information and assumptions that underpin the ratings process,
(v) the oversight framework should be consistent across states with appropriate sharing of information between national authorities, including through IOSCO, and
(vi) the Basel Committee should take forward its review on the role of external ratings in prudential regulation and determine whether there are any adverse incentives that need to be addressed.[565]

1.2.1.4 Standardisation of credit derivatives markets

The decision has also been taken to promote the standardisation and resilience of credit derivatives markets, in particular through the establishment of central clearing counterparties subject to effective regulation and supervision. The G20 Leaders called upon the industry, as appropriate, to develop an action plan on standardisation by autumn 2009 (not yet finalised).[566]

1.2.1.5 Enhancement of micro- and macro-prudential banking regulation

With regard to prudential banking regulation, the following decisions have been taken:

(i) Once economic recovery is assured, there is a need to improve the quality, quantity, and international consistency of capital in the banking system.

564 **G20 (2009b)**, paragraph 15, ninth indent.
565 **G20 (2009c)**, Section "Credit rating agencies".
566 Ibid., fourth section, seventh indent.

(ii) In future, regulation must prevent excessive leverage and require buffers of resources to be built in good times.[567]
(iii) The FSB, the Basel Committee and CGFS, working with accounting standard setters, should take forward, with a deadline of end-2009, implementation of the recommendations to mitigate procyclicality, including a requirement for banks to build buffers of resources in good times that they can draw down when conditions deteriorate.
(iv) Risk-based capital requirements should be supplemented with a simple, transparent, non-risk based measure which is internationally comparable, properly takes into account off-balance sheet exposures, and can help contain the build-up of leverage in the banking system.
(v) The Basel Committee and national supervisory and regulatory authorities should take forward work on improving incentives for risk management of securitisation, including considering due diligence and quantitative retention requirements, by 2010.
(vi) All G20 member states should progressively adopt the Basel II capital framework.
(vii) Finally, the Basel Committee and national supervisory and regulatory authorities should develop and agree by 2010 an international framework for promoting stronger liquidity buffers at financial institutions, including cross-border institutions.[568]

1.2.2 Micro-prudential supervision of international financial firms and other issues pertaining to international financial cooperation

Micro-prudential supervision of financial firms remains a competence of national authorities. Nevertheless, it has been agreed to establish 'supervisory colleges' by June 2009 for all 'significant cross-border financial firms' (i.e. financial firms whose presence in states all over the world may pose a threat to the stability of the international financial system), in addition to the 28 already in place.[569] In addition, it has been agreed:

- to implement the FSF principles for cross-border crisis management immediately, and that home authorities of each major international financial institution should ensure that the group of authorities with a common interest in that financial institution meet at least annually,
- to support continued efforts by the IMF, FSB, World Bank, and BCBS to develop an international framework for cross-border bank resolution arrangements, and
- to enhance international cooperation on the subject of exit strategies.[570]

567 **G20 (2009b)**, paragraph 15, sixth indent.
568 **G20 (2009c)**, Section "Prudential regulation", fourth indent et seq. .
569 Ibid., Section "International cooperation", first indent.
570 Ibid., second to fourth indents.

1.2.3 Macro-prudential oversight of the financial system

Another major policy area on which agreement was reached was the establishment of mechanisms, at an international level, for the enhancement of the macro-prudential oversight of the financial system. The aim of this proposal is to ensure, through cooperation between national monetary and supervisory authorities, the early assessment of imminent risks to the financial system, in order to take the necessary measures which may facilitate the prevention of the occurrence of generalised crises by:

- issuing 'risk warnings' concerning the macroeconomic level, and
- submitting proposals to meet the relevant risks.

In this respect it has been agreed that the FSB should collaborate with the IMF to provide early warnings of macroeconomic and financial risks and the actions needed to address them,[571] and that existing institutional frameworks need to be enhanced in order to allow relevant authorities to identify and take account of macro-prudential risks.[572]

1.2.4 Compensation systems

Another important issue on which there was agreement at the London Summit was the endorsement and implementation of the FSB's new principles on pay and compensation, as well as the provision of support to sustainable compensation systems and corporate social responsibility for all firms.[573] In this respect, the following principles should be respected:

- firms' boards of directors should play an active role in the design, operation, and evaluation of compensation systems,
- compensation arrangements, including bonuses, should properly reflect risk and the timing and composition of payments to be sensitive to the time horizon of risks,
- payments should not be finalised over short periods where risks are realised over long periods,
- firms should publicly disclose clear, comprehensive, and timely information about compensation, and
- stakeholders, including shareholders, should be adequately informed on a timely basis on compensation policies to exercise effective monitoring.[574]

571 **G20 (2009b)**, paragraph 15, second indent.
572 Ibid., paragraph 15, third indent.
573 Ibid., paragraph 15, fifth indent.
574 **G20 (2009c)**, section five, fourth sentence.

1.2.5 Tax havens and non-cooperative states

Finally, the G20 Leaders agreed to take action against non-cooperative states, including tax havens. As mentioned in the G20 Leaders Statement: *"We stand ready to deploy sanctions to protect our public finances and financial systems. The era of banking secrecy is over. We note that the OECD has today published a list of states assessed by the Global Forum (on Transparency and Exchange of Information) against the international standard for exchange of tax information"*.[575] In this respect the following decisions were taken:[576]

(a) In order to protect public finances and international standards against the risks posed by non-cooperative states, all states should adhere to the international standards with regard to micro-prudential supervision, taxation and combating the use of the financial system for the conduct of economic crimes. Accordingly, the appropriate institutions should conduct and strengthen objective peer reviews, based on existing processes, including the FSAP process of the IMF.

(b) States are called upon to adopt the international standard for information exchange endorsed by the G20 in 2004 and reflected in the UN Model Tax Convention. In this context, it is noted that the OECD published a list of states assessed by the 'Global Forum on Transparency and Exchange of Information' (hereinafter the 'Global Forum'), which operates under the auspices of the OECD, against the international standard for exchange of information.

(c) Action should be taken against states which do not meet international standards in relation to tax transparency. To this end, a toolbox of effective counter measures at the disposal of states should be developed, such as:

- increased disclosure requirements on the part of taxpayers and financial institutions to report transactions involving non-cooperative states,
- withholding taxes in respect of a wide variety of payments,
- denying deductions in respect of expense payments to payees resident in a non-cooperative jurisdiction,
- reviewing tax treaty policy,
- asking international institutions and regional development banks to review their investment policies, and
- giving specific weight to the principles of tax transparency and information exchange when designing bilateral aid programs.

(d) Consideration should also be given to further options relating to financial relations with these states.

(e) Proposals should be developed, by the end of 2009, to make it easier for economically developing states to secure the benefits of a new cooperative tax environment.

575 **G20 (2009b)**, paragraph 15, seventh indent.
576 **G20 (2009c)**, section six.

(f) It has also been agreed to take measures in order to strengthen adherence to international prudential regulatory and supervisory standards. To this end:

- on the one hand, the IMF and the FSB, in cooperation with international standard-setters, should provide an assessment of implementation by relevant states, building on existing FSAPs, where they exist, and
- on the other hand, the FSB should develop a toolbox of measures to promote adherence to prudential standards and cooperation with states.

(g) Finally, the FATF should revise and reinvigorate the review process for assessing compliance by states with AML/CFT standards, using agreed evaluation reports where available.

1.3 Implementation of the decisions taken

The G20 members instructed the Finance Ministers of participating states[577] to proceed with the implementation of these decisions in line with the timetable set out in the "Progress Report on the Actions of the Washington Action Plan".[578] Concurrently, the FSB and the IMF have been asked to:

- monitor progress, working with the FATF and other relevant international fora (notably the IASB), and
- provide a report to the following G20 Summit, at the level of Finance Ministers, that was held in Scotland, in November 2009.[579]

2. The G20 Pittsburgh Summit

2.1 Introductory remarks

On 24-25 September 2009, the G20 Meeting was held in Pittsburgh (PA), United States, at Summit level for the third consecutive time. The Summit:

- on the one hand, assessed progress achieved in strengthening the international financial system, as a follow-up to the London Summit in early April 2009,[580] and
- on the other, took decisions regarding actions that needed to be taken on the issue, in the immediate future.

577 **G20 (2009b)**, paragraph 16, first sentence.

578 **G20 (2009d)**: "*Progress Report on the Actions of the Washington Action Plan*", available at: http://www.g20.org/Documents/FINAL_Annex_on_ Action_Plan.pdf.

579 **G20 (2009b)**, paragraph 16, second sentence.

580 See subsection A, above.

It is worth noting that with regard to its own role, the Summit decided that the G20 should play a leading role in international economic cooperation, in relation to other international inter-governmental fora.[581]

According to the outcomes of the Summit, with regard to progress of work and initiatives already undertaken to address the causes of the financial crisis and strengthen the international financial system, the G20 found that substantial progress had been made with regard to:

- strengthening the prudential oversight of financial firms,
- improving risk management by such firms,
- strengthening transparency in both markets and transactions,
- promoting market integrity,
- establishing supervisory colleges regarding the supervision of cross-border financial groups, and
- reinforcing international cooperation.

The G20, which held its next meeting in Toronto, in June 2010, also found that the regulatory and supervisory framework for over-the-counter (OTC) derivatives, securitisation markets, credit rating agencies, and hedge funds had been enhanced.

In this context, the heads of the G20 member states called on Finance Ministers and Central Bank Governors to focus on the following aspects:[582]

(i) strengthening the framework for banks' prudential regulation (see under 2.2.1 below),
(ii) reforming compensation practices to support financial stability (under 2.2.2),
(iii) improving over-the-counter derivatives markets (under 2.2.3),
(iv) addressing cross-border resolutions and systemically important financial institutions: systemically important financial firms are called upon to develop internationally consistent firm-specific contingency and resolution plans (under 2.2.4),
(v) adjusting accounting standards (under 2.2.5),
(vi) addressing non-cooperative states and combating economic crime in the financial system (under 2.2.6), and
(vii) contribution of the financial system toward paying for any burdens associated with governmental interventions to repair the banking system's stability (under 2.2.7).

581 **Leaders' Statement: The Pittsburgh Summit**, 24-25 September 2009, available at: http://www.pittsburghsummit.gov/mediacenter/press/index.htm, Preamble, paragraph 19.
582 Ibid., main text, paragraphs 10-16.

2.2. The decisions taken

2.2.1 Strengthening banks' prudential regulatory system

The first decision concerns the need to strengthen the international regulatory framework governing banks' capital adequacy and other prudential oversight aspects. Specifically, rules should be adopted by end-2010 in order to:

(i) improve both the quantity and quality of bank capital,
(ii) discourage excessive leverage in banks' portfolios,
(iii) implement counter-cyclical capital buffers, i.e. higher-level and better-quality capital requirements in times of economic growth,
(iv) impose higher capital requirements on off-balance sheet activities, and
(v) strengthen the regulatory framework for controlling liquidity risk.

By adopting these measures, the G20 was aiming at fewer incentives for banks to take up excessive risk and therefore, contributing to a financial system that is better equipped to counter unfavourable conditions (like the recent ones).
In this context, the G20 welcomed the proposals submitted by the oversight body of the Basel Committee for strengthening the supervision and regulation of the banking sector.[583] Indeed, there was special reference to the introduction of a 'leverage ratio' as a supplementary measure to the existing regulatory framework governing banks' capital adequacy. Furthermore, to ensure comparability as well as a level playing-field, the G20 decided that leverage ratio calculation methodologies should be harmonised internationally, fully adjusting for differences in accounting.
These rules should be phased-in gradually, as financial conditions improve and economic recovery is assured, in order to be implemented by end-2012.

2.2.2 Reforming compensation practices to support financial stability

According to the G20, excessive compensation in the financial sector has both reflected and (also) encouraged excessive risk taking. Therefore, reforming compensation policies and practices is considered an essential part of the effort to increase financial stability. The G20 fully endorsed the implementation standards of the FSB[584] aimed at aligning compensation with long-term value creation, not excessive risk-taking, by:

583 On this see **Basel Committee on Banking Supervision (2009d)**: "*Comprehensive Response to the Global Financial Crisis*", Press release, September, available at: http://www.bis.org/press/p090907.htm.
584 **Financial Stability Board (2009d)** "*FSB Principles for Sound Compensation Practices,*" September, available at: http://www.financialstabilityboard.org/publications/r_090925c.pdf.

- avoiding multi-year guaranteed bonuses;
- requiring a significant portion of variable compensation to be deferred, tied to performance and subject to appropriate claw-back and to be vested in the form of stock or stock-like instruments, as long as these create incentives aligned with long-term value creation and the time horizon of risk;
- ensuring that compensation for senior executives and other employees having a material impact on the firm's risk exposure, align with performance and risk;
- making firms' compensation policies and structures transparent through disclosure requirements;
- limiting variable compensation as a percentage of total net revenues when it is inconsistent with the maintenance of a sound capital base, and
- ensuring that compensation committees overseeing compensation policies are able to act independently.

In this context, supervisors should have the responsibility to review firms' compensation policies and structures with institutional and systemic risk in mind and, if necessary to offset additional risks, apply corrective measures, such as higher capital requirements, to those firms that fail to implement sound compensation policies and practices. Supervisors should have the ability to modify terms governing compensation policies, in the case of firms that either fail, or require extraordinary public intervention. The G20 called on financial firms to implement these sound compensation practices immediately and tasked the FSB to monitor the implementation of FSB standards, and propose additional measures, as required, by March 2010.

2.2.3 Improving over-the-counter derivatives markets

The third issue handled by the G20 was improving trading and clearing terms for over-the-counter derivatives. In this context, it was decided that by end-2012 at the latest:

- all standardised OTC derivative contracts should be traded on exchanges or electronic trading platforms, where appropriate,
- these contracts should be reported to central depositories. and
- all relevant transactions should be cleared through central counterparties, otherwise financial firms with open positions on such transactions will be subject to higher capital requirements.

The G20 called on the FSB to regularly assess both implementation of the above, and whether such measures are sufficient to improve transparency in the derivatives markets, mitigate systemic risk, and protect against market abuse.

2.2.4 Addressing cross-border resolutions and systemically important financial institutions

With regard to cross-border resolutions and the systemically important financial institutions (SIFIs), the G20 decided the following:

(i) SIFIs should develop internationally-consistent firm-specific contingency and resolution plans.
(ii) The competent supervisory authorities should establish crisis management groups for the major cross-border SIFIs and a legal framework for crisis intervention, as well as improve information sharing in times of stress.
(iii) There is an imperative need for a specific legal framework for the effective resolution of SIFIs to help mitigate the disruption of financial institution failures and reduce moral hazard..[585]

The G20 asked the FSB to propose, by the end of October 2010, possible measures for adoption, including more intensive supervision and imposing additional micro-prudential measures (such as capital and liquidity requirements).

2.2.5 Adjusting accounting standards

The G20 called on the international fora issuing accounting standards, to redouble their efforts to achieve a single set of high quality, international accounting standards by June 2011. Furthermore, it called on the IASB to further strengthen its internal governance processes, enabling the involvement of more stakeholders.

2.2.6 Addressing non-cooperative states and combating economic crime in the financial system

The G20 Leaders stated the commitment to maintain the momentum in dealing with tax havens, money laundering, proceeds of corruption, terrorist financing, and developing relevant prudential standards. In this context:

(a) They welcomed the expansion of the Global Forum, including the participation of developing states, and welcomed the agreement to deliver an effective programme of peer review. It should be noted that the main focus of the Forum's work is to improve tax transparency and information exchange, so that states can fully enforce tax legislation to protect their tax base.

(b) They announced its readiness to use measures against tax havens as of March 2010.

585 See on this above under A 1.2.2 of this Section.

(c) They welcomed the progress made by the FATF in the fight against money laundering and terrorist financing and called upon the FATF to issue a public list of high risk states by February 2010.

(d) Finally, they called on the FSB to:

- submit a progress report with regard to international cooperation by these states and any progress made on information exchange in November 2009, and
- initiate a peer review process by February 2010.

2.2.7 The financial system's contribution toward paying for any burdens associated with governmental interventions to repair the banking system's stability

Finally, the G20 tasked the IMF to prepare a report for the next meeting with regard to the range of options states have adopted or are considering as to how the financial sector could make a fair and substantial contribution towards paying for any burdens associated with governmental interventions to restore the stability of the banking system.

3. The G20 Seoul Summit

According to the conclusions of the G20 Summit in Seoul, held on 12 November 2010,[586] important decisions were made regarding the readjustment of the international financial system and of public international financial law. On the basis of and further to the Action Plan for strengthening the financial sector announced at the G20 Washington Summit, the following were decided at the Seoul Summit:

(a) The members agreed to adopt the Basel Committee's new rules (known as 'Basel III') regarding capital adequacy, liquidity and leverage of banks, according to the timeline set, namely entry into force on 1 January 2013 and complete phasing-in by 1 January 2019. As will be discussed in detail in Section Six below (under B), the new rules are aimed at:

- strengthening banks' regulatory capital and liquidity,
- avoiding the build-up of leverage, and
- introducing capital buffers above the minimum requirements that can be used in times of crisis.

(b) The members reaffirmed the need to reduce moral hazard risks relating to Systemically Important Financial Institutions (SIFIs) and mitigate the 'too-big-to-fail' or 'too-interconnected-to-fail' problem. In this context, there was agreement on the need

586 **The G20 Seoul Summit Leaders Declaration**, November 2010, available at: http://www.seoulsummit.kr/outcomes.

to create a crisis management system with a resolution framework and other measures to ensure that all financial institutions can be resolved safely, quickly and without destabilising the financial system and exposing taxpayers to the risk of loss from government bailout interventions.

A proposal was also made to establish a stricter framework, initially only for financial institutions that are globally systemic (G-SIFIs), especially in terms of their capital adequacy and liquidity requirements, as well as for the exercise of supervision. The G20 asked the FSB and the Basel Committee to complete their remaining work in accordance with approved work processes and timelines in 2011 and 2012.

(c) There was a reaffirmation of implementation at national level of the Basel Committee's recommendations in relation to cross-border resolutions.

(d) The members endorsed the policy recommendations prepared by the FSB in consultation with the IMF on increasing supervisory intensity and effectiveness. In particular, an agreement was reached that supervision of the observance of the regulatory framework must be more rigorous and that supervisors should have a clear mandate, sufficient independence to act, appropriate resources and a full suite of tools enabling them to proactively identify risks and perform early interventions, if needed.

(e) There was also agreement on the need to enhance assessment processes to ensure consistency in the implementation of standards and codes.

(f) Members reaffirmed the commitment:

- on the one hand, to strengthen the regulatory framework supervision on hedge funds, OTC derivatives and credit rating agencies, and
- on the other hand, to fully implement the FSB's standards for sound compensation.

(g) Members requested the continuation of any work related to achieving convergence between the International Accounting Standards and the US accounting standards by end-2011.

(h) A decision was made to pursue the successful work on identifying non-cooperative states in cooperation with the FSB, the Global Forum and the FATF to combat money laundering and terrorism-financing.

(i) Looking further ahead, the members decided to carry out further work on the macro-prudential policy framework, reforming the regulatory framework for emerging markets and developing economies, strengthening regulation and supervision of shadow banking, improving integrity and transparency in capital markets, further regulating commodity derivatives markets and enhancing consumer protection.

Especially with regard to financial services consumer protection, G20 members asked the FSB to work with the OECD to provide information helping consumers make informed decisions, and as regards transparency, educating and protecting consumers against fraud.

4. The G20 Cannes Summit

As pointed out in the Communiqué issued at the end of the Summit, G20 Leaders agreed on the following with regard to the financial system:

(a) They agreed on measures to make sure that no financial corporation can be deemed 'too big to fail' or 'too interconnected to fail' and to protect taxpayers from bearing the cost of resolution.

(b) It was announced that the FSB published an initial list of global systemically important financial institutions (G-SIFIs). These will be submitted to strengthened supervision, a new international standard for resolution regimes as well as additional capital requirements from 2016.

(c) It was also decided to adopt a specific regulatory and supervisory framework on the 'shadow banking' sector.

(d) It was also decided that further measures would be taken in order to ensure the smooth operation and efficiency of capital markets, and IOSCO was tasked with evaluating the functioning of credit default swaps markets.

(e) Special mention was made to the G20 agreement on the adoption of the OECD's principles on the protection of financial services consumers, as well as granting legal status and greater financial independence to the FSB, given the expansion of its mission to include the coordination and checking whether the adopted standards are implemented by the competent, on a case-by-case basis, international fora.

Finally, it is worth mentioning that as regards the international governance the G20 members agreed with the proposal of the UK Prime Minister, David Cameron, for the G20 to remain an 'informal group'.

C. *Current supervisory and regulatory developments at international level: the Progress Report of the Financial Stability Board*

As mentioned above (under B.1.1), in 2008, the FSF issued a significant Report entitled "*Enhancing Market and Institutional Resilience*". This Report, which was lastly updated by the FSB in November 2011 with regard to the most recent implementation of its proposals, is structured in two parts:

(a) Firstly, it identifies the weaknesses of the financial system which contributed to the development of the recent (2007-2009) international financial crisis.

(b) On the basis of these weaknesses, the Report lists (in Annex A) a number of proposals pertaining to the following seven (7) categories of regulatory action, by identifying the regulatory measures to be adopted for each category, their content, the institutions and fora responsible for their adoption, as well as the timetable for their implementation:

- strengthened rules on the micro-prudential regulation of international banks and rules addressing Systemically Important Financial Institutions (SIFIs) (see below **Table 15**, under A),
- enhanced capital markets regulation (under B),
- rules on compensation practices in the financial sector (under C),
- enhanced international accounting standards and new rules on the valuation of financial standards (under D),
- rules on the macro-prudential oversight of the financial sector (under E),
- rules on the alignment of prudential regulation across the three sectors of the financial system (under F),
- a framework for strengthening adherence to international supervisory and regulatory standards and review of the FSB's Compendium (under G),
- rules on consumer protection in the financial sector (under H),
- initiatives concerning emerging markets and developing economies (under I), and
- rules on international cooperation and information exchange (under J).

Table 15: State-of-Play of Implementation of the G20 Recommendations for Strengthening Financial Stability – Report of the Financial Stability Board to G20 Leaders, 4 November 2011

Recommendation	Competent Authority/ Recipient of the Recommendation	Time Schedule	Progress / Report adopted
A1. Timely implementation of the Basel II capital framework (Basel II)	BCBS National states/ authorities	By 2011	Most G20 countries have already fully adopted Basel II. Implementation in remaining countries is still under way See also: BCBS "*Progress Report Table on the Basel II Adoption*"
A2. Enhancements to trading book exposures, complex securitisations and exposures to off-balance sheet vehicles	BCBS National states/ authorities	By end-2011	• BCBS "Enhancements to the Basel II Framework" • BCBS "Guidelines for Computing Capital for Incremental Risk in the Trading Book" • BCBS "Revisions to the Basel II Market Risk Framework" • BCBS "Interpretive Issues with respect to the Market Risk Framework"

Recommendation	Competent Authority/ Recipient of the Recommendation	Time Schedule	Progress / Report adopted
A3. Building high quality capital standards and mitigating procyclicality (Basel III) • definition of capital, • increase the level of capital, • requirement to build-up capital buffers, • requirement to build-up countercyclical buffers, and • introduction of a leverage ratio	BCBS National states/ authorities	Gradual implementation from 1.1.2013 up to 1.1.2019	BCBS "*Basel III: A Global Regulatory Framework for More Resilient Banks and Banking Systems*" See also: • BCBS "Basel III Definition of Capital - Frequently Asked Questions", and • BCBS "Final Elements of the Reforms to Raise the Quality of Regulatory Capital Issued by the Basel Committee" • BCBS "Results of the Comprehensive Quantitative Impact Study" • BCBS "Progress Report on Basel III Implementation"
A4. Introduction of global minimum liquidity standards (Basel III)	BCBS National states/ authorities	Observation period from 1.1.2011 Introduction of the Liquidity Coverage Ratio on 1.1.2015 and of the Net Stable Funding Ratio by 1.1.2018	BCBS "*Basel III: International framework for Liquidity Risk Measurement, Standards and Monitoring*" See also: BCBS "*Basel III Framework for Liquidity - Frequently Asked Questions*"

Recommendation	Competent Authority/ Recipient of the Recommendation	Time Schedule	Progress / Report adopted
A5. Addressing systemically important financial institutions (SIFIs) • a requirement that SIFIs and initially in particular global SIFIs (G-SIFIs) have higher loss absorbency capacity to reflect the greater risks that these institutions pose to the global financial system, • more intensive supervisory oversight, • robust core financial market infrastructures to reduce contagion risk from the failure of individual institutions, and • other supplementary prudential and other requirements as determined by the national authorities	FSB National states/ authorities	2011-2012	FSB Recommendations and Time Lines "*Reducing the Moral Hazard Posed by Systemically Important Financial Institutions*" See also: • FSB "Policy Measures to Address Systemically Important Financial Institutions (SIFIs) and Initial Group of Global SIFIs" • FSB "Key Attributes of Effective Resolution Regimes for Financial Institutions" • FSB "Report on Progress in Implementing the FSB's Recommendations on Intensity and Effectiveness of SIFI Supervision" • FSB "Intensity and Effectiveness of SIFI Supervision" • BCBS "Global Systemically Important Banks: Assessment Methodology and the Additional Loss Absorbency Requirement" • BCBS "Resolution Policies and Frameworks - Progress So Far" • BCBS "Report and Recommendations of the Cross-border Bank Resolution Group"

Recommendation	Competent Authority/ Recipient of the Recommendation	Time Schedule	Progress / Report adopted
			• IMF report "Resolution of Cross-border Banks – A Proposed Framework for Enhanced Coordination" • IMF, FSB, BIS "Guidance to Assess the Systemic Importance of Financial Institutions, Markets and Instruments: Initial Considerations" • CPSS, IOSCO "Principles for Financial Market Infrastructures"
A6. Ensuring the adequate use by the national supervisory authorities of the Pillar II (supervisory review process) flexibility (Basel II framework)	BCBS National supervisory authorities	2008-2009	BCBS "*Enhancements to the Basel II Framework*"
A7. Strengthening of the guidelines for sound stress testing practices	BCBS National supervisory authorities	2008-2009	BCBS "*Principles for Sound Stress-Testing Practices and Supervision*"
A8. Further enhancement of the Pillar III (market discipline) requirements (Basel II framework) including: • securitisation exposures in the trading book; • sponsorship of off-balance sheet vehicles; • resecuritisation exposures; and • pipeline and warehousing risks with regard to securitisation exposures	BCBS	2009	BCBS "*Enhancements to the Basel II Framework*"
A9. Strengthening deposit insurance	BCBS, IADI National states/ authorities	2011	BCBS, IADI "*Core Principles for Effective Deposit Insurance Systems*"
A10. Improvement of coordination and cooperation between supervisory authorities	BCBS IOSCO National supervisory authorities	2010	BCBS "*Good Practice Principles on Supervisory Colleges*" IOSCO "*Principles Regarding Cross-Border Supervisory Cooperation*"

Recommendation	Competent Authority/ Recipient of the Recommendation	Time Schedule	Progress / Report adopted
A11. Enhancement of the corporate governance	BCBS National supervisory authorities	2010	BCBS "*Principles for Enhancing Corporate Governance*"
A12. Enhancement of risk management	BCBS Senior Supervisors Group - FSB National supervisory authorities	2009	• BCBS "Operational Risk - Supervisory Guidelines for the Advanced Measurement Approaches" • BCBS "Principles for the Sound Management of Operational Risk" • BCBS "Sound practices for backtesting counterparty credit risk models" • Senior Supervisors Group "Risk Management Lessons from the Global Banking Crisis of 2008"
A13. Expanding the regulatory perimeter – Shadow banking	FSB National states/ authorities	2011	FSB "*Shadow Banking: Strengthening Oversight and Regulation*" See also: • FSB "Securities Lending and Repos: Market Overview and Financial Stability Issues" • FSB "Shadow Banking: Scoping the Issues"
A14. Enhancement of banking supervision	BCBS National supervisory authorities / Banks	2011	BCBS Consultative Paper on revised "Core Principles for Effective Banking Supervision"
B1. Objectives and Principles of Securities Regulation	IOSCO National states/ authorities	2010	IOSCO "*Objectives and Principles of Securities Regulation*" See also: IOSCO "*Methodology for Assessing Implementation of the IOSCO Objectives and Principles of Securities Regulation*", which replaces the February 2008 version

Recommendation	Competent Authority/ Recipient of the Recommendation	Time Schedule	Progress / Report adopted
B2. Improving the OTC derivatives markets	FSB National states/ authorities	2011-2012	FSB "*Implementing OTC Derivatives Market Reforms*" See also: • FSB "*Progress Report on Implementing OTC Derivatives Markets Reforms*" • IOSCO "Report on OTC Derivatives Data Reporting and Aggregation Requirements – Consultative Report" • IOSCO "Report on Trading of OTC Derivatives" • CPSS, IOSCO "Considerations for Trade Repositories in OTC Derivatives Markets – Consultative Report"
B3. Enhancement of the oversight of Central Counterparties	CPSS, IOSCO National states/ authorities	2010	• CPSS, IOSCO "Guidance on the Application of the 2004 CPSS-IOSCO Recommendations for Central Counterparties to OTC Derivatives CCPs – consultative report"
B4. Hedge funds	IOSCO National states/ authorities	2010	• IOSCO "International Regulators publish Systemic Risk Data Requirements for Hedge Funds" • IOSCO "Hedge Funds Oversight"
B5. Commodity derivatives	IOSCO National states/ authorities	2010	IOSCO "*Principles for the Regulation and Supervision of Commodity Derivatives Markets*"

Recommendation	Competent Authority/ Recipient of the Recommendation	Time Schedule	Progress / Report adopted
B6. Credit rating agencies	IOSCO FSB National states/ authorities	2010-2011	• IOSCO "Regulatory Implementation of Statement of Principles Regarding the Activities of Credit Rating Agencies" • FSB "Principles for Reducing Reliance on CRA Ratings" • IOSCO "Code of Conduct Fundamentals for Credit Rating Agencies" (revised in May 2008)
B7. Exchange-Traded Funds	FSB National states/ authorities	2011	FSB "*Potential Financial Stability Issues Arising from Recent Trends in Exchange-Traded Funds (ETFs)*"
B8. Transparency requirements for public offerings and asset-backed securities	IOSCO National states/ authorities	2009	IOSCO "*Disclosure Principles for Public Offerings and Listings of Asset-Backed Securities*"
B9. Transparency requirements for listed entities	IOSCO National states/ authorities	2010	IOSCO "*Periodic Disclosure by Listed Entities*"
B10. Transparency requirements on point of sale	IOSCO National states/ authorities	2011	IOSCO "*Principles on Point-of-Sale Disclosure*"
B11. Addressing the impact of technological changes on market integrity and efficiency	IOSCO National states/ authorities	2011	• IOSCO "Regulatory Issues Raised by the Impact of Technological Changes on Market Integrity and Efficiency" • IOSCO "Principles for Dark Liquidity"

Recommendation	Competent Authority/ Recipient of the Recommendation	Time Schedule	Progress / Report adopted
C1. Reforming compensation practices to support financial stability	FSB National states/ authorities	2009-	• FSF "Principles for Sound Compensation Practices" • FSB "Principles for Sound Compensation Practices. Implementation Standards" See also: FSB: "*2011 Thematic Review on Compensation*"
C2. Range of methodologies for risk and performance alignment of remuneration	BCBS National supervisory authorities	2010-	BCBS "*Range of Methodologies for Risk and Performance Alignment of Remuneration*"
D1. Adoption of IASB standards (International Financial Reporting Standards)	IASB National states/ authorities	2010-2012	Nearly all FSB member states have either adopted or have programmes underway to converge with, or consider adoption of IFRS by 2012
D2. Convergence of IASB and FASB standards	IASB and FASB Boards	By end-2011	Progress toward FSB recommendations for improved, converged accounting standards can be seen in four main areas: • measurement of loans, • impairment of financial assets, • addressing valuation uncertainty in fair value measurement guidance, • derecognition and disclosures about off-balance sheet special purpose entities, • balance sheet netting of derivatives and other financial instruments, • leasing, and • revenue recognition
D3. Enhancement of the IASB standards for offsetting financial instruments	IASB	2008-2009	BCBS "*Guiding Principles for the Replacement of IAS 39*"

Recommendation	Competent Authority/ Recipient of the Recommendation	Time Schedule	Progress / Report adopted
D4. Enhancement of the IASB standards for the improvement of disclosures relating to the evaluation and the methodologies used	IASB	2008-2009	BCBS "*Guiding Principles for the Replacement of IAS 39*"
D5. Enhancement of the guidelines for the fair value of financial instruments in markets that are no longer active	IASB	2008-2009	IASB "*Measuring and Disclosing the Fair Value of Financial Instruments in Markets that are no longer Active*"
D6. Adoption of stringent procedures of evaluation and disclosure	IASB	2008	BCBS "*Fair Value Measurement and Modelling: An Assessment of Challenges and Lessons Learned from the Market Stress*" BCBS "*Guiding Principles for the Replacement of IAS 39*"
D7. Guidelines for the enhancement of assessing banks' financial instruments fair value practices	BCBS National supervisory authorities	2008	BCBS "*Supervisory Guidance for Assessing Banks' Financial Instrument Fair Value Practices*"
D8. Enhancement of guidelines relating to auditing fair value accounting estimates for complex or illiquid financial instruments and the relevant disclosures	IAASB Important standard-setters of auditing standards National states/ authorities	2008-2009	IAASB "*Challenges in Auditing Fair Value Accounting Estimates in the Current Market Environment*"
D9. Timely disclosure by regulatory and supervisory authorities to the Board of Directors and bank management of concerns regarding their exposure to risks and to the quality of risk management	BCBS National supervisory and regulatory authorities	2008-	BCBS "*External Audit Quality and Banking Supervision*"

Recommendation	Competent Authority/ Recipient of the Recommendation	Time Schedule	Progress / Report adopted
E1. Developing macro-prudential frameworks and tools	FSB, IMF, BIS, CGFS	2010-	• FSB, IMF, BIS "Macro-prudential Policy Tools and Frameworks" • IMF "Macro-prudential Policy: an Organizing Framework" See also: CGFS "*Macro-prudential Instruments and Frameworks: a Stocktaking of Issues and Experiences*"
E2. The role of margin requirements and haircuts in procyclicality	CGFS/BIS	2010-	CGFS "*The Role of Margin Requirements and Haircuts in Procyclicality*"
E3. Macro-prudential analysis of the risks in the financial system	IMF, FSB National states/ authorities	2010-	• FSB "Understanding Financial Linkages: A Common Data Template for Global Systemically Important Banks" • IMF, FSB "The Financial Crisis and Information Gaps"
F. Recommendations for addressing the gaps due to the differentiated nature of regulatory intervention in the banking sector the capital markets and the insurance sector	Joint Forum / BIS	2010-	• Joint Forum "Principles for the Supervision of Financial Conglomerates" • Joint Forum "Review of the Differentiated Nature and Scope of Financial Regulation. Key Issues and Recommendations"
G1. Framework for strengthening adherence to international supervisory and regulatory standards	FSB National states/ Authorities	2010-	FSB "*Framework for Strengthening Adherence to International Standards*" FSB Peer Reviews: by state and subject area
G2. Review of the Compendium of Standards of the Financial Stability Board	FSB National states/ authorities	2011	Review of the FSB "*Compendium of Standards*"

Recommendation	Competent Authority/ Recipient of the Recommendation	Time Schedule	Progress / Report adopted
H. Consumer Protection	OECD FSB National states/ authorities	2011-	• OECD: "G20 High-Level Principles on Financial Consumer Protection" • FSB: "Consumer Finance Protection with Particular Focus on Credit" • FSB: "Principles for Sound Residential Mortgage Underwriting Practices"
I. Emerging Markets and Developing Economies	FSB/IMF/World Bank IOSCO National states/ authorities	2011-	• FSB, IMF, World Bank: "Financial Stability Issues in Emerging Markets and Developing Economies" • IOSCO, World Bank: "Development of the Corporate Bond Markets in Emerging Countries"
J. International Cooperation and Information Exchange	FSB National states/ authorities	2011-	FSB: "*Global Adherence to Regulatory and Supervisory Standards on International Cooperation and Information Exchange*"

SECTION SIX THE MAIN SOURCES OF PUBLIC INTERNATIONAL BANKING LAW

A. *The regulatory framework of the Basel Committee on the exercise of micro-prudential supervision to international banks and on the cross-border cooperation between supervisory authorities*

1. The sources of relevant provisions

1.1 The original Basel Concordat (1975)

As a result of the above-mentioned Herstatt Bank crisis, the need to enhance international cooperation on micro-prudential banking supervision became imperative, leading to the establishment of the Basel Committee.[587] The first report of the Committee, known as the Basel Concordat,[588] was issued in early 1975 and contained recommendations on the division of responsibilities between:

- the parent (or home) state supervisory authorities (hereinafter the 'parent authorities'), namely the authorities of the state, in which a bank is legally incorporated, which have granted the operating license, and
- the host state supervisory authorities (hereinafter the 'host authorities'), namely the authorities of the state in which an international bank's foreign establishments are operating, a concept used extensively in the Basel Committee's reports and deemed to include both foreign branches and foreign subsidiaries.[589]

It is worth mentioning at this point the essential difference between branches and subsidiaries:

(a) *Branches are a place of business which form a legally dependent part of a bank and carry out directly all or some of the transactions inherent in a bank's business.*

(b) *Subsidiaries, on the contrary, are independent legal institutions controlled financially and operationally by their parent companies.*

587 See under B 2.2.1 in Section Four above.

588 The Basel Concordat was not disclosed until 1981 when it was published as an appendix to a book by **Williams and Johnson (1981)**. This is indicative of the purely informal character of the Basel Committee's operation until 1983.

589 The prevalent term under international economic law for such establishments is 'commercial presence' (see Article XXVIII(d) of the General Agreement on Trade in Services).
By contrast, under EU banking law, 'host' competent authorities are defined as the national authorities of the member state in which an EU-based credit institution has a foreign branch (and not a subsidiary) or in which it provides services (Directive 2006/48/EC, Article 4, points (4) and (8).

The report also stresses the need for host authorities to cooperate with parent authorities on exchanging information and to assign responsibility to the latter to conduct direct or indirect supervision over their banks' foreign establishments.

The Basel Committee does not define the term 'international bank'; it is deemed to mean any bank that is legally incorporated in one state and operates in another state through branches and banking subsidiaries. International banks are referred to as:

- *institutions with foreign banking establishments,*
- *banks undertaking significant cross-border business,*
- *banks conducting significant international business,*
- *banks engaged in cross-border banking,*
- *internationally active banks, or*
- *institutions with cross-border banking establishments.*

1.2 The revised Basel Concordat (1983)

In 1983, the Basel Committee amended the 1975 Concordat by issuing a revised Concordat entitled "*Principles for the supervision of banks' foreign establishments*". This revision process was triggered by misgivings regarding certain provisions of the original Concordat following the bankruptcy of the Luxembourg-based holding company *Banco Ambrosiano Holding*, subsidiary of the Italian bank *Banco Ambrosiano*. The Revised Concordat:

- clearly reaffirms that the action and cooperation of supervisory authorities should be aimed at ensuring that no international banking activity escapes effective prudential supervision,
- complements and clarifies the content of the Basel Concordat's recommendations, by laying down specific values governing the division of responsibilities between parent and host authorities of international banks
- establishes the principle of consolidated supervision of foreign subsidiaries to be performed by the parent authorities,[590] and
- sets forth guidelines for the supervisory treatment of investment holding companies and other non-banking financial companies that are parent or subsidiary companies of international banks.

The supervisory problem laid bare by the Banco Ambrosiano scandal was that when the Institut Monétaire Luxembourgois, i.e. the competent banking supervisory authority in Luxembourg, revoked the operating license of Banco Ambrosiano Holding in 1982, no supervisory authority would assume responsibility for resolving the problem, as:

590 Adoption of the consolidated supervision principle had been proposed by the Basel Committee as early as 1976, and had been adopted by the G10 Central Bank Governors in 1978.

- *on the one hand, the Italian authorities considered that the matter fell within the competence of Luxembourg's supervisory authorities, since the company was registered in Luxembourg,*
- *on the other hand, the Luxembourg authorities did not exercise such supervision, given that, according to national legislation, a holding company was not considered a bank and as a result, the supervision of Banco Ambrosiano Holding did not come under their jurisdiction.*[591]

1.3 Subsequent supplements to the Revised Concordat

1.3.1 The "Information flows between banking supervisory authorities" report (1990)

In 1990, the Basel Committee complemented the principles of the revised Basel Concordat with the text *"Information flows between banking supervisory authorities (Supplement to the Basel Concordat of May 1983)"* (hereinafter 'the 1990 report').[592] The main objective of this instrument is to specify the implementation of the Revised Concordat's principles relating to the exchange of information between parent and host authorities in performing micro-prudential supervision over international banks with foreign establishments, by recommending practical solutions for the elaboration of a framework for regular and structured cross-border cooperation, and taking into account the need to improve the quality and completeness of supervision over cross-border banking activities.

1.3.2 The "Minimum standards for the supervision of international banking groups and their cross-border establishments" report (1992)

In July 1992, following yet another banking crisis – the scandal involving the international banking group BCCI – the Basel Committee revisited the issue of cross-border cooperation between banking supervisory authorities. The Committee's reaction to the problems raised by the crisis was reflected in the report entitled "*Minimum standards for the supervision of international banking groups and their cross-border establishments*" (hereinafter 'the 1992 report').

591 For a detailed analysis of this case, see **Dale (1984)**, pp. 156-167, and **Kapstein (1994)**, pp. 53-57.

592 This report is based on an unpublished 1987 report entitled *"The Implementation of the Basle Concordat: Practical aspects of international collaboration between banking supervisory authorities"*, prepared by the Basel Committee in collaboration with the Offshore Group of Banking Supervisors.

This report reaffirms the content of certain main principles of the Revised Concordat, raising them to standards to be upheld by every supervisory authority participating in the Basel Committee. Indeed, since then, the Committee itself has been systematically monitoring its members' compliance with these standards.

1.3.3 "The Supervision of Cross-border Banking" report (1996)

The Basel Committee's latest initiative in this context dates back to October 1996, when a very detailed report was published on the issue of cross-border banking supervision, entitled "*The Supervision of Cross-border Banking*" (hereinafter 'the 1996 report'). This report, which was drawn up by a special working group with the participation of members from the Basel Committee and the Offshore Group of Banking Supervisors:

- identifies the practical problems ensuing from implementation of the 1992 report, and
- makes recommendations for removing all existing obstacles impeding supervisory authorities from performing effective prudential supervision of international banks.

2. Division of responsibilities between supervisors relating to the micro-prudential supervision of international banks

2.1 Prudential supervision of international banks' foreign branches

According to the provisions of the 1975 Concordat, parent and host supervisors should jointly bear responsibility for supervising the foreign branches of international banks. Specifically:

- according to the 'principle of equity', parent authorities should retain responsibility for supervising the solvency of international banks' foreign branches, whereas,
- in accordance with the 'principle of neutrality' established therein, supervision of their liquidity should the primary responsibility of host supervisors, with the obligation to notify parent authorities.[593]

With a view to ensuring that the activity of all international banks with foreign establishments would not, in any event, go beyond the scope of supervisors' authority (either parent or host), the Revised Concordat complemented and further specified the abovementioned rules, as follows:

593 On these two principles, see in details **Key (1993)**, pp. 89-103.

(a) The supervision of the solvency of foreign branches should be performed by parent authorities. However, host authorities shall have the right to impose on the said branches the obligation to pay an 'endowment capital' as guarantee for proper fulfilment of obligations in their jurisdiction.

(b) The liquidity of foreign branches shall be mainly supervised by host authorities. However, parent authorities shall also be entitled to conduct additional controls.

(c) Moreover, the Revised Concordat establishes special rules on the supervision of branch transactions and open foreign-exchange positions, which partly come under solvency supervision. It follows, therefore, that supervision of such positions falls, as a rule, within the joint competence of parent and host authorities, and concurrently:

- parent authorities should verify the suitability of the systems used by the bank to manage such positions, so as to be able to assess its overall exposure (including the one resulting from foreign branch transactions) to foreign exchange risk, and
- host authorities should, on the one hand, ascertain the suitability of supervisory procedures for foreign branch exposure to foreign exchange risk, and, on the other, have full knowledge of the respective procedures used by parent authorities.

2.2 Prudential supervision of international banks' foreign subsidiaries

2.1.1 Division of responsibilities

According to the 1975 Concordat, host authorities were primarily responsible for supervising the solvency and the liquidity of foreign subsidiaries of international banks, with the obligation to fully inform parent authorities. The Revised Concordat introduced major amendments:

(a) The supervision of the solvency of foreign subsidiaries of international banks is a responsibility of both parent and host authorities, i.e.:

- parent authorities perform supervision on a consolidated basis, and
- host authorities perform prudential supervision on an individual basis over the subsidiaries incorporated within their jurisdiction.

(b) Host authorities are responsible for the supervision of the liquidity of foreign subsidiaries of international banks. However, host authorities should ensure that parent authorities are kept informed, as the latter have a legitimate interest in being informed about the facilities that parent banks provide to their subsidiaries.

(c) Finally, the above-mentioned provisions (under 2.1 (c)) also apply to open foreign exchange operations and positions.

2.2.2 In detail: the principle of exercising supervision on a consolidated basis

In accordance with the principle of consolidated supervision, risk exposure of banks and banking groups should be controlled on the basis of their overall activity, irrespective of the state where such activity is exercised. Consequently, the activity of international banks, including activity of foreign subsidiaries, shall be treated as a whole and thus made subject to prudential supervision by the parent authorities.

Consolidated supervision extends the responsibility of the parent authorities to monitoring the risk exposure of domestic banks with foreign establishments, without, however, downgrading the role of host authorities, given that they:

- exercise individual supervision over subsidiaries, and
- provide host authorities with the required information aimed at efficient consolidated supervision.

2.3 Prudential supervision of banking joint ventures

The Revised Concordat also touches upon the issue of prudential supervision of banking joint ventures for the first time. More specifically, it is stipulated that as far as banking joint ventures are concerned, supervisory authorities of the state where the joint venture is established are responsible, as a rule, for its supervision. However, the involvement of the supervisory authorities of the states where banks are established, especially banks with increased holdings in the joint venture, is also deemed necessary.

3. Cross-border cooperation and information flows between supervisory authorities

3.1 The 1990 report

3.1.1 Overall examination of recommendations

The need for closer cooperation and flows of information between authorities exercising supervision over international banks with foreign establishments, as above, was ascertained both in the 1975 Concordat and in the 1983 Revised Concordat. However, it was the 1990 Report that specified the implementation terms for this request, as it contains best practice recommendations regarding the following five (5) issues:

- conditions necessary for a foreign bank's authorisation by host authorities (see under 3.1.2 below),
- information that the parent authorities will need to be in a position to secure (under 3.1.3.1),

- information that host authorities will need to be in a position to secure (under 3.1.3.2),
- abolition of restrictions on the flow of information between supervisory authorities from the existence of regulatory provisions safeguarding banking secrecy (under 3.1.4), and
- the role of external auditors (under 3.1.5).

3.1.2 Conditions for authorisation of foreign establishments of international banks

The 1990 report is based on the assumption that the initial field of collaboration between parent and host authorities emerges before a host supervisory authority authorises the foreign establishment of an international bank. During this period, the foundations for an efficient information provision mechanism from the foreign establishment to the parent enterprise or, as appropriate, the bank's head office. In view of this, the report addresses the following recommendations to the parent and host authorities:

(a) Host authorities should, as a matter of principle, ensure that parent authorities have no objection before authorising the foreign establishment of international banks. Where a host authority is unable to obtain a positive response from the parent authority, it should consider:

- either refusing the application, or
- imposing conditions on the provision of the authorisation and informing the host authorities thereon.

(b) If the supervision of parent authorities is not adequate, pursuant to the Revised Concordat's rules on division of responsibilities, the foreign establishment shall be authorised only if host authorities are in a position to substitute for parent authorities.[594]

(c) The parent authorities should take all the necessary measures to prevent banks within their jurisdiction from establishing a presence in states where supervision by competent authorities is not adequate, or from acquiring banking enterprises in such states (and should notify host authorities accordingly).

594 The same applies in the case of banking joint ventures, for which the supervisory authorities of the state of major stakeholder banks do not assume responsibility, contrary to the Revised Concordat's principles.

3.1.3 Information needs of supervisory authorities

3.1.3.1 Parent supervisory authorities

In order to ensure effective supervision by parent authorities over the totality of an international bank's business, parent and host authorities should verify whether the bank has adequate internal control mechanisms ensuring a regular flow of information:

- from the foreign establishment to the parent enterprise or, as appropriate, to the head office, and
- through the above, to the parent authorities.

This channel is instrumental for the parent authorities to collect information that will enable them to effectively exercise prudential supervision of international banks' foreign establishments, according to the Revised Concordat. Moreover:

(a) Host authorities should inform parent authorities on any material problems identified in the operation of foreign establishments.

(b) Parent authorities have the right to perform audits on the accuracy of data submitted by foreign establishments.

(c) If a foreign establishment faces problems, host authorities should consult the parent authorities and provide them with prior warning if they intend to revoke the foreign establishment's authorisation or take any other similar action.

3.1.3.2 Host supervisory authorities

Similarly to rules applicable to parent authorities, effective supervision by host authorities of international banks' foreign establishments requires them to collect information on the international bank's business and possible problems. They should also be aware of parent authorities' ability to supervise the foreign establishments of their domestic banks according to the Revised Concordat's principles.

To comply with these conditions, the report makes the following recommendations to authorities:

(a) Parent authorities should inform host authorities of amendments in supervisory measures having a significant impact on the operations of their banks' foreign establishments.

(b) Where a parent authority has doubts about the standard of host supervision in a particular state and, as a result, envisages action that will affect foreign establishments in the territory concerned, advance consultation is recommended so that the host authority can correct any inadequacies.

(c) Where an international bank with foreign establishments faces problems or changes of ownership are impending, parent authorities should communicate such information to host authorities.

(d) If a parent authority intends to take action to protect the interests of depositors with an international bank having foreign establishments, such action should be subject to coordination with host authorities of the bank's foreign establishments to the extent possible.

3.1.4 Removal of secrecy constraints

The report also addresses the issue of doing away with banking secrecy restrictions, so as to ensure the exchange of information between parent and host authorities, as above. Recognising the existence of national rules on banking secrecy aimed at protecting the interests of banks' depositors, the report recommends that states should review and amend any legislative provisions that limit or prohibit the exchange of information between supervisory authorities, setting, in any case, specific terms on the use of information exchanged.

3.1.5 The role of external auditors

Finally, the report contains detailed recommendations on dealing with problems associated with external audits of international banks with foreign establishments.

(a) Firstly, the report recommends host authorities not to authorise branches and/or subsidiaries if the adequacy of external audits is not verified in advance.

(b) It is preferable that the same external auditors inspect the foreign establishments and the parent company or, as appropriate, the head office of the international bank.

(c) Finally, the report recommends that supervisory authorities should monitor the quality of performed audits and, where deemed necessary, replace external auditors.

3.2 The 1992 report

3.2.1 The four minimum standards of supervision

In 1992, the Basel Committee converted the above-mentioned recommendations of the 1990 Report on foreign establishment authorisation by host authorities into the following four (4) minimum standards of supervision:

(a) All international banking groups and international banks should be supervised by a parent state authority that capably performs consolidated supervision.

(b) The creation of a foreign banking establishment should receive the prior consent of both the host supervisory authority and the bank's or banking group's parent supervisory authority.

(c) Supervisory authorities should have the right to collect information on the foreign establishments of banks or banking groups for which they are parent state supervisor.

(d) If a host authority ascertains that any of these minimum standards is not sufficiently met, it may impose restrictive measures in order to satisfy its prudential concerns in accordance with these minimum standards.

3.2.2 Obligations of host supervisory authorities

Pursuant to the above-mentioned standards, before authorising a branch or subsidiary of an international bank, host authorities must take the following actions:

(a) First of all, they need to verify whether both the applicant bank and the group to which it belongs are subject to consolidated supervision by administrative authorities that are capable in practice to supervise it. Assessment of the ability of host authorities to exercise effective prudential consolidated supervision is performed on the basis of the following criteria:

- the ability to collect and evaluate consolidated information,
- the ability to prevent the creation of inappropriate organisational structures or business links, and
- the ability to prevent a bank or banking group from establishing a presence in states where the banking supervision regime is particularly lax.

(b) They should also examine whether parent authorities expressly consent to the bank's cross-border expansion and, if otherwise, refuse to grant an operating license. During the approval process for such an operating license, parent and host authorities should, in particular, take the following into account:

- the financial robustness of both the bank (and the group to which it belongs), and in particular its capital adequacy,
- the suitability of its internal organisation and operating procedures for managing risk exposure,[595] and
- observance of the rules stipulated in the Revised Concordat on the division of responsibilities between parent and host authorities, in terms of supervision of the solvency and the liquidity of international banks' foreign establishments.

(c) Moreover, they need to ensure that, along with parent authorities, they collect the necessary information on the business of foreign establishments in view of effective supervision. They are also called to cooperate with parent authorities to mutually abol-

595 Authorities should also examine the amount of financing extended to foreign establishments from the parent enterprise or, as appropriate, the head office.

ish any (actual and legal) obstacle to the collection of information on foreign establishments operations in their jurisdiction.

(d) Finally, if any of the above-mentioned conditions are not sufficiently met, the host authorities shall be called upon to impose the restrictive measures that they deem appropriate in order to ensure effective prudential supervision of the international bank's foreign establishment. Such restrictive measures include the refusal to grant an operating license, but only as a last resort.

3.3 The 1996 report

The 1996 report contains a list of 29 conclusions and recommendations *"on the improvement and facilitation of exercising prudential supervision of the risks to which banks are exposed, with a view to ensuring the integrity of individual banks and the stability of the financial system as a whole"*. These recommendations are aimed at ensuring:

- the ability of the parent authorities exercising consolidated supervision to obtain all the necessary information from foreign branches and foreign subsidiaries of international banks operating on their territory, and
- the necessary conditions so that host authorities of banks' foreign establishments can have access to essential information that is required for prudential supervision to be efficient.

Moreover, it is explicitly stipulated that if the parent authorities do not apply the above guiding principles, the host authorities shall be entitled to either revoke the authorisation of foreign establishments or refuse to grant such an authorisation, as appropriate.

B. The regulatory framework of the Basel Committee on the micro-prudential and macro-prudential regulation of international banks

1. 'Basel III': the sources of the new regulatory framework and the rationale for reform

1.1 The Basel Committee reports constituting the sources of 'Basel III'

On 16 December 2010, the Basel Committee adopted and published two important reports entitled:

- "Basel III: A global regulatory framework for more resilient banks and banking systems",[596] and
- "Basel III: International framework for liquidity risk measurement, standards and monitoring".[597]

These reports, endorsed politically by the GHOS in November 2010 and subsequently by the G20 Seoul Summit,[598] are the result of extensive consultations that have taken place since 2008,[599] namely amidst the recent (2007-2009) international financial crisis. Both are *quasi* final, since, there may be amendments and/or additions to their provisions in upcoming months, according to the Basel Committee's agenda. On 13 January 2011, the Committee issued a press release entitled *"Basel Committee issues final elements of the reforms to raise the quality of regulatory capital"*.[600]

These two reports are collectively known as the 'Basel III regulatory framework' (hereinafter 'Basel III'), and probably constitute the Basel Committee's most important reaction to the recent crisis.[601] They provide for a new regulatory framework for international banks reforming the one that is currently in force.

The purpose of the reform is to strengthen the stability of the banking system, internationally:[602]

- on the one hand, by enhancing bank-level or micro-prudential regulations that will help raise the resilience of individual banking institutions during periods of stress, and
- on the other, by introducing macro-prudential regulations, addressing system-wide risks that can build up across the banking (and, more generally, the financial) sector, as well as the procyclical amplification of these risks over time.

Accordingly, 'Basel III' seeks to significantly strengthen the content of the provisions of the currently applicable regulatory framework and introduce novel means of micro-prudential regulation. Nevertheless, the fundamental novelty of 'Basel III' is the adoption of rules on macro-prudential regulation. In this sense, Hannoun's remark that 'Basel III' is an *"enhanced Basel II plus a macro-prudential overlay"* is very accurate.[603]

596 **Basel Committee on Banking Supervision (2010a)**, available at: http://www.bis.org/publ/bcbs189.htm. This document has been updated in 1 June 2012, available under the same internet address.
597 **Basel Committee on Banking Supervision (2010b)**, available at: http://www.bis.org/publ/bcbs188.htm.
598 For a summary overview of the Summit's findings, see B 3 under Section Five above.
599 For a compilation of all the relevant preparatory texts and speeches of high-ranking Committee officials, visit: http://www.bis.org/list/basel3/index.htm.
600 **Basel Committee on Banking Supervision (2011)**, January, available at: http://www.bis.org/press/p110113.htm.
601 For an overview of the Committee's work in response to the crisis, see http://www.bis.org/bcbs/fincriscomp.htm.
602 **Basel Committee on Banking Supervision (2010a)**, paragraph 6.
603 See **Hannoun (2010)**, p. 9.

For more details on the distinction between the micro- and macro-prudential policies in the banking sector (and, more generally, the financial system), which make up the two pillars of 'Basel III' (see under B 3.2 in Section Two above).

Finally, the Basel Committee is also pursuing an extensive reform of the currently applicable regulatory framework on capital requirements for international banks to cover against exposure to market risks (known as 'Basel 2.5'), based on the report "*Revisions to the Basel II market risk framework*".[604] It is remarkable that this is not included, in terms of regulatory consistency, in the 'Basel III' framework, although it obviously pertains to the same subject-area.[605]

At the EU level, adoption of this work by the Basel Committee is already under way and will be completed in 2012 with the adoption of the proposed legislative acts (a Regulation and a Directive) of the European Parliament and the Council, introducing extensive amendments and adding new chapters to Directives 2006/48/EC and 2006/49/EC (which will be repeated).[606]

1.2 The rationale for reform

1.2.1 From 'Basel I' to 'Basel II'

1.2.1.1 Introductory remarks

'Basel III' is (as its name suggests) the second major amendment of the regulatory framework developed by the Basel Committee. Indeed, in the context of its work on micro-prudential banking regulation, dating back to the mid-1980s, the Basel Committee undertook initiatives for international convergence of rules on the calculation and fulfilment of bank capital adequacy requirements to cover against their exposure to various risks.

604 **Basel Committee on Banking Supervision (2009c)**, July, available at: http://www.bis.org/publ/bcbs158.htm. Interpretative issues of the Basle Committee with regard to the revisions to the market risks framework are contained in a document of the Committee of November 2011, available at: http://www.bis.org/publ/bcbs208.htm.

605 On the progress report of the Basel Committee with regard to the implementation of 'Basel II', 'Basel 2.5', and 'Basel III', see **Basel Committee on Banking Supervision (2012)**, April, available at: http://www.bis.org/publ/bcbs215.htm.

606 See on this **Gortsos (2012c)**, Sections B, D and E.

1.2.1.2 'Basel I'

(I) Initial provisions

The first relevant report of the Basel Committee was the 1988 *'Basel Capital Accord'*, known as 'Basel I'.[607] The provisions of this accord concerned the following:

- establishing a uniform method for calculating the capital requirements of international banks to cover against their exposure to credit risk (and 'country risk'), both for balance-sheet items and off-balance-sheet items, based on specific, predefined risk weights (the 'standardised approach'), and
- specifying the elements of regulatory capital that banks can use to meet their capital requirements to cover against those risks. [608]

In 1996, the Basel Committee issued a report entitled *"Amendment to the Capital Accord to incorporate market risks"*. Contrary to what the title suggests, the provisions of this report did not amend, but rather complemented 'Basel I'[609] by establishing:

- uniform methods based on a 'standardised approach', and, for the first time, an internal ratings-based approach ('IRBA') for the calculation of their capital requirements to cover against exposure to market risks, and
- an alternative definition of regulatory capital used exclusively for meeting these capital requirements.

607 **Basel Committee on Banking Supervision (1988)**: *"International convergence of capital measurement and capital standards"*, July, available at: http://www.bis.org/publ/bcbsc111.htm. Prior to this report, a bilateral agreement had been concluded between the United States and the United Kingdom, known as the US/UK Accord, that was the catalyst for the report's adoption. On this, see **Norton (1995)**, pp. 186-190.

608 On this, see **Norton (1995)**, pp. 193-198, and **Haussmann (1995)**, pp. 230-237.

609 From 1991 until 1995, 'Basel I' was amended on five (5) occasions in terms of individual technical points by means of the following reports:

- **(1991)**: "Amendment of the Basel capital accord in respect of the inclusion of general provisions/general loan-loss reserves in capital", November,
- **(1994a)**: "Amendment to the Basel Capital Accord of July 1988", July,
- **(1994b)**: "Basel Capital Accord: the treatment of the credit risk associated with certain off-balance-sheet items", July,
- **(1994c)**: "Basel Committee Amendment to the 1988 Capital Accord: Recognition of Collateral", December, and
- **(1995)**: "Basel Capital Accord: treatment of potential exposure for off-balance-sheet items", April.

(II) Amendment to the Basel Capital Accord (1996)

In January 1996, the Basel Committee issued a report entitled "Amendment to the Capital Accord to incorporate market risks" (hereinafter the 'Amendment to the Accord'). The report in question:[610]

- supplements the regulatory framework on capital adequacy by imposing capital requirements on internationally active banks also for the market risks to which they are exposed, and
- proposes an alternative definition of regulatory capital which banks are permitted by the supervisory authorities to maintain in order to meet market risk capital requirements.

1.2.1.3 'Basel II'

'Basel I' was strongly criticised both by supervisory authorities and supervised banks:[611] In 1999 the Basel Committee, having identified the need to amend individual provisions and (mainly) enhance its content, conducted extensive consultations with market stakeholders on its amendment. The final report entitled *"The New Basel Capital Accord"*, known as 'Basel II', was adopted in June 2004.[612] The main objectives of the new Accord were the following:[613]

(a) Supervisory authorities recognised the internal ratings-based approach (IRBA) – alternatively to the standardised approach – as an acceptable method for calculating the value of banks' portfolios also in terms of credit risks (as they did in 1996 for market risks) provided that certain conditions are met. [614]

(b) Rules were introduced for banks to cover against exposure to operational risk.

(c) A supervisory review process was introduced (the second pillar of 'Basel II'), whereby supervisory authorities have the power to exercise individualised supervision

610 Concurrently, the Basel Committee issued two additional texts entitled: "*Overview of the amendment to the Capital Accord to incorporate market risks*", and "*Supervisory framework for the use of back-testing in conjunction with the internal models approach to market risk capital requirements*".

611 See, *inter alia*, **Macht (2007)**, pp. 63-66.

612 **Basel Committee on Banking Supervision (2004)**: *"Basel II: International Convergence of Capital Measurement and Capital Standards, A Revised Framework"*, June, available at: http://www.bis.org/publ/bcbs107.htm. The provisions of 'Basel I' and 'Basel II', as applicable in 2006, were codified into one single text entitled *"International Convergence of Capital Measurement and Capital Standards, A Revised Framework – Comprehensive Version"*, **Basel Committee on Banking Supervision (2006)**, June, available at: http://www.bis.org/publ/bcbs128.htm.

613 For a detailed presentation of the 'Basel II' provisions, see **Sigrist (2006)**, **Macht (2007)**, pp. 67-100, and **Gleeson (2010)**.

614 For a detailed presentation of these provisions (mainly at a technical level), see the individual contributions in the collective work edited by **Ong (2004)**, pp. 1-293.

over banks with operations entailing greater systemic risk. The Pillar is based on four (4) main principles:[615]

- provision for procedures by banks for internal assessment of their capital adequacy and the adoption of a strategy for the maintenance of the level of own capital,
- establishment of the power of supervisory control over the efficiency of the risk management procedures of banks,
- the possibility of the imposition by the competent authorities on specific banks of capital requirements for cover against credit risk in excess of the minimum limit (8%), and
- establishment of the power of timely intervention of the supervisory authorities in the event of a deterioration in the capital adequacy ratio of a bank.

It is reasonable to suggest that by adopting this process, macro-prudential elements were introduced for the first time in the Basel Committee's regulatory framework on banks' capital adequacy.

(d) It established a – qualitative and quantitative – obligation for banks to disclose information in order to reinforce market discipline with sound risk management rules. Its justification rests upon the extensive freedom which the New Accord gives to banks as to the methods of internal ratings, since some of the obligations of disclosure are a condition for the use of advanced methods. Disclosure obligations concern, in general, information in connection with:[616]

- the risks to which banks are exposed;
- their management procedures;
- the quality of the items of own funds used to cover risks.

(e) Finally, 'Basel II' also introduced amendments to some of the provisions that concern capital adequacy requirements to cover against market risks.[617] On the contrary, the provisions regarding the composition of their regulatory capital remained unchanged.

615 **Basel Committee on Banking Supervision (2004)**, Part 3, pp. 159-165.
616 Ibid., Part 4, pp. 177-190.
617 **Basel Committee on Banking Supervision (2006)**, Part 2, section VI.

1.2.2 From 'Basel II' to 'Basel III'

1.2.2.1 The causes of the recent international financial crisis and the rationale behind the 2010 reform

When the international financial crisis broke out in 2007, banks were adequately capitalised in most states whose banking system was affected,[618] undoubtedly also due to the fact that most had transposed the provisions of 'Basel II' into their national law. But this proved insufficient to prevent either the onset of the crisis or the occurrence of ensuing problems, as a result of several factors. Specifically:

(a) As the Basel Committee points out,[619] one of the most important causes of the crisis was the banking system's excessive leverage in many states, both for on- and off-balance sheet items of a significant number of banks. Although these banks initially had very robust capital adequacy ratios, leveraging led to their gradual deterioration. This leverage was, at least partly, the result of the regulatory framework currently in force on bank capital adequacy, since banks resorted to regulatory capital arbitrage, mainly through excessive securitisation of assets, in an effort to reduce the cost of implementation of the relevant rules, thus increasing their lending activity with the same level of regulatory capital.[620]

(b) At the same time, many banks had inadequate – as subsequently proven – liquidity buffers. According to the Basel Committee, during the initial liquidity phase of the recent financial crisis, many banks encountered problems despite having sufficient capital adequacy, as a result of the non-prudent management of their liquidity. This fact demonstrated the importance of adequate liquidity buffers for the smooth operation of markets and the banking system.[621]

More specifically, before the crisis, banks raised adequate funds at low cost (on the interbank market and by issuing short-term debt). When the crisis broke out, the rapid shift in market conditions clearly demonstrated the speed at which the banking system's liquidity could dry out. Affected banks then turned to their central banks for financial

618 This remark does not apply to 'investment banks' in the United States, which were at the heart of the recent crisis. Note that these enterprises were not banks within the meaning of the Basel Committee's provisions, as they did not have an administrative license to accept deposits from the public (they were not 'depository institutions' according to United States law) and were not subject to binding rules regarding their capital adequacy. On this, see **Posner (2010)**, pp. 55-60, and **Tirole (2010)**, pp. 24-26.
Here, it should also be noted that in the context of European financial law European investment firms (and not investment banks) have been subject to a micro-prudential regulatory framework since 1993 (by virtue of the provisions of **Directive 93/6/EEC** of the Council, OJ L 141, 11.6.93, pp. 1-27), which is similar to the one applicable to European credit institutions.

619 **Basel Committee on Banking Supervision (2010a)**, paragraph 4.

620 On this, see **Tirole (2010)**, pp. 19-21 and 28-32, **Lastra and Wood (2010)**, p. 540, and **Goodhart (2011)**, pp. 7-8. Nevertheless, it is worth mentioning that securitisation *per se* is, in principle, a particularly useful technique, which allows banks to improve their liquidity position and (conditionally) limit their exposure to interest-rate income risk. See **Albertazzi et. al. (2011)**.

621 **Basel Committee on Banking Supervision (2010b)**, paragraph 2.

support, leading the latter to adopt policies known as 'non-standard monetary policies'.[622]

(c) Although there is no doubt that during the recent crisis the systemic risk facing the financial system was very high, it is also clear that the regulatory framework currently in force does not contain any rules for the prevention of systemic risk, neither in its time nor in its cross-sectional dimension.[623] On the contrary, the regulatory framework currently in force on capital adequacy, especially based on IRB calculation of capital requirements, was considered to be one of the factors exacerbating pro-cyclicality[624] by creating incentives for banks:

- to contribute to further credit expansion in times of economic growth, under more lax capital requirements on the supply of credit, and
- to limit financing during times of recession, as relevant capital requirements become stricter.[625]

1.2.2.2 The impact of the crisis and the Basel Committee's reaction

As a result of the above-mentioned factors, many international banks (small and large, some even systemically important) were not able to absorb the losses generated as a result of the crisis. At its peak in 2008, markets exerted pressure on banks to reduce their leverage, thus making them:

- reduce the value of their assets further, and subsequently,
- increase their losses, reduce regulatory capital, and diminish their capacity to provide financing to businesses and households.[626]

At the same time, they encountered major liquidity problems for an extended period of time.

Consequently, the Basel Committee proceeded with the adoption of the new international regulatory framework, known as 'Basel III', in order to address the above-mentioned failures. In particular, the Committee deemed that 'Basel II' was not adequate, pointing out that its shortcomings and some of its provisions contributed (to a certain

622 See on this **Committee on the Global Financial System (2008)**, and **Borio and Disyatat (2009)**. With regard to international cooperation between central banks on liquidity provision to the financial system amidst the crisis, see **Allen and Moessner (2010)**.

623 It is worth noting that academics, international organisations and international fora dealing with the issue of financial stability had pointed out, as early as 2000, the need for macro-prudential policies. As for the reasons why the relevant proposals were not extensively adopted before the recent crisis, see **Borio (2006)**, pp. 18-20 (with extensive further references).

624 The same applies for the current bank accounting standards (see **Lastra and Wood (2010)**, p. 539).

625 See on this **Tirole (2010)**, pp. 32-33, and **Goodhart (2011)**, p. 8.

626 **Basel Committee on Banking Supervision (2010a)**, paragraph 151.

extent) to the outbreak of the crisis and the subsequent negative effects on the real economy.

2. The regulatory framework currently in force

2.1 Calculation of capital requirements

2.1.1 Capital requirements for credit risk

2.1.1.1 Portfolio for calculation

Since 1988 banks' capital requirements for credit and country risk have been calculated on the basis of total assets and off-balance sheet items, with the exception of those in banks' trading books (since 1997, when the 1996 Accord entered into force).[627] The value to which banks are exposed to credit risk as a result of positions in these items is calculated thereafter in accordance with the provisions on the specific position risk.

2.1.1.2 Calculation of value exposed to risk

(I) The original provisions

In order to determine the extent to which a bank is exposed to credit risk from items representing assets on its balance sheet, the 1988 Accord established a standardised approach. In accordance with this approach, the credit risk-weighted value is determined on the basis of one of four risk weights (0%, 20%, 50% or 100%) applied to the value of each asset.[628]

The calculation procedure for the credit risk-weighted value of off-balance-sheet items is more complex, since counterparty risk-weighting is preceded by the conversion of these items into asset equivalents by means of specific 'credit conversion factors'. Moreover, the procedure differs in the case of:

- positions in over-the-counter (OTC) derivative instruments on interest rates and foreign exchange, or
- other off-balance sheet items (i.e. commitments and contingent claims).[629]

627 Basel Committee (1988), part 1, paragraph 28.
628 Ibid., part 1, paragraphs 28-41, and Annex 2.
629 Ibid., part 1, paragraphs 42-43, and Annex 3.

(II) The provisions of the New Accord

The First Pillar of the New Accord (2004) introduced substantial amendments to the framework for the calculation of capital requirements to cover against credit risk. More specifically:

(a) It amended the standardised approach for the calculation of the value of a bank's exposure to credit risk from its assets.[630] Although the new standardised approach retains the methodology of applying predetermined risk weights to assets, it is marked by greater risk sensitivity, to the extent that the (new) risk weights are determined depending on the external rating (where applicable) of the counterparty.[631]

(b) It recognised the calculation method of the value exposed to risk on the basis of internal systems of rating developed by each bank (internal ratings-based approach). Depending upon the level of development of internal risk-rating systems, banks have two alternative methods of calculation at their disposal:[632]

- the foundation IRB approach, and
- the advanced IRB approach.

Within this framework, banks were allowed to use specific parameters of credit risk for each exposure; more specifically:

- the probability of the counterparty defaulting on the undertaken obligation (Probability of Default, PD),
- the loss in the event of counterparty default (Loss Given Default, LGD),
- exposure as against the counterparty (Exposure At Default, EAD), and
- the term remaining to maturity (Maturity, M).

In the case of the foundation method, banks determine only the Probability of Default (PD) parameter, whereas in the advanced approach they determine all of the parameters.[633]

(c) It adopted (for the first time) a specific, detailed framework for the calculation of capital requirements to cover against credit risk from securitised assets.[634]

(d) On certain conditions, the various methods for the mitigation of credit risk (such as collateral, guarantees and credit derivatives, as well as netting of off-balance-sheet items) are taken into account in the calculation of capital requirements.[635]

630 On the other hand, the provisions regarding off-balance sheet items have not been amended.
631 **Basel Committee (2004),** Part 2(II), pp. 15-47.
632 Ibid., Part 2(III), pp. 55-57. It should be noted that in the case of the retail banking portfolio (consumer and housing loans), banks may use only the advanced approach (Part III, pp. 69-71).
633 Ibid., Part 2(III), pp. 55-57.
634 Ibid., Part 2(IV), pp. 113-136.
635 Ibid., Part 2(II), pp. 26-47.

2.1.1.3 Level of capital requirement

The minimum solvency ratio (which is defined as regulatory capital to risk-weighted assets in accordance with the above) to be maintained by banks has been set at 8%, and has remained unchanged.[636]

2.1.2 Capital requirements for market risks

2.1.2.1 Portfolio for calculation

Capital requirements to cover banks against all market risks, except those related to foreign exchange, are calculated on the basis of their trading book positions.[637] On the other hand, the calculation of capital requirements to cover against the risk to which they are exposed from changes in nominal exchange rates and gold prices is made on the basis of all their assets and liabilities, both on- and off-balance sheet.[638]

2.1.2.2 Determination of the value which is exposed to risk

(I) Position risk

In order to measure the value of their portfolio which is exposed to risk from open positions in debt securities, equities and derivatives on these, banks may use two alternative methods:

(a) Using the standardised approach,[639] calculation is based on specific weights applied uniformly to all banks. This method can be broken down into three successive stages:

(aa) An initial evaluation of open positions in debt securities, (equity and non-equity) derivatives on debt securities, interest and foreign exchange rates, equities and derivative instruments on shares or stock indices included in the trading book.

(ab) A subsequent calculation, separately for each of the four categories of these financial instruments, of the net open positions by offsetting positive and negative open positions.

(ac) Finally, net open positions are weighted in accordance with the 'building-blocks approach', whereby the value of the trading book exposed to risk is calculated separately for the specific and the general position risk – and by means of a different method for each of these constituents, in relation to the risk from positions in debt securities

636 **Basel Committee (1988)**, part III, paragraph 44.
637 **Basel Committee (1996)**, Introduction, part I, paragraph 2.
638 Ibid., Introduction, part 1, paragraph 6.
639 Ibid., Part A.1 and A.2.

and derivatives on these, on the one hand, and the risk from positions in shares and derivatives on these, on the other.

(b) Banks are also allowed to calculate the value of their trading book's exposure to position risk using a method based on internal risk models.[640] According to this method, the value which is exposed to position risk (specific or general) may be calculated on the basis of the results produced by the models that they themselves use internally for the measurement and management of the risk to which they are exposed, on condition, *inter alia*, that:

- the models in question are recognised by the competent authorities;[641]
- specific qualitative criteria concerning the adequacy of their administrative and technical infrastructure and the existence of adequate internal procedures are met;[642]
- procedures for the specification of the parameters affecting open positions in the trading book are put in place, and[643]
- specific quantitative criteria are met.[644]

(II) Foreign exchange risk

In order to measure the value of banks' portfolio that is exposed to foreign exchange risk, two alternative methods are also available:

(a) According to the standardised method of calculation, a two-phase procedure is followed:[645]

(aa) First of all, the net open positions in currencies and gold are calculated.

(ab) Subsequently, the overall net open foreign-exchange position is calculated as the sum of two amounts:

- of the positive or negative net open positions in foreign exchange, whichever the greater, or
- of the positive or negative net open position in gold.

(b) In accordance with the method based on internal risk models, a bank may measure value–at-risk on the basis of results of its internal model for the measurement and management of risk, provided that they meet the same criteria which apply to the general position risk.[646]

640 Ibid., Part B.
641 Ibid., Part B.1.
642 Ibid., Part B.2.
643 Ibid., Part B.3.
644 Ibid., Part B.4.
645 Ibid., Part A.3.
646 Ibid., Part B. The difference from the position risk lies in the determination of the parameters that affect open positions, given that it is reasonable to set different criteria for each risk.

(III) Risk from open positions in commodities

In order to measure the value of their portfolio which is exposed to risk from open positions in commodities and derivatives on these, banks may use two alternative methods, as in the case of the two market risks mentioned above:

(a) In accordance with the two alternative versions of the standardised method, a bank is allowed to use:

- either the method dependent upon the maturity of the positions, which is similar to that used for the determination of the value exposed to general position risk from debt securities; or
- a simplified method,[647] according to which the value exposed to risk is determined as the sum by which the bank's positive positions exceed its negative positions in the same commodity in identical futures contracts and options, or in identical contracts with a right of option.[648]

(b) As regards the method based on internal risk measurement models, the same applies by analogy as in relation to the calculation of the value of the portfolio exposed to general position risk and foreign exchange risk.[649]

2.1.2.3 Level of capital requirement

The level of own capital which is required to cover banks against their exposure to market risks is determined by category of risk, as is explained in brief below. However the minimum level of the total capital adequacy ratio, for cover, that is, against both credit risk and market risks (and by 2007 operational risk), may not be lower than 8%.

(I) Position risk

The level of own capital required for position risk differs depending upon the method used for value-at-risk measurement. More specifically:

(a) If the standardised method is followed, the level of the capital requirement is equal to the sum of all the standardised net positions, positive and negative, as explained above. For its measurement, the four individual constituents (specific and general risk for debt securities and derivatives on these, on the one hand, and equities and derivatives on these, on the other) are calculated separately.[650]

647 Ibid., Part A.4, paragraphs 7-11.
648 Ibid., Part A.4, paragraphs 12-13.
649 Ibid., Part B. In this case the only difference between the two above-mentioned risks lies in the specification of the parameters, which affect open positions.
650 Ibid., Part A.1, paragraph 1, and A.2, respectively.

(b) In accordance with the method based on internal risk models, the level of capital requirements is equal to the greater of two sums:[651]

- the first is the value at risk (VaR) of the previous day, calculated on the basis of specific minimum criteria already set, and
- the second is the VaR aggregate for the past 60 business days, weighted by the sum of two factors: a scaling factor with a minimum level 3,[652] and a complementary factor which takes on values from 0 to 1, depending upon the number of times this has been exceeded in the previous 250 business days.[653]

(II) Foreign exchange risk

In the case of foreign exchange risks, the level of own funds required for banks to cover against such risks also differs depending on the method used for measuring value–at-risk. Consequently:

(a) In accordance with the standardised method, the capital requirement amounts to 8% of their total net open position. Specific provisions govern the measurement of the capital requirement when alternative calculation methods are used, as described above.[654]

(b) If the internal risk models method is opted for, the level of the capital requirement for foreign exchange risk is determined in accordance with the same procedure as in the case of general position risk (as described above).

(III) Risk from open positions in commodities

The provisions on position risk and foreign exchange risk also apply to the determination of the level of capital requirements to cover against the risk from open positions in commodities. More specifically:

(a) In accordance with the standardised method and if maturity calculation is used, the capital requirement is calculated separately for each commodity as the sum of individual weighted positions.[655] If use is made of the simplified method, the capital requirement is calculated as the sum of: a 15% rate of the net position in each commodity to the current market price, and a 3% rate of the gross position in each commodity to

651 Ibid., Part B.4, point (i).
652 Ibid., Part B.4, point (j).
653 Special provisions apply in connection with the capital requirements for cover against special position risk.
654 Ibid., Part A.3, paragraph 12.
655 Ibid., Part A.4, paragraphs 7-11.

the current market price.[656] In both cases, total capital requirement is the sum of capital requirements for each individual commodity.

(b) If the internal risk model method is opted for, the level of capital requirement to cover against the risk from open positions in commodities is determined in accordance with the same procedure as in the case of general position risk and foreign exchange risk (as described above).

2.1.3 Capital requirements for operational risk

The New Accord (2004) establishes capital requirements for banks to cover against their exposure to operational risk for the first time. Falling within the concept of this risk are losses attributable to the inadequacy/unsuitability of internal procedures and systems or to human factors or to external causes.[657] The Basel Committee proposes three (3) alternative methods for the calculation of the capital requirements in question:

- the 'basic indicator approach',[658]
- the 'standardised approach' and the 'alternative standardised method', only for retail banking operations,[659] and
- the 'advanced measurement approach'.[660]

2.2 Fulfilment of capital requirements

2.2.1 The main definition of own funds

The above-mentioned capital requirements are governed by the provisions of the 1988 Accord, which specify the items eligible as own funds. These items are divided into two categories: core and supplementary capital. The importance of this distinction is that total supplementary own funds cannot exceed 100% of core capital.[661]

(a) Core capital comprises common and preference shares (excluded are cumulative preference shares), paid-in surplus, disclosed reserves (with the exception of revaluation reserves), profit and loss carried forward, retained profits of the current year, as well as general provisions.[662]

(b) Supplementary capital includes revaluation reserves (following revaluation of fixed assets), instruments with no fixed maturity date issued by the bank (under certain con-

656 Ibid., Part A.4, paragraphs 12-13.
657 **Basel Committee (2004)**, Part 5, p. 137.
658 Ibid., Part 2(V), pp. 137-138.
659 Ibid., Part 2(V), pp. 139-140.
660 Ibid., Part 2(V), pp. 140-144.
661 **Basel Committee (1988)**, part 1, paragraph 14.
662 Ibid., Part 1, paragraphs 12-14, and Annex 1.

ditions), cumulative preference shares (which provide a right to a cumulative dividend for previous years), as well as subordinated term debt (on condition that certain criteria are met).[663]

2.2.2 The alternative definition of own funds

Since 1996, for the fulfilment of the capital requirements concerning cover against market risks, banks may use at their discretion either the main or the alternative definition laid down in the 1996 Report. According to the latter, own funds include the following:

- items under the main definition, as above,
- net earnings in the trading book, and
- subordinated debt which fulfils certain criteria (more flexible compared to the debt included in the main definition).[664]

2.3 Pillars II and III of the New Accord

2.3.1 The provisions of Pillar II

The supervisory review process of the Second Pillar is one of the main innovations of the New Accord, reflecting the shift of interest of the supervisory authorities away from micro-prudential towards macro-prudential supervision, thus enabling the individualised supervision of banks whose operations involve greater systemic risk. The Pillar revolves around four (4) principles:[665]

- provision for an Internal Capital Adequacy Assessment Process ('ICAAP') and adoption of a strategy to maintain the level of own funds;
- power of supervisory review over the efficiency of banks' risk management processes;
- competent authorities may impose capital requirements on specific banks in excess of the minimum limit (8%) so that all credit risks are adequately covered;
- power of supervisory authorities to timely intervene in the event of deterioration of a bank's capital adequacy ratio ('CAR').

The provisions of Pillar II focus on the following three (3) issues:[666]

663 Ibid., Part 1, par. 15-27, and Annex 1.
664 **Basel Committee (1996)**, Introduction, part II.
665 **Basel Committee (2004)**, Part 3, pp. 159-165.
666 Ibid., Part 3, pp. 165-168.

(i) Managing risks which are not handled within the framework of Pillar I (e.g. interest rate risk, large exposure risk, liquidity risk, strategic risk).
(ii) Dealing with factors that are not under the bank's control (fluctuations in the economic cycle).
(iii) Monitoring whether conditions for the adoption of the advanced methods (both for credit and operational risk) are met.

2.3.2 The provisions of Pillar III

The Third Pillar of the New Accord concerns the obligation of banks to disclose – both qualitative and quantitative – information with a view to reinforcing market discipline with sound risk management rules. Its justification rests upon the extensive freedom provided by the New Accord to banks in terms of internal ratings methods, since certain disclosure obligations are a prerequisite for the use of the advanced methods. The obligations of disclosure concern, in general, information in connection with:

- the risks to which banks are exposed,
- their management processes,
- the quality of own funds items used to cover against risks.[667]

3. The provisions of 'Basel III': an overview

3.1 Overall examination

3.1.1 Systematic classification

From a systematic point of view, the provisions of 'Basel III' can be classified into two categories:[668]

(a) The first category includes the provisions amending the regulatory framework currently in force on the capital adequacy of international banks (namely 'Basel II'), as well as additions thereto (see under 3.1.2 below).

(b) The second category includes the provisions introducing 'innovative elements', which can be further divided into:

- provisions introducing new rules on micro-prudential regulation (under 3.1.3.1),[669]
- provisions introducing rules on macro-prudential regulation (under 3.1.3.2).

667 Ibid., Part 4, pp. 177-190.
668 For an overall examination of the provisions from the Committee's point of view, see **Basel Committee on Banking Supervision (2010a)**, pp. 7-39.
669 At a secondary level, these provisions also have a macro-prudential function.

The innovative nature of the above-mentioned elements is found in two factors:

(a) The first is the fact that for the first time there will be international convergence of the above-mentioned micro-prudential rules, although many states have already adopted relevant provisions in their domestic legislation.

(b) The second factor concerns macro-prudential rules, most of which are introduced for the first time in public international financial law, without any prior experience of their implementation at national level.

The provisions of the new regulatory framework are expected to be phased in, starting from 1 January 2013 until 1 January 2019 (final deadline for full implementation). For a brief overview of all the transitional provisions introduced, see Table in Annex 4 (in the first of the reports constituting 'Basel III').[670]

3.1.2 Amendments and additions to the regulatory framework currently in force on banks' capital adequacy

3.1.2.1 Rules on banks' minimum regulatory capital

The most important amendment to the Basel Committee's regulatory framework on banks' capital adequacy has to do with the definition of their regulatory capital. The new provisions aim at:

- improving the quality of regulatory capital (namely through a new, stricter definition of Tier 1 capital), and
- strengthening their overall regulatory capital (although the capital adequacy ratio remains at 8%).

This aspect will be discussed in further detail below under B 4.

3.1.2.2 Rules on banks' cover against exposure to credit risk

(I) Essential provisions

During the recent financial crisis, it turned out that some banks suffered significant losses from exposures not covered by capital adequacy rules. For this reason, the new regulatory framework seeks to strengthen banks' cover against their exposure to credit risk from items in their portfolio (on- and off-balance sheet), such as OTC derivatives,

670 **Basel Committee on Banking Supervision (2010a)**, Annex 4: Phase-in arrangements.

repurchase agreements and loans for the purchase of securities and positions in derivatives.[671]

Furthermore, provisions are also introduced as follows:

(a) In calculating their capital requirements to cover against credit risk according to the standardised approach, banks should:

- assess the credit risk of their exposures themselves, irrespective of whether there is a rating by a credit rating agency, and
- determine whether the risk weights applied to such exposures are appropriate or not.[672]

(b) In order to recognise a credit rating agency as 'eligible', national supervisory authorities should verify whether such an agency meets the appropriate criteria, using as reference the 2008 revised IOSCO code *(Code of Conduct Fundamentals for Credit Rating Agencies, Report of the Technical Committee)*.[673]

(II) Implementation schedule

These provisions will take effect on 1 January 2013.[674]

3.1.3 The 'innovative' elements

3.1.3.1 New rules relating to micro-prudential regulation

(I) Leverage ratio

(A) Content of the ratio

As already mentioned, one of the underlying causes of the crisis was the build-up of excessive leverage in the banking system. Therefore, and with a view to preventing any such build-up in future (namely as a result of major negative impact of deleveraging processes on the real economy in periods of stress), the 'Basel III' provisions introduce a simple, non-risk based leverage ratio (namely assets and off-balance sheet items of

671 Ibid., paragraphs 97-117. Similar provisions had also been established in July 2009, especially with regard to risk weights for positions from securitisation, by way of the above-mentioned report: **Basel Committee on Banking Supervision (2009c)**.

672 **Basel Committee on Banking Supervision (2010a)**, paragraphs 118-119.

673 Ibid., paragraphs 120-121. The IOSCO Code is available at: http://www.iosco.org/library/pubdocs/ pdf/IOSCOPD271.pdf.

674 Ibid., paragraph 97.

banks are not risk-weighted) that is calibrated to act as a credible supplementary measure to the risk-based capital requirements (as a backstop measure).[675]

The leverage ratio, amounting to 3%, is defined, according to the detailed provisions of the new regulatory framework,[676] as:

- Tier 1 regulatory capital (according to the new definition)[677] as numerator, and
- 'non-risk weighted' on- and off-balance-sheet exposures as denominator, based on their book value and (initially) without right to net assets and liabilities (as is in the case of calculating capital requirements).

In view of the above, many assets weighted at 0% in the measurement of capital requirements (thus not placing any burden on capital), shall be taken into account in the calculation of the leverage ratio. Accordingly, the scope for regulatory arbitrage, by substituting low-risk for high risk weighted assets, will be reduced.

(B) Implementation schedule

Given that there are still doubts about the suitability of the decisions on the leverage ratio's numerator and denominator (especially in terms of their implementation during a full economic cycle and for the totality of banks), they shall be reviewed by the Basel Committee in the course of a two-year 'supervisory monitoring period' (January 2011-December 2012), to be followed by a four-year 'parallel-run period' (January 2013-December 2016). On the basis of this review's findings and any subsequent adjustments made, the final leverage ratio should become effective on 1 January 2018. In any event, banks will be required to disclose their leverage ratio and its components as of 1 January 2015.[678]

(II) Liquidity ratios

(A) Introductory remarks

The new regulatory framework introduces, for the first time at international level, two liquidity ratios for banks:

675 Ibid., paragraph 152.
676 Ibid., paragraph 153-164.
677 See on this below under B 4.1.2.
678 **Basel Committee on Banking Supervision (2010a)**, paragraph 165-167.

- a short-term'liquidity coverage ratio', ('LCR', see under (B) below), and
- a long-term 'net stable funding ratio' ('NSFR', under (C)).[679]

(B) Liquidity coverage ratio

This standard aims at ensuring that a bank maintains an adequate level of high-quality liquid assets that can be converted into cash to meet its liquidity needs.[680] This standard, which should be equal to or in excess of 100%, is defined as the ratio of:

- the stock of high-quality liquid assets to total net cash flows over the next 30 calendar days,[681]

as laid down in the extensive and detailed provisions of the new regulatory framework.[682]

(C) Net stable funding ratio

The net stable funding ratio was introduced in order to address the problem caused by liquidity mismatches of assets and liabilities in banks' balance sheets and create incentives for banks to use stable funding sources for their assets (including loans) with a maturity in excess of one year.[683] This standard, which must be over 100%, is defined as the ratio of the available amount of stable funding to the required amount of stable funding,[684] as stipulated in detail in the new regulatory framework.[685]

Banks are expected to meet the liquidity requirements on a continuous basis.[686] The LCR should be reported to the supervisory authority at least monthly, with the operational capacity to increase the frequency to weekly or even daily in stressed situations at the discretion of the supervisor. The NSFR should be calculated and reported at least quarterly.[687]

679 The failure to achieve thus far international convergence on the content of rules regarding liquidity ratios is due to the fact that banking liquidity is linked to monetary policy elaborated and implemented by national central banks. This is why there has been no harmonisation of the relevant provisions at the level of the European Union, since the rules on European banking law concern member states of the European Union and not only member states whose currency is the euro (which follow of course a single monetary policy).
680 **Basel Committee on Banking Supervision (2010b)**, paragraph 15.
681 Ibid., paragraphs 16-17.
682 Ibid., paragraphs 20-118.
683 Ibid., paragraphs 119-120.
684 Ibid., paragraphs 121-122.
685 Ibid., paragraphs 124-136.
686 Ibid., paragraph 185.
687 Ibid., paragraph 186.

(D) Tools for the supervisor's monitoring of liquidity risk

In order to ensure proper monitoring and evaluation of the liquidity risk on the part of supervisory authorities in a uniform manner, the Basel Committee has established five (5) monitoring tools:

- 'contractual maturity mismatch',
- 'concentration of funding',
- 'available unencumbered assets',
- 'LCR by significant currency', and
- 'market-related monitoring tools'.[688]

Supervisory authorities should use these tools on a continuous basis in order to obtain adequate and specific information on liquidity conditions in the banking system as a whole, but also in individual banks.[689]

(E) Implementation schedule

An observation period was put in place for both ratios in 2011, in order for the implications of these standards on banking activity, financial markets, credit extension and economic growth to be monitored. The liquidity coverage ratio ('LCR') should enter into force on 1 January 2015, and the net stable funding ratio on 1 January 2018.[690]

3.1.3.2 Rules with regard to macro-prudential regulation

(I) Introductory remarks

As already mentioned, the second part of Basel III's innovative elements includes provisions establishing, for the first time at international level, rules on macro-prudential regulation. These rules can be broken down as follows (in terms of the two dimensions of systemic risk discussed in Section Two above (under B 2.4.1):
(a) The new regulatory framework includes special provisions to address the systemic risk's time dimension, namely limiting procyclicality. In this context, banks are called:

(i) to create a 'capital conservation buffer' in smooth periods (see under (II) below),
(ii) to create a 'countercyclical buffer' in times of excessive credit expansion (under (III)),

688 Ibid., paragraph 139-183.
689 Ibid., paragraph 137.
690 Ibid., paragraph 196-197.

(iii) to make strong forward-looking provisions, based on anticipated losses from on-balance and off-balance sheet items,[691] and
(iv) to cover against excessive procyclicality of their minimum capital requirements.[692]

(b) On the contrary, no special provisions are introduced to address the systemic risk's cross-sectional dimension. The Basel Committee considers that some of the rules established for banks' coverage for credit risk exposure arising from specific items in their portfolio (according to the above-mentioned), will also help to address this dimension on systemic risk as well.[693]

For instance, the Basel Committee considers that provisions giving banks incentives to clear their transactions in OTC derivatives through central counterparties will also contribute to limiting the systemic risk's cross-sectional dimension (as lower capital requirements will be imposed).[694]

(II) Capital conservation buffer

(A) Content of the capital conservation buffer

According to the new regulatory framework, in addition to their minimum capital requirements, banks shall also be required to hold a capital conservation buffer. This buffer will be created outside periods of stress (namely during times of economic growth and credit expansion), and may be used in order to absorb losses generated in times of stress of the economic cycle.[695]

The 2.5% capital conservation buffer of banks' total risk-weighted assets (according to provisions on the capital adequacy ratio) shall exclusively comprise common equity Tier 1 capital (according to the new definition),[696] and may be used to avoid recourse to other regulatory capital elements for absorbing losses.[697] If buffers are withdrawn, banks should rebuild them promptly by reducing dividend payments, sharing buy-backs and staff remuneration payments.[698]

691 **Basel Committee on Banking Supervision (2010a)**, paragraph 23-25.
692 Ibid., paragraph 20-22. The correlation between these four (4) categories of macro-prudential policy rules is clearly demonstrated in paragraph 31 of the report (ibid).
693 **Basel Committee on Banking Supervision (2010a)**, paragraph 33.
694 Ibid., paragraph 13.
695 Ibid., paragraph 28 and 123.
696 For further details, see below under B 4.1.2.
697 **Basel Committee on Banking Supervision (2010a)**, paragraph 129.
698 Ibid., paragraph 124.

(B) Implementation schedule

The capital conservation buffer will be phased in between 1 January 2016 and 1 January 2019 (it should start at 0.625% of risk weighted assets on 1 January 2016 and increase annually by an additional 0.625%, to reach its final level of 2.5% of risk weighted assets in 2019).

The Basel Committee considers that states experiencing excessive credit growth during the transition period should consider accelerating the adoption of the provisions at the discretion of national supervisory authorities.[699]

(III) Countercyclical buffer

(A) Content of the buffer

As already mentioned, losses incurred in the banking sector can be extremely severe when an economic downturn is preceded by a period of excess credit growth. To address this problem, 'Basel III' introduces an obligation for banks to create an additional buffer, in exceptional cases, i.e. the 'countercyclical capital buffer' in order to ensure that capital requirements take into account the macro-financial environment in which banks operate.

National authorities will enact this obligation and determine the size of the buffer when excess aggregate credit growth is deemed to be associated with a build-up of systemic risk. In this context, authorities are called upon to:

- monitor credit growth and other indicators that may signal a build-up of systemic risk, and
- assess whether (and to what extent) credit growth is excessive and is leading to the build-up of systemic risk. Based on this assessment, a countercyclical buffer requirement will be put in place when the circumstances warrant it.[700]

The size of the countercyclical buffer will vary, at the competent authorities' discretion, between 0 and 2.5% of risk-weighted assets (according to the provisions of the capital adequacy framework).[701] The buffer shall:

699 Ibid., paragraph 133.
700 Ibid., paragraph 139-140.
701 Ibid., paragraph139, last passage.

- be implemented through an extension of the capital conservation buffer discussed above,[702] and
- include exclusively, at least initially, common equity Tier 1 capital (according to the new definition).[703]

In particular, internationally active banks (with foreign subsidiaries in a number of states) must create this buffer on the basis of a weighted average of the buffers applied for states to which they have exposures (given that the economic cycle in individual states may not be (and usually is not) synchronised).[704]

In December 2010, the Basel Committee published guidelines addressed to the national authorities, which lays down the general principles to be upheld in terms of how the countercyclical capital buffer will be imposed and calculated.[705]

(B) Implementation schedule

The countercyclical buffer regime will be phased in concurrently with the capital conservation buffer between 1 January 2016 and 1 January 2019. The Basel Committee considers that states recording excessive credit growth during this transition period should consider accelerating the adoption of the relevant provisions. In addition, states may choose to implement more stringent countercyclical buffer requirements.[706]

4. Specifically: the new provisions on banks' minimum regulatory capital

4.1 Definition of minimum regulatory capital

4.1.1 Introductory remarks

The most important amendment to the Basel Committee's capital adequacy framework currently in force is undoubtedly associated with regulatory capital. As already discussed, this amendment is aimed at improving the quality of regulatory capital after evaluating the (negative) experience gained during the recent financial turmoil in terms of banks' ability to absorb the losses sustained as a result of their risk exposure. In this context, it is necessary to make the following two remarks:

702 Ibid., paragraphs146-148.
703 Ibid., paragraph 142. See footnote 53 of the report on the possibility of expanding the range of equity capital elements that banks may use to meet this obligation.
704 Ibid., paragraphs 143-144.
705 **Basel Committee on Banking Supervision (2010c)**: *"Guidance for national authorities operating the countercyclical capital buffer"*, December, available at: http://www.bis.org/publ/ bcbs187.htm.
706 **Basel Committee on Banking Supervision (2010a)**, paragraph 150. Note also that these buffers shall be initially calculated on a consolidated basis (ibid., footnote 52).

(a) The total regulatory capital of banks, now known as 'minimum capital' in light of the introduction of these two buffers will still be[707] the product of:

- 'Tier 1 Capital' which is classified in two categories,[708] a distinction that is important in terms of relevant quantitative limits (see under 4.1.2 below), and
- 'Tier 2 Capital' (under 4.1.3).[709]

On the contrary, the alternative definition of regulatory capital (Tier 3 Capital), that banks could use in accordance to the current regulatory framework, in order to fulfil their capital requirements for market risks,[710] is repealed.[711]

(b) The amendments introduced pertain to the items of each category of regulatory capital, as well as eligibility criteria for elements to be included in each category.

4.1.2 The rules on Tier 1 capital

According to 'Basel III', Tier 1 capital shall comprise two categories of elements:

- common equity Tier 1 capital (see under 4.1.2.1 below), and
- additional Tier 1 capital (under 4.1.2.2).

4.1.2.1 Common equity Tier 1 capital

Common equity Tier 1 capital consists of the following elements (subject to specific criteria):[712]

(a) The value of paid-in share capital in terms of common shares (with or without voting rights), excluding preferred shares.[713]

(b) Retained profits, including interim profits or losses.

(c) Disclosed reserves.

707 Ibid., paragraph 9.

708 According to the terminology of the Basel Committee, equity capital of banks still conducting their business ("going-concern capital") (ibid., paragraph 49, item 1).

709 According to the terminology of the Basel Committee, equity capital of banks no longer conducting their business ("gone-concern capital") (ibid., paragraph 49, item 2).

710 This category includes subordinated short-term loans (**Basel Committee on Banking Supervision (2006)**, paragraph 49 (xiii)-(xiv)).

711 **Basel Committee on Banking Supervision (2010a)**, paragraph 9.

712 Ibid., paragraph 52.

713 For these fourteen (14) conditions see ibid., paragraph 53. Special rules apply for banks that do not have the legal form of a joint-stock company (e.g. cooperative banks) and hence no share capital.

(d) Subject to specific conditions, common shares which have been issued by consolidated subsidiaries of the bank and held by third parties ('minority interest shares').[714]
(e) Share premiums from the issuance of these common shares.

4.1.2.2 Additional Tier 1 capital

Additional Tier 1 capital consists of the following elements:[715]
(a) Preferred shares and bonds mainly complying with the following conditions:[716]

- no maturity date,
- issued and paid-up,
- subordinated to depositors and general creditors,
- no step-up or redeem clause,
- callable/redeemable at the option of the issuer only following a minimum of five (5) years and provided that certain conditions are met.[717]

According to the Annex attached to the above-mentioned (under B 1.1) Basel Committee' press release of 13 January 2011,[718] preferred shares and bonds included in Tier 1 or Tier 2 capital should also comply with the terms indicated therein, thus ensuring optimum loss absorbance.
(b) Subject to specific conditions, instruments with the above characteristics which:

- have been issued by consolidated subsidiaries of the bank,
- are held by third parties, and
- are not included in common equity Tier 1 capital.[719]

(c) Share premiums from the issuance of preferred shares under this category.[720]
Consequently, notwithstanding other modifications introduced:

(i) Perpetual, non-cumulative preferred shares are still included in banks' Tier 1 capital but under quantitative restrictions.
(ii) Innovative instruments which, according to the current regulatory framework, are included in Tier 1 capital up to 15%[721] shall no longer be eligible for inclusion.

714 For these conditions, see **Basel Committee on Banking Supervision (2010a)**, paragraphs 62-65 and Annex 3.
715 **Basel Committee on Banking Supervision (2010a)**, paragraph 54.
716 For these also fourteen (14) conditions see ibid., paragraph 55.
717 Ibid., paragraph 55, point 5.
718 **Basel Committee on Banking Supervision (2011)**.
719 For these conditions, see **Basel Committee on Banking Supervision (2010a)**, paragraph 62-65 and Annex 3.
720 Ibid., paragraph 56.
721 **Basel Committee on Banking Supervision (2006)**, Annex 1.

4.1.3 The rules on Tier 2 capital

Under 'Basel III', Tier 2 capital comprises the following:[722]

(a) Preferred shares and bonds complying, primarily, with the above-mentioned terms on additional Tier 1 capital, but have a minimum original maturity of at least five (5) years.[723]

(b) Subject to specific conditions, instruments with the above characteristics which:

- have been issued by consolidated subsidiaries of the bank,
- are held by third parties, and
- are not included in Tier 1 capital.[724]

(c) Share premiums from the issuance of preferred shares included in this category.[725]

(d) Certain loan-loss provisions.

Consequently, undisclosed reserves, as well as revaluation reserves, which, according to the current regulatory framework, are included in Tier 2 capital,[726] *shall no longer be eligible for inclusion.*

4.1.4 Specific provisions

Detailed provisions have been introduced on the deduction of instruments from individual elements of banks' regulatory capital, which are certainly stricter than the regulatory framework currently in force.[727] Also, the new regulatory framework significantly strengthens the regime that governs the obligation of banks to disclose information regarding the composition of their regulatory capital.[728]

4.2 New quantitative limits

The Basel Committee has set the following new quantitative limits regarding the minimum capital requirements of banks that should be observed on a continuous basis:[729]

(a) Common Equity Tier 1 capital must be at least 4.5% of risk-weighted assets and off-balance sheet items.

722 **Basel Committee on Banking Supervision (2010a)**, paragraph 57.
723 Ibid., paragraph 58.
724 For these conditions see ibid., paragraphs 64-65 and Annex 3.
725 Ibid., paragraph 59.
726 **Basel Committee on Banking Supervision (2006)**, paragraph 49 (iv)-(vi).
727 **Basel Committee on Banking Supervision (2010a)**, paragraphs 66-90.
728 Ibid., paragraph 91-93.
729 Ibid., paragraph 50.

(b) Tier 1 capital must be at least 6.0% of risk-weighted assets and off-balance sheet items (as opposed to 4.0% under the regulatory framework currently in force).[730]

(c) Total (Tier 1 plus Tier 2) capital must be at least 8.0% of risk-weighted assets and off-balance sheet items. Consequently, the amount of Tier 2 capital should not exceed 2.0%.

It should also be noted that funds for general banking risks (which, in view of the above, are included in Tier 2 capital) shall not exceed 1.25% of risk-weighted assets and off-balance sheet items,[731] as is the case under the regulatory framework currently in force.[732]

4.3 Implementation schedule

Implementation of the new rules should start on 1 January 2013, and banks should adjust gradually. In particular:

(a) As far as the above new quantitative limits are concerned, the following transitional arrangements have been made:[733]

(i) As of 1 January 2013, minimum capital requirements shall be:
- for common equity Tier 1 capital 3.5%, and
- for total Tier 1 capital 4.5%.

(ii) As of 1 January 2014, minimum capital requirements shall be:
- for common equity Tier 1 capital 4.0%, and
- for total Tier 1 capital 5.5%.

(iii) Full implementation of the new provisions should commence on 1 January 2015.

(b) Implementation of the provisions regarding instruments that can be deducted from regulatory capital (see under 4.1.4 above) should begin on 1 January 2014, with full implementation due on 1 January 2018.[734]

(c) Finally, transitional provisions, to be enacted on 1 January 2013, have been introduced on the treatment of instruments that will no longer, according to the new regulatory framework, meet requirements for inclusion:

- in the common equity Tier 1 capital,[735] and
- in the additional Tier 1 capital and Tier 2 capital.[736]

730 **Basel Committee on Banking Supervision (2006)**, Annex 1a, section B (i).
731 **Basel Committee on Banking Supervision (2010a)**, paragraph 60(c).
732 **Basel Committee on Banking Supervision (2006)**, Annex 1a, section B(iv).
733 **Basel Committee on Banking Supervision (2010a)**, paragraph 94, points (a) and (b), and Annex 4.
734 Ibid., paragraph 94(c) - (e) and Annex 4.
735 Ibid., paragraph 95.
736 Ibid., paragraph 94(g.).

These provisions shall only apply with regard to instruments issued prior to 12 September 2010.[737]

Table 16: Minimum regulatory capital of international banks according to the provisions of the regulatory framework currently in force and the new regulatory framework

Regulatory framework currently in force	New regulatory framework (as of 1 January 2015, subject to transitional arrangements)
1. Tier 1 capital: • common shares • preferred shares with no maturity without accumulated dividend entitlement • share premium from the issue of these categories of shares • retained earnings • disclosed reserves • innovative instruments (max 15% of Tier 1 capital)	**1. Tier 1 capital:** **(a) Common equity Tier 1 capital**: • common shares • share premium from the issue of common shares • retained earnings • disclosed reserves **(b) Additional Tier 1 capital**: • preferred shares and bonds with no maturity (subject to conditions) • share premium from the issue of this category of shares
2. Tier 2 capital: • undisclosed reserves • fixed assets and financial instruments revaluation reserves • funds for general banking risks (with qualitative restriction) • hybrid instruments • preferred shares with no maturity with accumulated dividend entitlement • subordinated loans (max 50% of Tier 1 capital)	**2. Tier 2 capital:** • preferred shares and bonds with specific maturity (subject to conditions) • share premium from the issue of this class of shares • funds for general banking risks (subject to conditions and with quantitative restriction)
3. Tier 3 capital (max 250% of Tier 1 capital used to cover against market risks)	–

737 Ibid., paragraph 96.

Table 17: Total capital requirements that will be imposed on banks in accordance with the new regulatory framework of the Basel Committee at the end of the transitional periods (*)
(% in relation to total risk-weighted assets and off-balance sheet items)

	Common Equity Tier 1 capital	**Total Tier 1 capital**	**Total capital requirement (Tier 1 and Tier 2 capital)**
1. Minimum regulatory capital (as of 1.1.2015)	4.5% (from 2%)	6.0% (from 4%)	8.0% (unchanged)
2. Capital conservation buffer (as of 1.1.2019)	2.5% (new)		
3. Sum 1 + 2 (as of 1.1.2019)	7.0%	8.5%	10.5%
Countercyclical buffer (as of 1.1.2019)	0 – 2.5% (new)		
(*) For systemically important banks, there will be an additional capital requirement.			

5. Assessment

5.1 Introductory remarks

As clearly demonstrated above, 'Basel III' introduces a significant revision of the currently applicable international regulatory framework with a view to safeguarding banking (and, more generally, financial) stability. This revision, in the aftermath of the recent international financial crisis, introduces a clearly stricter regulatory framework, seeking:

- on the one hand, to address the problems that ensued from implementation of certain 'Basel II' provisions, and
- on the other, to fill the gaps, especially with regard to banks' liquidity management and macro-prudential regulation.

In conclusion, an initial assessment, focusing on three (3) main issues, can be made.

5.2 Benefits and costs from the phasing-in of the new rules

According to the above overview, the phasing-in of the 'Basel III' provisions will begin in 2013 and extend over a six-year period, while some provisions will almost certainly be amended during the supervisory monitoring transitional periods that are provided for. This leads to a positive and a negative conclusion.

(a) The reason behind the phasing-in of the new rules is that, if they were to be fully and cumulatively implemented, the resulting cost would impact heavily on the operation of banks. Their capital requirements will increase significantly (especially in times of economic growth), while implementation of liquidity ratio requirements will lead to a redefinition of their business model. It was thus deemed necessary to introduce an adjustment period.

(b) On the contrary, the fact that some of the provisions of 'Basel III' will almost certainly be amended, creates a climate of ambiguity which may lead to delays in adoption of the rules, especially given that adoption is at the national authorities' discretion (see under 5.4 below).

5.3 Risks from implementation of the new rules

The new regulatory environment will limit banks' profitability margins, as well as their rate of return on equity ('ROE') (irrespective of the extent to which they are able to roll over the cost to their clients or the extent of operational cost cuts).[738] This is quite true taking into account that 'Basel III' is merely one of the 'building-blocks' of regulatory intervention in terms of the operation of banks underway.

This, of course, is the price to be paid for protecting the international banking system's stability against the risk of another major financial crisis.[739] *Even if it is true (as in the author's view) that the new environment is overregulated, the experience of the recent crisis justifies politically (but not always adequately) the decision to adopt stricter measures.*

In this context, however, there are (at least) three risks, the importance of which should not be undermined:

(a) Implementation of the new rules can, at least in certain cases, lead to a decline in bank financing, with negative consequences on the real economy and growth. Consequently, it is critical to have accurate and reliable assessments regarding the expected impact of the above factors on banks' lending activity (especially smaller and spe-

738 In this context, it is interesting to note the remark made by a member of the banking supervisory community, Mr Jochen Sanio, President of Bafin (the supervisory authority of the German financial system), that there is a clear risk of the banking sector being turned into a "low-return industry" (**Sanio (2011)**, p. 39).

739 In any case, the view that the potential of future crises outbreaks may be eliminated is probably not realistic. See studies by **Caprio and Klingebiel (1999)**, **Laeven and Valencia (2008)** and **Reinhart and Rogoff (2008)** relating to financial crises (especially 'systemically important' ones) that have taken place to date.

cialised – mortgage, savings and cooperative – banks), both at times of economic growth and economic recession.[740]

(b) Given that the banking system as a whole will be called upon to raise huge amounts of equity capital from the markets (albeit with a six-year horizon), primarily by issuing common shares, the expected drop in the rate of return on equity ('ROE') will place them at a competitive disadvantage vis-à-vis enterprises in other sectors of the economy, whose ROE ratio will remain stable or even increase.

It is noteworthy that systemically important banks may even uphold an additional capital requirement (apart from the above), amounting to 2% of their risk-weighted assets and off-balance sheet items: This requirement must also be covered by common equity Tier 1 capital. As a result, the equity capital of large international banks may, in extremis, may need to increase even eightfold in the coming years.[741]

Consequently, in order to comply with the requirements of the new regulatory framework, banks that fail to raise the necessary capital from markets will be forced to:

- deleverage and thus curtail their credit supply, and/or
- resort to restructuring that will increase the degree of concentration in the banking sector, without any obvious positive synergies therefrom.

(c) Finally, the need for banks to cut spending as a result of the implementation of the new regulatory framework may lead to:

- a new cycle of regulatory arbitrage, mainly by shifting activities to parts of the financial system that will still escape regulation and supervision (the 'shadow banking system', which, as already mentioned, played a catalytic role in the outbreak of the crisis), as well as to states with more relaxed supervisory and regulatory regimes, and
- financial innovations that may expose banks to risks that today are non-identifiable.[742]

Assuming that implementation of 'Basel III' will mark the end of regulatory arbitrage is at best risky, no matter how detailed the provisions may be. Experience has shown that, following the introduction of new regulations, regulated enterprises typically move faster than regulators.[743]

This makes the need to upgrade the role of supervisory authorities (who, in any case, will shoulder a heavier burden following the new regulatory framework's introduction)

740 A first positive step in this direction (albeit overtly optimistic in its assumptions) is the report of the **Basel Committee on Banking Supervision (2010d)** entitled "*Results of the comprehensive quantitative impact study*", December, available at: http://www.bis.org/publ/bcbs186.htm. See also, **Angelini et. al. (2011)**, and **Slovik and Cournède (2011)**.

741 For further details, see **Sanio (2011)**, p. 39.

742 It should be borne in mind that the level of nominal interest rates still remains at low levels, after the recent financial crisis, ,internationally, and, consequently, if there is no shift in the monetary policy trend, then there is a risk of seeing new speculative activities, as was the case before the recent financial crisis.

743 **Kane (1987)** makes reference to the existence of a 'regulatory dialectic', pp. 114-116.

even more imperative, in order to enable them to constantly monitor developments and timely submit adjustment proposals. [744]

5.4 The problem of competitive equality

Last but not least, it should be pointed out that the Basel Committee rules, in general, are not legally binding and enforceable, as mentioned above. Consequently, adopting the provisions of 'Basel III', fully or in part, remains at the discretion of national legislators (and in the case of the EU, the European Parliament and the Council).

Accordingly, one of the most important issues that arise concerns to what extent states – and in particular which states – will implement 'Basel III' so as to ensure a level playing field especially among banks with international activities faced with international competition (which, *inter alia*, is also affected by the relative regulatory cost on competitors). The precedent set with the refusal by certain Basel Committee members to transpose 'Basel II' is recent and surprising.[745]

744 According to **Sanio (2011**, p. 37): *"Als "Vorwegnehmer" müssen Regulatoren ein Gespür für die Entstehung neuer Risiken entwickeln. Und sie müssen präventiv Regeln entwickeln, mit denen sich die neuen Risiken unter Kontrolle halten lassen, auf dass sie sich nie zu einer systemischen Krise aufwachsen können"* (note that with the term 'Regulatoren' the author obliously refers to the supervisory authorities, which usually also have regulatory powers).

745 The case of the United States is quite indicative. Although the US monetary and banking supervisory authorities which are members of the Basel Committee strongly supported the adoption of banks' capital requirements on the basis of the Internal Ratings-Based Approach (IRBA), they have not yet managed to ensure the transposition of relevant provisions in their national legislation.

AN OVERALL ASSESSMENT

A. Extent and scope of adequate regulatory intervention in the financial system

1. Introductory remarks

The current political, academic and, more generally, public debate focuses on the readjustment of the applicable public financial law at international, regional and/or national level, in the aftermath of the recent international financial crisis. The method of strengthening the regulatory framework is definitely not a novelty, given that such measures are used every time there is a crisis in the financial system of one or more states, whether it is a banking crisis – like the current one – a foreign-exchange crisis or a 'twin' crisis.

In the context of this debate, it would be necessary, *inter alia*, to evaluate the extent of such a readjustment, given than it is often argued (quite strongly today because of the crisis) that the financial system operates either 'unregulated' or merely through 'self-regulation', without any binding rules in place to protect the public or any safety valves to ensure stability. Indeed, supporters of this view identify the main causes of the crisis in the lack of regulatory intervention.

2. The true meaning of 'financial system deregulation'

The view that the financial system operates in a regulatory vacuum could not be further from the truth. This misconception is mainly due to the fact that objectives of regulatory intervention that were mostly established after World War II (based on the logic of using savings to achieve government-led economic growth and social policy targets) were abandoned as ineffective little by little – starting in the late 1970s – by all of the economically developed, but also many of the developing states.

In this context, a process known as 'financial system deregulation' was put in place (and completed in many states around the world). The term 'deregulation' refers to completely eliminating regulatory intervention in terms of direct state intervention in the operation of financial systems. This process is mainly aimed at the following:

- relieving the financial system of its dependency on state ownership control, and abolishing administrative price fixing measures, and
- liberalising international trade in financial services, within the context of the World Trade Organisation.

The rapid growth in international economic prosperity during the period that followed the financial system's deregulation in those states, even with the observed asymmetries in the distribution of wealth (which, anyway, cannot by any means be attributed to deregulation itself), ultimately justifies this decision as an accurate one.

Here, a theoretical observation is necessary. According to neoclassical theory, regulatory intervention is needed if its purpose is to eliminate 'market failures'. The main market failures observed in the financial system concern the existence of information asymmetry between providers (of goods and services) and consumers, and conditions favouring negative externalities.[746] *By contrast, the financial system is not a natural monopoly.*[747]

The abolition of restrictive financial regulations has been thought by several agents, including members of the academia, to be tantamount to the lack of any regulatory intervention in the financial system. This is incorrect. The financial system in general does not operate in a 'regulatory vacuum', as is often wrongly argued. On the contrary, immediately after the deregulation process, and as a matter of fact on account of it, it operates under vigorous regulatory intervention of unprecedented extent (with the adopted rules having a very structured internal cohesion):

- both at international level within the existing international architecture of the financial system and all relevant international financial law rules, as outlined in the present study, and
- at European level (and, by extension, in the national law of EU member states) according to the provisions of applicable European financial law, with a view to achieving European financial integration.

This process, on the opposite end of the one described above (that is, the 'deregulation process'), is known in academic literature as the 're-regulation process'.

However, note needs to be made of the fact that in certain economically developing states, deregulation was not accompanied by the appropriate measures to shield the system's stability and the results were made painfully visible in previous decades when such states all over the world experienced crises. Certainly, there are also gaps in the financial system's regulatory planning in economically developed states as well.

3. The gaps and ineffectiveness of the existing framework

Despite the significant amplitude of the international and European institutional and regulatory framework that was gradually developed in the course of the last thirty years, the outbreak of the recent (2007-2009) international financial crisis, given its extent and intensity, has revealed gaps in the framework, and thus, rendered necessary the initiatives aimed at its readjustment.

746 See on this under A 3.1 in Section Two above.
747 See **Gorton (1988b)**, p. 5-7.

As already mentioned, the analysis of the causes of this crisis clearly is beyond the scope of this study. In this context, it would be useful to point out the following problems, which are considered to be extremely important:

(a) First of all, in offshore centres, financial regulatory intervention and supervision do not, in principle, exist even as concepts.

(b) In recent years, certain markets and various categories of financial firms in developed states (the 'shadow banking sector') have been operating without any regulatory intervention.

(c) Note, finally, that the rules adopted proved ineffective, including, but not limited to:

- the rules on banks' capital adequacy which intensify 'pro-cyclicality', namely, by encouraging banks to grant more loans during economic upturns and to be more hesitant in their credit activity at times of recession, and
- rules with implementation costs exceeding the benefits of their adoption, at least in some aspects (the most striking example being rules on the protection of financial services consumers).

On a more theoretical level, we need to point out the following:

(1) The adoption of regulatory rules provides companies with an incentive – across the board and at all times – to minimise the ensuing cost, by urging them to roll their activity over to services subject to lower/no regulatory intervention or to states that have lower/no regulatory intervention. Recourse to such regulatory arbitrage is a lesson learned from economic (and financial) history and is the basis of the 'dialectical relationship' constantly forged between supervisory authorities and supervised parties (establishment of rules – transgression of rules – establishment of new, stricter rules, usually with a time lag), and is made even easier nowadays thanks to IT technology advances. All the more so, given that the supervised firms operate faster than the supervisors and regulators.

The existence of regulatory arbitrage between states (combined with the tendency of certain states to adopt laxer rules, so as to attract greater business activity to the territory of their jurisdiction (known as competitive deregulation or competition in laxity) is indeed the main policy objective for the need to establish harmonised rules at national or regional level.

(2) While market failures are the policy objective for regulatory intervention in modern economies, administrative interventions may also sometimes present failures (regulatory failures). Rules and supervisory processes do not always serve their purpose as best as possible. Public choice theory is rife with relevant examples.[748] As **Norberg (2009)** points out correctly: *"It is pointless to compare the real-life market economy, in all its imperfection, with an ideal image of how hypothetical, perfect authorities*

748 For a review of this theory, see **Mercuro and Medema (2006)**, pp. 156-207.

would govern the economy. It goes without saying that we must compare it with the real, imperfect authorities that we actually have".[749]

(3) Public choice theory is important in the framework of this discussion from another perspective too, namely the actual conditions under which political decisions are taken. Contrary to the above-mentioned (and prevailing) approach that regulatory intervention in the financial system aims at satisfying specific policy objectives (according to the 'public interest' approach),[750] this theory professes that regulatory intervention is the result of actions taken by politicians, bureaucrats or lobbyists to use the legal preparatory process in order to satisfy their own interests.

This approach raises, *inter alia*, the issue of the influence of companies affected by regulatory intervention rules on those who adopt them (regulatory capture).

(4) Another important issue that needs to be addressed relates to the *ex post*, in the event of a crisis, unequal treatment of large financial firms (albeit not exclusively), considered to be "systemically important" because their failure is politically untenable (referred to as 'too big to (be left to) fail'). In this context, extensive distortions occur given that:

- smaller financial firms are at a comparatively disadvantaged position in terms of competition,
- market discipline is less effective where it is most needed, namely large financial firms with low capital adequacy, due to exposure to moral hazard, and
- the cost of bailing out the latter group of financial firms through state subsidies in periods of crisis is extremely high.

(5) At times of crisis, regulatory intervention and the concomitant supervision in every segment of economic and social activity usually overshoots its purpose. This is a reasonable reaction on the part of the intervening body to – at least – appease society as a whole, and common in areas such as:

- air transport, in case of accidents,
- healthcare, in case of epidemics, or
- in the financial system, in case of financial firm insolvencies.

In due course, 'excessive' intervention measures become lax, inert or are transgressed by the market itself. A striking example would be the (post-crisis) security measures imposed on those who flew to London on the day following the July 2005 bombings and those who fly to London today.

A final remark. It has been argued that a thorough and detailed analysis of the root causes should be the sine qua non for any adequate proposal as part of the current 'readjustment process' of public international financial law. In periods of crisis there is always an unwarranted risk of overregulation (and all kinds of financial crises have taken place in the course of history). In this context, it should be argued that, in realistic

749 See **Norberg (2009)**, p. 134.
750 See under A 1 in Section Two above.

terms, expectations regarding current policy initiatives should be to minimise the eventuality of future crises of the magnitude and extent that we are experiencing today, and not to eliminate financial crises completely.

B. The future of public international financial law

Despite having attained a very significant level of international financial integration since the early 1970s, financial regulation (for the most part) and financial supervision (in its entirety) are still carried out by national authorities. Nevertheless, the last three decades have seen the establishment of several international fora, which, along with a limited number of international organisations, make up the current institutional governance of the international financial system's architecture. These institutions may be divided, depending upon their legal nature and composition, into five categories:

(i) three inter-governmental fora: Group of Ten (G10), Group of Seven (G7), and Group of Twenty (G20),
(ii) four (4) international economic organisations: IMF, BIS, WTO (in matters relating to the liberalisation of international trade in financial services), and OECD (in matters of corporate governance),
(iii) various international fora of:
  - national supervisory and regulatory authorities (Basel Committee on Banking Supervision, IOSCO, IAIS, and Joint Forum on Financial Conglomerates),
  - experts from national central banks (Committee on Payment and Settlement Systems, Committee on the Global Financial System),
  - enlarged composition (notably the Financial Action Task Force on Money Laundering), and
  - agencies managing national deposit guarantee systems (International Association of Deposit Insurers),
(iv) two private professional associations, notably the International Accounting Standards Board in matters of corporate accounting, and the International Federation of Accountants in matters of corporate auditing, and
(v) the FSB, composed, among others, by the above-mentioned international organisations and international fora.

It is worth mentioning that none of these international bodies has been assigned any supervisory power over financial firms. Nevertheless, most of the international fora participating in the FSB have issued guidelines and recommendations over the last three decades, most of which have been internationally accepted in broad terms, by economically developed and developing states, as necessary for the preservation of the globalised financial system's soundness and stability. However, these legal acts are 'soft law' instruments and, hence, not legally binding.

The current structure is definitely characterised both by specialisation and by compartmentalisation. This is mainly due to the fact that states assign the various aspects of financial regulation to different authorities. Even when financial supervision is based on the 'integrated approach', there are aspects of financial regulation, supervision and oversight that cannot be assigned to a single authority, even if this is the central bank (which is definitely responsible for the oversight of payment systems).

In light of the above remarks, which briefly summarise the *status quo* in the international financial architecture, any reform proposal should be based on the assumption that it is rather impracticable to conceive – in terms of political realism – the creation of international authorities (which is, in any case, unprecedented). In particular, the creation of a fully-fledged supervisory authority would require the creation of a supranational organisation with global participation (in order to prevent regulatory arbitrage), based on international convention, to which the signatory parties would assign the power to:

- supervise their national financial institutions and markets (or, at least, those considered as 'systemically important'),
- issue binding legal norms on their regulation, and
- impose sanctions on these financial institutions.[751]

The difficulties arising in the context of discussions within the EU on the possibility of establishing a regional, supranational financial supervisory authority manifestly reflect the problems that would arise on an international scale.

Accordingly, the main issue that should be addressed in the context of the current debate is not international supervisory reform, but rather international regulatory reform. International supervisory reform should be confined to enhancing international supervisory cooperation, mainly through effective operation of 'colleges of supervisors' for globally active financial institutions (and, in particular, banking groups).

Overall, the design of the existing international institutional structure governing financial regulation is, in broader terms, adequate. This assessment is based on the following considerations:

(a) It is of primary importance for rules on international financial regulation to be discussed and adopted by institutions with the decisive (and not merely advisory) participation of national supervisory authorities (which are concurrently regulatory ones). The same applies, *mutatis mutandis*, to rules on payment systems oversight (under the remit of central banks), on combating money laundering (under the remit of governments, judiciary and supervisory authorities), or on accounting and auditing standard-setting.

751 With regard to the conditions for such a development, see **Schreiber (2005)**, pp. 241-242. An international organisation cannot have such powers. According to **Stein-van Buttlar (2009)** (p. 9): *"Ein grundlegender Unterschied zwischen der Völkerrechtsordnung und staatlichen Rechtsordnungen liegt im Fehlen internationaler Gesetze als Rechtsquellen des Völkerrechts. Den zwischenstaatlichen Rechtsbeziehungen fehlt ein Gesetzgebungsorgan, das mit Wirkung für alle Staaten Recht setzen kann".*

Accordingly, it is difficult to envisage the substitution of international fora, such as the Basel Committee, the IOSCO, the CPSS or the FATF, by any new constellation. It is open, however, to discuss amendments with regard to the composition of certain of these fora in order to reflect the most appropriate representation of the international community, as it has already happened with the broadening of membership of the FSB.

(b) It is the responsibility of these international fora to address the relevant issues and propose appropriate solutions for the problems arising amidst the current financial turmoil, in close cooperation with the FSB.

(c) The FSB is, indeed, an appropriate forum for the comprehensive synthesis and coordination of international financial regulatory initiatives and decision-making on prioritising new rules to be adopted. This is due to the fact that in it is participated in by all the international organisations and fora which deal, as already mentioned, with the various aspects related to financial regulation and oversight. It is not by coincidence that the current agenda of the FSB covers the entire range of the issues brought to the fore as a regulatory response to the causes of the recent financial turmoil.

(d) The IMF plays a significant role within the current international financial architecture, which is based on:

- its supervisory task over national economies (revised Article 4 of its Articles of Association), under which it carries out its Financial Sector Assessment Programs for all its member states, and
- its role to provide financial assistance, subject to conditionality, to less-developed economies.

In this sense, the IMF has the power to encourage its member states – directly and indirectly – to adopt a significant portion of the rules contained in guidelines and recommendations issued by the above-mentioned international fora, which, as already argued, are not legally binding.

Nevertheless, the existing international regulatory *apparatus* should definitely be enhanced. To the author's opinion, this enhancement should be pursued along the following lines:

(a) The main shortcoming of the regulatory structure is the room it leaves for regulatory arbitrage among institutions, markets and states. In order to be addressed, the work of international standard-setters should focus on:

- closing the existing gap between heavily regulated financial firms and markets (such as commercial banks and equity markets) and non-/less-regulated ones (debt markets, OTC derivative markets, hedge funds, credit-rating agencies),
- dealing effectively with the regulation and supervision of activities in offshore financial centres.

(b) As mentioned above, the rules to be adopted should enact a thorough 'cost-benefit analysis' in order to be effective and avoid unintended spillovers. The pro-cyclicality of the existing capital adequacy regulations under the 'Basel II framework' is an obvious example – especially under the current adverse economic conditions worldwide – of potential serious negative effects of measures adopted for legitimate reasons.

Finally, a question arises as to the need for a new 'Bretton Woods' Agreement.

(a) Taken literally, the answer to this question would be that there are currently no official plans for the international community to resort to an international monetary system of fixed, but adjustable, foreign exchange rates, like the one established in 1945 by the Bretton Woods Agreement and abandoned in the early seventies. On the contrary, the current trend is toward the creation of regional currency unions around the globe.[752]

(b) A broader reading of this question raises the issue of the need for an international agreement, like Bretton Woods, which would lay the foundations for a new international organisation responsible for safeguarding the stability of the internationalised financial system.

The case against creating such an international organisation in the capacity of an international financial supervisor has already been discussed. The creation of an international organisation – even if its powers are confined to the adoption of regulatory norms – is not necessary for the reasons indicated above. On the contrary, what is imperative is:

- to bolster the content of regulatory norms adopted at international level by the existing standard-setting bodies, and
- to ensure their proper implementation by national authorities, whereby the IMF should (and definitely could) play an increasingly substantial role.

Accordingly, in the author's view, there is an immediate need for the adoption of sound and adequate international principles (and their implementation on a global scale), rather than new international institutions.

752 See **Vicuña (2008)**.

SECONDARY SOURCES

A

Äberli, R.W. (1989): *Risikopolitische Analyse der Ausserbilanzgeschäfte,* Bankwirtschaftliche Forschungen, Band 119, Verlag Paul Haupt, Bern und Stuttgart

Aggarwal, R. (2002): Demutualization and corporate governance of stock exchanges, *Journal of Applied Corporate Finance*, Spring

Ainley, M. (1984): *The General Arrangements to Borrow*, Pamphlet Series No. 41, International Monetary Fund, Washington D.C.

Albertazzi, U., Eramo, G., Gambacorta, L., and C. Salleo (2011): *Securitization is not that Evil after all*, BIS Working Papers, No. 341, Monetary and Economic Department, Bank for International Settlements, March

Aliber, R. (1980): International banking: a survey, *Journal of Money, Credit and Banking,* 16, November, pp. 661-668

Allen, F. (2001): *Do Financial Institutions Matter?*, Financial Institutions Center, Wharton, Working Paper Series, 01-04

Allen, F. and A.M. Santomero (1999): *What Do Financial Intermediaries Do?*, Financial Institutions Center, Wharton, Working Paper Series, 99-30-B

Allen, F. and D. Gale (2001): *Comparative Financial Systems: A Survey,* Financial Institutions Center, Wharton, Working Paper Series, 01-15

Allen, F. and E. Carletti (2008a): The Role of Liquidity in Financial Crises, Jackson Hole Symposium: *Maintaining Stability in a Changing Financial System*, Federal Reserve Bank of Kansas City, September

Allen, F. and E. Carletti (2008b): The Roles of Banks in Financial Systems, in A. Berger, Ph. Molyneux and J. Wilson (editors): *Oxford Handbook of Banking*, Oxford University Press, Oxford – New York

Allen, F. and E. Carletti (2011): *New Theories to Underpin Financial Reform*, Financial Institutions Center, Wharton, Working Paper Series, 11-40

Allen, F. and R.J. Herring (2001): *Banking Regulation versus Securities Market Regulation*, Financial Institutions Center, Wharton, Working Paper Series, 01-29

Allen, F., Babus, A. and E. Carletti (2009): *Financial Connections and Systemic Risk*, National Bureau of Economic Research, Working Paper, No. 16177, July

Allen, F., Capie, F., Fohlin, C., Miyajima, H., Sylla, R., Wood, G. and Y. Yafeh (2010): *How Important Historically were Financial Systems for Growth in the U.K., U.S., Germany, and Japan?*, paper prepared for the World Bank Project on Financial Structure, October

Allen, W. and R. Moessner (2010): *Central Bank Co-operation and International Liquidity in the Financial Crisis of 2008-2009*, BIS Working Papers no. 310, Monetary and Economic Department, Bank for International Settlements, June

Amtenbrink, F. (1999): *The Democratic Accountability of Central Banks - A Comparative Study of the European Central Bank*, Hart Publishing

Angelini, P., Clerc, L., Cúrdia, V., Gambacorta, L., Gerali, A., Locarno, A., Motto, R., Roeger, W., Van den Heuvel, S., and J. Vlček (2011): *Basel III: Long-term Impact on Economic Performance and Fluctuations*, BIS Working Papers, No. 338, Monetary and Economic Department, Bank for International Settlements, February

Árvai, Z., Driessen, K. and İ. Ötker-Robe (2009): *Regional Financial Interlinkages and Financial Contagion within Europe*, IMF Working paper, WP/09/06, January

Ashcraft, A.B. and T. Schuermann (2007): *Understanding the Securitization of Subprime Mortgage Credit,* Financial Institutions Center, Wharton, Working Paper Series, 07-43

Athanassiou (2012, editor): *Research Handbook on Hedge Funds, Private Equity and Alternative Investments*, Research Handbooks in Financial Law, Edward Elgar, Cheltenham-NorthHampton

Avgouleas, E. (2008): International financial regulation, access to finance, systemic stability, and development, *LAWASIA Journal*, pp. 62-76

Avgouleas, E. (2009): The global financial crisis, behavioural finance and financial regulation: In search of a new orthodoxy, *Journal of Corporate Law Studies*, JCLS073, vol. 9, April, pp. 121-157

Avgouleas, E., Goodhart, Ch. and D. Schoenmaker (2010): *Bank Recovery and Resolution Plans (living Wills) as the Catalyst of Global Reform*, Financial Institutions Center, Wharton, Working Paper Series, 10-09

B

Bagehot (1873): *Lombard Street*, new edition of 1901, Kegan Paul, Trench, Trumber & Co., London

Baldwin, S. (1907): The international congresses and conferences of the last century as forces working towards the solidarity of the world, *American Journal of International Law*, 1, p. 565

Baltensperger, Er. and J. Dermine (1987): The Role of Public Policy in Ensuring Financial Stability: A Cross-country, Comparative Perspective, in R. Portes and A.K. Swoboda (editors): *Threats to International Financial Stability*, Cambridge University Press, Cambridge, pp. 67-90

Bank for International Settlements (2008): *Financial System and Macroeconomic Resilience, Sixth BIS Conference 18-19 June 2007*, Monetary and Economic Department, BIS Papers, No. 41, July

Bank of England (2009): *The Role of Macroprudential policy*, discussion paper, Bank of England, D0066A, November

Banque de France (2008): *Observations on Risk Management Practices during the Recent Market Turbulence,* Senior Supervisors Group, March

Barro, R.J. (1990): *Macroeconomics*, John Wiley & Sons, third edition, New York – Chichester – Brisbane Toronto – Singapore

Barth, J.R., Caprio, G. and R. Levine (2006): *Rethinking Bank Regulation – Till Angels Govern*, Cambridge University Press, Cambridge, New York, Melbourne, Madrid, Cape Town, Singapore, São Paolo

Basel Committee on Banking Supervision (2011): *The transmission channels between the financial and real sectors: a critical survey of the literature*, Working Paper No. 18, February

Bauer, K.A. (1985): *Das Recht der Internationalen Bankenaufsicht*, Nomos Verlagsgesellschaft, Baden- Badens

Baxter, T.C. Jr. and J.H. Sommer (2001): Liquidity Crises, in Lastra R.M. (editor): *The Reform of the International Financial Architecture*, International Banking, Finance and Economic Law Series, Kluwer Law International, The Hague - London - New York, pp. 211-233

Baxter, T.C. Jr. and D. Gross (2010): The Federal Reserve's Response to the Crisis: Doing Whatever it Takes Within its Legal Authority, in Giovanoli M. and D. Devos (editors): *International Monetary and Financial Law: The Global Crisis*, Oxford University Press, Oxford-New York, pp. 293-304

Becker, G.S. (2009): *The Free Market's Trial by Fire*, Mont Pelerin Society Conference: The End of Globalising Capitalism – Classical Liberal responses to the Global Financial Crisis, March, at: http://www.montpelerin.org/nyc2k9.cfm

Benjamin, J. (2007): *Financial Law*, Oxford University Press, Oxford - New York

Benston, J., Eisenbeis, R.A., Horvitz, P.M., Kane, E. and G.G. Kaufman (1986): *Perspectives on Safe and Sound Banking: Past, Present and Future*, The MIT press, Cambridge

Berger, A.N., Klapper, L.F. and R. Turk-Ariss (2008): *Banking Structures and Financial Stability*, World Bank Policy Research Working Paper 4696

Berger, K.P. (2010): *The Creeping Codification of the New Lex Mercatoria*, 2nd edtion, Alphen aan den Rijn, Kluwer, The Netherlands

Bergsten, F. (2000): *Reforming the International Financial Architecture*, Committee on Banking and Financial Services, United States House of Representatives, Washington, at: www.iie.com/papers/cfbergsten.htm

Bernanke, B.S. (2008): *Economic Outlook*, Testimony before the Joint Economic Committee, US Congress, Washington D.C., September

Bernanke, B.S. (2010): *Statement by Ben S. Bernanke by the Chairman Board of Governors of the Federal Reserve System before the Financial Crisis Inquiry Commission,* Washington, D.C., September

Binning, T. and S. Willey (2008): The MiFID Regime for Trading Venues; Regulated Markets, Multilateral Trading Facilities and Systematic Internalisers, in E. Avgouleas (general editor): *The Regulation of Investment Services in Europe under MiFID:* Implementation and Practice, Tottel Publishing, West Sussex, pp. 73-100

Bizzozero, A. and Ch. Robinson (2010): *Activités financières cross-border vers et depuis la Suisse*, Bizzozero & Robinson - BRlegal, Bulle, Switzerland

Blair, M., Walker, G. and R. Purves (2009, editors): *Financial Services Law*, second edition, Oxford University Press, Oxford - New York

Blair, W. (2010): Standards and the Rule of Law after the Global Financial Crisis, in Giovanoli M. and D. Devos (editors): *International Monetary and Financial Law: The Global Crisis*, Oxford University Press, Oxford – New York, pp. 96-103

Blanchard, O.J. (2008): *The Tasks Ahead*, IMF Working Paper, WP/08/262, November

Blumer, A. (1996): *Bankenaufsicht und Bankenprüfung: Grundkonzepte, Problembestand und Perspektiven der Iinstitutionellen Ausgestaltung Ausgewählter Bankenübewachungssysteme*, Bank- und finanzwirtschaftliche Forschungen, Band 217, Verlag Paul Haupt, Bern – Stuttgart – Wien

Boorman, J. (2001): *Ownership and Conditionality*, IMF Survey, Vol. 30, No 13, p. 220 ff.

Bordo, M. and H. James (2010): The past and future of IMF reform: a proposal, in Wyplosz, Ch. (2010, editor): *The New International Monetary System - Essays in honor of Alexander Swoboda*, Routledge International Studies in Money and Banking, Rutledge, USA - Canada, pp. 9-28

Borio, C. (2003): *Towards a Macro-Prudential Framework for Financial Supervision and Regulation?*, Bank for International Settlements, Working Papers, No 128, Basel, February

Borio, C. (2006): *Monetary and Prudential Policies at a Crossroads? New Challenges in the New Century*, BIS Working Papers, No. 216, Monetary and Economic Department, Bank for International Settlements, September

Borio, C. (2008): *The Financial Tturmoil of 2007-?: A Preliminary Assessment and Some Policy Considerations*, BIS working Papers, No 251, Bank for International Settlements, March, pp. 1-13

Borio, C. (2009): *Ten Propositions about Liquidity Crises,* Bank for International Settlements, Working Papers, No 293, Basel, November

Borio, C. (2010): *Implementing a Macroprudential Framework: Blending Boldness and Realism*, keynote address for the BIS-HKMA research conference on Financial Stability: Towards a Macroprudential approach, Honk Kong SAR, July, at: http://www.bis.org/repofficepubl/hkimr201007.12c.pdf

Borio, C. and M. Drehmann (2009): Assessing the risk of Banking Crises-revisited, *BIS Quarterly Review*, March, pp. 29-46

Borio, C. and P. Disyatat (2009): *Unconventional Monetary Policies: An Appraisal*, BIS Working Papers No. 292, Monetary and Economic Department, Bank for International Settlements, November

Boyle, A. and Ch. Chinkin (2007): *The Making of International Law*, Oxford University Press, Oxford - New York

Brakman, S., Garretsen, H., van Marrenwijk, Ch., and Ar. van Witteloostuijn (2006): *Nations and Firms in the Global Economy – An Introduction to International Economics and Business*, Cambridge University Press, Cambridge

Bremmer, I. and N. Roubini (2011): A G-Zero World, *Foreign Affairs*, Volume 91, Number 2 (March/April), pp. 2-7

Broadman, H. (1994): GATS: The Uruguay Round Accord on International Trade and Investment in Services, *The World Economy*, Vol. 17, No. 3, pp. 281-292

Brummer, C. (2010): Why soft law dominates international finance - and not trade, *Journal of International Economic Law,* Vol. 13, No. 3, September, Oxford University Press, Oxford, September, pp. 623-644

Brunnermeier, M., Crockett, A., Goodhart, Ch., Persaud, A.D. and H. Shin (2009): *The fundamental principles of financial regulation*, Geneva Reports on the World Economy 11, International Center for Monetary and Banking Studies (ICMB), Geneva, Switzerland

Bryant, R.C. (1987): *International Financial Intermediation*, Brookings Institution, Washington, D.C.

Buchheit, L.C. (2001): A Lawyer's Perspective on the New Financial Architecture, in Lastra, R.M. (2001, editor): *The Reform of the International Financial Architecture*, International Banking, Finance and Economic Law Series, Kluwer Law International, The Hague - London - New York, pp. 235-245

Buser, S.A, Chen, A.H, and E. Kane (1981): Federal deposit insurance, regulatory policy, and optimal bank capital, *The Journal of Finance*, Vol. xxxv, No. 1, pp. 51-60

C

Calais-Aulay, J. and F. Steinmetz (2006): *Droit de la Consummation*, 7éme édition, Dalloz, Paris

Calomiris, Ch.W. (1999): The IMF' s impudent role as lender of last resort, *Cato Journal*, Vol. 17, No 3, p. 21ff.

Calomiris, Ch.W. (2008): The Subprime Turmoil: What's Old, What's New, and What's Next, Jackson Hole Symposium: *Maintaining Stability in a Changing Financial System*, Federal Reserve Bank of Kansas City, August

Calomiris, Ch.W. and B.G. Gorton (1990): *The Origin of Banking Panic Models: Facts and Banking Regulation*, The Wharton School, University of Pennsylvania, No. 11

Caprio, J. and D. Klingebiel (1996): *Bank Insolvencies: Cross-Country Experience*, World Bank Policy Research Working Paper, No. 1620, World Bank, Washington

Caprio, J. and D. Klingebiel (1999): *Episodes of Systemic and Borderline Financial Crises,* World Bank database

Carisano, R. (1992): *Deposit Insurance; Theory, Policy and Evidence*, Luiss, Dartmouth

Carmassi, J., Luchetti, E. and St. Micossi (2010): *Overcoming too-big-to-fail: A Regulatory Framework to Limit Moral Hazard and Free Riding in the Financial Sector*, Report of the CEPS-Assonime Task Force on Bank Crisis Resolution, Centre for European Policy Studies, Brussels

Carmassi, J., and St. Micossi (2012): *Time to set banking regulation right*, Centre for European Policy Studies, Brussels

Carreau, D. et P. Juillard (2005): *Droit International Economique,* Dalloz, Paris

Cartwright, P. (2004): *Banks, Consumers and Regulation*, Hart Publishing, Oxford

Caruana, J. (2009): *The International Policy Response to Financial Crises: Making the Macroprudential Approach Operational*, panel remarks AT Jackson Hole, August

Caruana, J. (2010a): *Macroprudential Policy: Working Towards a New Consensus*, Speech at the high level meeting on The emerging framework for financial regulation and monetary policy, jointly organized by the BIS's Financial Stability Institute and IMF Institute, Washington, DC, April

Caruana, J. (2010b): *Macroprudential Policy: What we Have Learned and Where we are Going*, Keynote speech at the Second Financial Conference of the International Journal of Central Banking, Bank of Spain, Madrid, June

Caruana, J. (2010c): *Basel III: Towards a Safer Financial System*, speech at the 3rd Santander International Banking Conference, Madrid, September

Caruana, J. (2011): *Why central bank balance sheets matter*, Keynote address at the Bank of Thailand - BIS conference on "Central bank balance sheets in Asia and the Pacific: the policy challenges ahead", Chiang Mai, Thailand, December (all this author's articles are available through a search engine in the internet address of the BIS)

Cecchetti, St.G. (2009): *Financial System and Macroeconomic Resilience: Revisited*, opening remarks at the eights BIS Annual Conference, Basel, June

Cecchetti, St.G. (2010): *Financial Reform: A Progress Report*, remarks prepared for the Westminster Economic Forum, National Institute of Economic and Social Research, London, October

Cecchetti, St.G., Disyatat, P. and M. Kohler (2009): *Integrating Financial Stability: New Models for a New Challenge*, Bank for International Settlements, Working Paper, at: http://www.bis.org/publ/othp06.pdf?noframes=1

Cecchetti, St.G., Fender, I. and P. McGuire (2010): *Towards a Global Risk Map*, Bank for International Settlements, Working Papers, No 309, Basel, May

Central Bank Governance Group (2009): *Issues in the Governance of Central Banks*, Report, Bank for International Settlements, May

Central Bank Governance Group (2011): *Central Bank Governance and Financial Stability*, Report, Bank for International Settlements, May

Chan, N., Getmansky, M., Haas, S.M. and A.W. LO (2006): Do hedge funds increase systemic risk?, *Economic Review*, fourth quarter, Federal Reserve Bank of Atlanta, pp. 49-80

Charnovitz, S. (2010): Addressing government failure through international financial law, *Journal of International Economic Law,* Vol. 13, No 3, September, Oxford University Press, Oxford, pp. 743-761

Chow, J.T.S. and J. Surti (2011): *Making Banks Safer: Can Volcker and Vickers Do It?,* IMF Working Paper, WP/11/236, October, at: http://www.imf.org/external/ pubs/ft/wp/20011/wp11236.pdf

Čihák, M. and P.K. Brooks (2009): *From Subprime Loans to Subprime Growth? Evidence fro the Euro Area*, IMF Working Paper, WP/09/69, March

Claessens, St., Herring, R.J. and D. Schoenmaker (2010): *A Safer World Financial System: Improving the Resolution of Systemic Institutions*, Geneva Reports on the World Economy 12, International Center for Monetary and Banking Studies (ICMB), Geneva, Switzerland

Clement, P. (2010): The term 'macroprudential': origins and evolution, *BIS Quarterly Review*, March

Coffee, J.C., Jr (2010): *Bail-Ins Versus Bailouts: Using Contingent Capital to Mitigate Systemic Risk*, The Center for Law and Economic Studies, Working Paper, no. 380, Columbia University School of Law, October, at: http://www.law.columbia.edu/ lawec

Cole, R.T., Feldberg, G. and D. Lynch (2007): Hedge funds, credit risk transfer and financial stability, *Financial Stability Review, Special Issue Hedge Funds,* No. 10, April, Banque de France, pp. 7-17

Commission of Experts appointed by the Swiss Federal Council (2010): *Final Report of the Experts for Limiting the Economic Risk Posed by Large Companies,* October

Committee on the Global Financial System (2008): *Central bank operations in response to the financial turmoil*, CGFS Papers, No. 31, Bank for International Settlement

Committee on the Global Financial System (2010a): *The role of margin requirements and haircuts in procyclicality*, CGFS Papers, No. 36, March

Committee on the Global Financial System (2010b): *Macroprudential Instruments and Frameworks: A Stocktaking of Issues and Experiences*, CGFS Papers, No. 38, May

Committee on the Global Financial System (2010c): *Long-term Issues in International Banking,* Bank for International Settlements, CGFS Papers, No. 41, Basel, July

Committee on the Global Financial System (2011): *The impact of sovereign credit risk on bank funding conditions*, CGFS Papers, No. 43, Basel, July

Conthe, M. and S. Ingves (2001): *Financial Sector Assessment Program,* at: http:// www.imf.org/ external/np/fsap/fsap.asp

Cooper, N. (1987): Sterling, European Monetary Unification and the International Monetary System, in N. Cooper (editor): *The International Monetary System-Essays in World Economics,* The MIT Press, Cambridge, Massachusetts, London, England

Cox, J.C. and M. Rubinstein (1985): *Options markets*, Prentice-Hall, New Jersey

Craig, P. and G. de Búrca (2011, editors): *The Evolution of EU Law*, 2nd edition, Oxford University Press, Oxford – New York

Crocket, A. (2002): Thoughts on the New Financial Architecture, in D.G Dickinson and W.A. Allen (editors): *Monetary Policy, Capital Flows and Exchange Rates*, London-New York, pp. 78 ff.

Crocket, A. (2007): The evolution and regulation of hedge funds, *Banque de France, Financial Stability Review, Special Issue Hedge Funds,* No. 10, April, pp. 19-28

D

Dale, R. (1984): *The Regulation of International Banking*, Woodhead-Faulkeur, Cambridge

Dale, R. (1994): International Banking Regulation, in B. Steil (editor): *International Financial Markets Regulation*, Wiley Publishers, Chichester-New York-Brisbane-Toronto-Singapore, pp. 167-196

Dale, R. (1996): *Risk and Regulation in Global Securities Markets*, Wiley Publishers, Chichester-New York-Brisbane-Toronto-Singapore

Danielsson, J. and J.-P. Zigrand (2007): Regulating hedge funds, *Banque de France, Financial Stability Review, Special Issue Hedge Funds*, No. 10, April, pp. 29-36

Davies, H. and D. Green (2010): *Global Financial Regulation. The Essential Guide*, Polity Press, Cambridge, UK – Malden, USA

De Haan, J., Oosterloo, S. and D. Schoenmaker (2009): *European Financial Markets and Institutions*, Cambridge University Press, Cambridge (and other)

De Meester, B. (2010): The global financial crisis and government support for banks: What role for GATS, *Journal of International Economic Law*, Volume 13, No. 1, March, Oxford University Press, Oxford, pp. 27-63

Dermine, J. and D. Schoenmaker (2010): In Banking, is small beautiful?, *Financial Markets, Institutions & Instruments,* Volume 19, Issue 1, February, New York University Salomon Center and Wiley Periodicals, Inc., pp. 1-19

Dewatripont, M., and J. Tirole (1994): *The Prudential Regulation of Banks*, The Walras-Pareto Lectures, No. 1, The MIT Press, Cambridge-London

Dewatripont, M., Rochet, J.-Ch. and J. Tirole (2010): *Balancing the Banks. Global Lessons from the Financial Crisis*, Princeton University Press, Princeton and Oxford

Diamond, D. (1984): Financial intermediation and delegated monitoring, *Review of Economic Studies*, 51, August, pp. 393-414

Diamond, D. and P. Dybvig (1983): Bank runs, deposit insurance and liquidity, *Journal of Political Economy*, 91, July, pp. 401-419

Diatta, M.L. (2007): *Les Unions monétaires en droit international*, Publications de l' Institut Universitaire de Hautes Etudes Internationales, Genève, Presses Universitaires de France, Paris

Dierick, F. (2004): *The Supervision of Mixed Financial Services Groups in Europe*, European Central Bank, Occasional Paper Series, No. 20, European Central Bank, August

Draghi, M. (1997): Hedge funds and financial stability, *Financial Stability Review, Special Issue Hedge Funds*, No. 10, Banque de France, April, pp. 37-43

Draghi, M. (2008a): *The Current Crisis and Beyond*, Remarks at the Federal Reserve Bank of Kansas City Symposium, Jackson Hole, August

Draghi, M. (2008b): *How to Restore Financial Stability*, Lecture at the 5th Bundesbank Lecture, Berlin-Brandenburgische Akademie der Wissenschaften, Berlin, September

Drehmann, M., Borio, Cl., Gamacorta, L., Jimenez, G. and C. Trucharte (2010): *Countercyclical capital buffers: exploring options*, Bank for International Settlements, Working Papers, No. 317, Basel, July

Dupuis-Danon, M.Ch. (2005): Blanchiment d'argent: illusions, réalités, impact, *Rapport moral sur l'argent dans le monde*, pp. 91. ff

Dwyer, G.P.JR. (2006): Preface-hedge funds: Creators or risk?, *Economic Review*, Fourth Quarter, *Federal Reserve Bank of Atlanta*, pp. v-vi

E

Eatwell, J. and L. Taylor (2000): *Global Finance at Risk – The case for international banking regulation*, New York

Edwards, F.R. (2006): Hedge funds and investor protection regulation, *Economic Review*, Fourth Quarter, Federal Reserve Bank of Atlanta, pp. 35-48

Eichengreen, B. (1994): *International Monetary Arrangements for the 21st Century*, Integrating National Economies, The Brookings Institution, Washington, D.C.

Eichengreen, B. (2008a): *Securitization and Financial Regulation: Pondering the New Normal*, Fixed Income Forum, Santa Barbara, California, July

Eichengreen, B. (2008b): *Thirteen Questions about the Subprime Crisis*, Conference of the Tobin Project: Toward a new Theory of Financial Regulation, While Oak Conference and Residency Center, February

Eichengreen, B. and M. Bordo (2002): Crises Now and Then: What Lessons from the Last Era of Financial Globalization?, NBER Working Paper No. 8716

Eichengreen, B. and R. Borio (2008a): *Rescuing our Jobs and Savings: What G7/8 Leaders Can Do to Solve the Global Credit Crisis*, Centre for Economic Policy Research (CEPR), at: http://www.VoxEU.org

Eichengreen, B. and R. Borio (2008b): *What G20 Leaders Must Do to Stabilise our Economy and Fix the Financial System*, VoxEU.org, November

Eichengreen, B., Feldmann, R., Liebman, J., von Jürgen, H. and Ch. Wyplosz (2011): Public Debts: Nuts, Bolts and Worries, Geneva Report on the World Economy 13, International Center for Monetary and Banking Studies (ICMB), Geneva, Switzerland

Eilenberger, G. (1986): Bankbetriebswirtschaftslehre, Oldenbourg Verlag, München-Wien, pp. 108-157

Einsele, D. (2006): Bank- und Kapitalkarktrecht, Mohr Siebeck, Tübingen

Eisenbeis, R.A. (2009): *The Financial Crisis: Miss-Diagnosis and Reactionary Responses*, paper presented at the International Atlantic Economic Society Conference on Misframing and mismanagement of the Financial Engineering Crisis: The wasted years, held at Boston, MA, October

Elul, R. (2005): *The Economics of Asset Securitization*, Business Review, Q3, at: http://www.philadelphiafed.org

European Central Bank (2002a): Recent developments in international cooperation, *Monthly Bulletin*, February, pp. 53-65

European Central Bank (2002b): International supervisory cooperation, *Monthly Bulletin*, May, pp. 55-64

European Central Bank (2007): The EU arrangements for financial crisis management, *ECB Monthly Bulletin*, February, pp. 80-81

European Central Bank (2008a): *The incentive structure of the 'originate and distribute' model*, European Central Bank, December

European Central Bank (2008b): *Financial Stability Review*, December, European Central Bank

European Central Bank (2010): Recent regulatory initiatives to address the role of systemically important financial institutions, *Financial Stability Review*, June, pp. 147-154,

European Central Bank (2011): *Eurosystem oversight policy framework*, July, European Central Bank

European Commission (1995): *GATS: The General Agreement on Trade in Services*, European Commission, Brussels – Luxembourg

European Commission (2000): *Institutional Arrangements for the Regulation and Supervision of the Financial Sector*, Internal Market Directorate General, January

Evans, H. (2001): An International Financial Regulator?, in Lastra R.M. (editor): *The Reform of the International Financial Architecture*, International Banking, Finance and Economic Law Series, Kluwer Law International, The Hague - London - New York, pp. 109-117

F

Felton, A. and C.M. Reinhart (2008): *The First Global Financial Crisis of the 21st Century, Part II June-December 2008*, Centre for Economic Policy Research (CEPR), VoxEU.org, January

Fender, I., Ho, C. and P. Hördahl (2009): Overview: Investors ponder depth and duration of global growth, *BIS Quarterly Review*, March, pp. 1-17

Ferguson, R.W., Jr, Hartmann, Ph., Panetta, F. and R. Portes (2007): *International Financial Stability*, Geneva Reports on the World Economy 9, International Center for Monetary and Banking Studies (ICMB), Geneva, Switzerland

Fernandez-Bollo, E. et G. Tabourin (2007): Les établissements de crédit, in Commentaire J. Megret : *Integration des marchés financiers*, Direction Dominique Servais, Institut d' Etudes Européennes, Editions de l' Université de Bruxelles, Bruxelles, pp. 91-148

Fikentscher, W. (1983): *Wirtschaftsrecht, Band I.: Weltwirtschaftsrecht und Europäisches Wirtschaftsrecht*, Verlag C.H.Beck, München

Financial Stability Board, International Monetary Fund and Bank for International Settlements (2011): *Macroprudential policy tools and frameworks*, February 14, at: http://www.financialstabilityboard.org/publications/ r_1103.pdf.

Finlay, St. (2009): *Consumer Credit Fundamentals*, second edition, Palgrave Macmillan, Hampshire, New York

Fischer, S. (1995): The IMF and the World Bank at the Fifty, in H. Genberg (editor): *The International Monetary System* – Its Institutions and its Future, Springler Verlag, Berlin – Heidelberg

Flannery, M.J. (1982): Deposit insurance creates a need for bank regulation, *Federal Reserve Bank of Philadelphia*, January/February, pp. 17-26

Folkerts-Landau, D. (1991): *The Case for International Coordination of Financial Policy,* in W. Branson, J. Frenkel and M. Goldstein (editors): *International Policy Coordination and Exchange Rate Fluctuations*, The University of Chicago Press, Chicago and London, pp. 279-306

Footer, M.E. (1994): Global and regional approaches to the regulation of trade in services, *International and Comparative Law Quarterly*, Vol. 43, pp. 661-678

Fox, E.M. (2003): Competition Law, in A.F. Lowenfeld, (editor): *International Economic Law*, International Economic Law Series, paperback, Oxford University Press, Oxford - New York, pp. 340-383

Frankel, A.B. (2009): *The Risk of Relying on Reputational Capital; A Case Study of the 2007 Failure of New Century Financial,* Bank for International Settlements, Working Papers, No 294, Basel, December

Freedman, C. (1987): Discussion on Guttentag and Herring (1987a: Emergency Liquidity Assistance for International Banks), in Portes, R. and A.K. Swoboda (1987, editors): *Threats to International Financial Stability*, Cambridge University Press, Cambridge, pp. 189-194

Fried, J.T. and J.A. Haley (2010): Crisis Prevention: Lessons from Emerging Markets for Advanced Economics, in Giovanoli, M. and D. Devos (2010, editors): *International Monetary and Financial Law: The Global Crisis*, Oxford University Press, Oxford-New York, pp. 69-95

Frieden, J., Pettis, M., Rodrik, D. and E. Zedillo (2012): *After the Fall: The Future of Global Cooperation*, Geneva Report on the World Economy 14, International Center for Monetary and Banking Studies (ICMB), Geneva, Switzerland (forthcoming)

Furceri, D. and A. Mourougane (2009): *Financial Crises: Past Lessons and Policy Implications*, OECD, Paris, January

G

Galati, G. and R. Moessner (2011): *Macroprudential Policy – A Literature Review*, BIS Working Papers No. 337, Monetary and Economic Department, Bank for International Settlements, February

Garbaravicius, T. and F. Dierick (2005): *Hedge Funds and their Implications for Financial Stability,* European Central Bank, Occasional Paper Series, No. 34, European Central Bank, August

Garicano, L. and R.M. Lastra (2010): Towards a new architecture for financial stability: seven principles, *Journal of International Economic Law,* Vol. 13, Number 3, September, Oxford University Press, Oxford, pp. 551-574

Genberg, H. (1995): *The International Monetary System, its Institutions and its Future*, Springer Verlag, Berlin – Heidelberg

Genberg H. and A.K. Swoboda (1991): *The Provision of Liquidity in the Bretton-Woods System*, Discussion Papers in International Economics, The Graduate Institute of International Studiers, Geneva

Gerlach, P. (2010): The dependence of the financial system on central bank and government support, *BIS Quarterly Review*, March

Geva, B. (2008): TARGET2: Transfer of funds and harmonisation of EU payment law, *Uniform Commercial Code Law Journal*, Vo. 41, No. 2, pp. 113-123

Gianviti, F. (2000): The Prevention and Resolution of International Financial Crises: A Perspective from the International Monetary Fund, in Giovanoli M. (editor): *International Monetary Law: Issues for the new Millennium*, pp. 97-109

Gianviti, F. (2001): The Reform of the International Monetary Fund (Conditionality and Surveillance), in Lastra R.M. (editor): *The Reform of the International Financial Architecture*, International Banking, Finance and Economic Law Series, Kluwer Law International, The Hague - London - New York, pp. 93-106

Gianviti, F. (2010): The Objectives of Central Banks, in Giovanoli, M. and D. Devos (editors): *International Monetary and Financial Law: The Global Crisis*, Oxford University Press, Oxford-New York, pp. 449-483

Giovanoli, M. (2000a, editor): *International Monetary Law – Issues for the New Millennium*, Oxford University Press, Oxford-New York

Giovanoli, M. (2000b): A New Architecture for the Global Financial Market: Legal Aspects of International Financial Standard Setting, in Giovanoli M. (editor): *International Monetary Law - Issues for the New Millennium*, Oxford University Press, Oxford-New York, pp. 3-59

Giovanoli, M. (2010): The International Financial Architecture and its Reform after the Global Crisis, in Giovanoli M. and D. Devos (editors): *International Monetary and Financial Law: The Global Crisis*, Oxford University Press, Oxford-New York, pp. 3-39

Giovanoli, M. and D. Devos (2010, editors): *International Monetary and Financial Law: The Global Crisis*, Oxford University Press, Oxford-New York

Gleeson, S. (2010): *International Regulation of Banking – Basel II: Capital and Risk Requirements*, Oxford University Press, Oxford – New York

Goldstein, M. (1997): *The Case for an International Banking Standard*, Institute for International Economics, Policy Analyses in International Economics, 47 Washington, DC, April

González-Páramo, J.M. (2008a): Central banks and the financial turmoil, Speech at eleventh Annual International Banking Conference on *Credit market Turmoil in 2007-2008: Implications for the Public Policy*, Chicago, September

González-Páramo, J.M. (2008b): *Financial Turmoil, Securitisation and Liquidity*, Speech at Global ABS Conference, Cannes, June

González-Páramo, J.M. (2008c): Globalisation, macroeconomic stability and monetary policy at a time of financial turmoil, Speech at FCAVN Conference on *Globalisation in the XXI Century: Challenges and Dilemmas*, San Sebastián, September

González-Páramo, J.M. (2008d): Some lessons from the global financial turmoil, Speech at IIF Conference on *Global Financial Turmoil: Next Steps for the Industry*, London, September

González-Páramo, J.M. (2008e): *Sub-prime Crisis, Liquidity Tensions and Central Banks: One Year on*, Speech at 2nd Spanish Capital Markets Forum, Madrid, September

González-Páramo, J.M. (2009a): *Financial Market Failures and Public Policies: A Central Banker's Perspective on the Global Financial Crisis*, Closing Remarks at XVI Meeting of Public Economics, Granada, February

González-Páramo, J.M. (2009b): *The Financial Market Crisis, Uncertainty and Policy Response*, Speech at IE Business School Annual Alumni Conference, Madrid, November

Goodhart, C.A.E. (1988): *The Evolution of Central Banks*, The MIT Press, Cambridge Massachussets

Goodhart, C.A.E. (1995): *The Central Bank and the Financial System*, Macmillan Press Ltd., Houndmills et.al.

Goodhart, C.A.E. (2000a): *The Organizational Structure of Banking Supervision*, Financial Stability Institute, Bank for International Settlement, No. 1, Basel, October

Goodhart, C.A.E. (2000b, editor): *Which Lender of Last Resort for Europe?*, Central Banking Publications, London

Goodhart, C.A.E. (2009): *The Regulatory Response to the Financial Crisis*, Edward Elgar, Cheltenham, UK – Northhampton, MA, USA

Goodhart, C.A.E. (2010): *The Changing Role of Central Banks*, BIS Working Papers No. 326, Monetary and Economic Department, Bank for International Settlements, November

Goodhart, C.A.E. and D. Schoenmaker (1993): Institutional Separation between Supervisory and Monetary Agencies, in C.A.E. Goodhart (editor): *The Central Bank and the Financial System*, Macmillan Press, London

Goodhart, C.A.E. and R.M. Lastra (2010): Border problems, *Journal of International Economic Law,* Vol. 13, No. 3, September, Oxford University Press, Oxford, pp. 705-718

Gorton, G.B. (1988a): Banking panics and business cycles, *Oxford Economic Papers*, 40, pp.751-781

Gorton, G.B. (1988b): Why are Banks Regulated? Comments, *Paper presented for the Conference on the Perspectives of Banking Regulation*, Cleveland Federal Reserve Bank

Gorton, G.B. and A. Metrick (2010): Regulating the shadow banking system, *Brookings Papers on Economic Activity 2*, Fall, pp. 261-312

Gorton, G.B. and A. Winton (2002): *Financial Intermediation*, Financial Institutions Center, Wharton, Working Paper Series, 02-28

Gortsos, C.V. (1996): *Supranational and International Regimes for the Prudential Regulation of International Banks*, Graduate Institute of International Studies, University of Geneva, Geneva

Gortsos, C.V. (2009a): Legislative initiatives in response to the Financial Turmoil, Briefing Paper for the House of Lords Report: *The Future of EU Financial Regulation and Supervision*, European Union Committee, 14th Report of Session 2008-2009, Volume II: *Evidence*, pp. 214-219

Gortsos, C.V. (2009b): Assessment of the Banking "Rescue" Packages and "Recovery" Plans of the Member States in the European Union, in: *Banking Rescue Measures in the EU Member States – Compilation of Briefing Papers*, Report, European Parliament, Policy Department, Economic and Scientific Policy, IP/A/ECON/RT/2008-29, pp. 9-46

Gortsos, C.V. (2010): The Proposals of the Larosière Group on the Future of Financial Supervision in the European Union, in Giovanoli, M. and D. Devos (editors): *International Monetary and Financial Law: The Global Crisis*, Oxford University Press, Oxford – New York, pp. 127-145

Gortsos, C.V. (2011a): European Financial Integration: Economic Aspects, the Existing Legal Framework and the Way ahead, in Jovanovich M. (editor): *International Handbook of the Economics of Integration*, Volume II, Edward Elgar Hehlthahn, pp. 394-425

Gortsos C.V. (2011b): Basel III: The reform of the existing regulatory framework of the Basel Committee on Banking Supervision for strengthening the stability of the international banking system, in Meng, W., Ress, G. and T. Stein (Hrsg.): *Europäische Integration und Globalisierung*, Festschrift zum 60-jährigen Bestehen des Europa-Instituts, Schriften des Europa-Instituts der Universität des Saarlandes – Rechtswissenschaft, Band 84, Nomos Verlagsgesellschaft, Baden-Baden, pp. 167-183

Gortsos, C.V. (2011c): *The European Banking Authority within the European System of Financial Supervision*, ECEFIL Working Paper Series, No. 2011/1, August, at: http://www.ecefil.eu//UplFiles/wps/WORKING%20PAPER%20SERIES%202011_1.pdf

Gortsos, C.V. (2012a): Greek Responses to the Sovereign Debt Crisis, in C. Stephanou and C.V. Gortsos (ediotrs): *Containing the Sovereign Crisis: European and Greek Responses*, ECEFIL Working Paper Series, No. 2012/4, pp. 47-72, May, at: http://www.ecefil.eu//UplFiles/wps/WORKING%20PAPER%20SERIES%2020124.pdf, pp. 45-72

Gortsos, C.V. (2012b): *European Banking Law*, Notes for the post-graduate program of the Europa Institut, Universität des Saarlandes, second edition, updated, June, at: http://www.ecefil.eu//UplFiles/monographs/European%20Banking%20Law_Saarland_June2012.pdf

Gortsos, C.V. (2012c): *Current Developments in European Banking Law*, ECEFIL Working Paper Series, No. 2012/5, July, at: http://www.ecefil.eu//UplFiles/wps/ WORKING%20PAPER%20SERIES%202012_5.pdf

Grabbe, J.O. (1986): *International Financial Markets*, Elsevier, New York, Amsterdam, London

Gross, D. (2007), UNCITRAL at 40: An overview of current achievements and challenges, *Uniform Law Review 12*, p. 178 ff.

Group of Thirty (2008): *The Structure of Financial Supervision – Approaches and Challenges in a Global Marketplace*, Group of Thirty, Washington, D.C.

Grubel, H.G. (1979): *A Proposal for the Establishment of an International Deposit Insurance Corporation*, Essays in International Finance, No. 133, Princeton, N.J., Princeton University, International Finance Section

Gudmundsson, M. (2008): *How might the Current Financial Crisis Shape Financial Sector Regulation and structure?*, Keynote address at the Financial Technology Congress, Boston, September

Guillén M.F. (2008): *International Banking crises: A Dossier*, The Lauder Institute, Wharton Arts & Sciences, University of Pennsylvania

Guillén M.F. (2009): *The Global Economic and Financial Crisis: A Timeline*, The Lauder Institute, Wharton Arts & Sciences, University of Pennsylvania

Guttentag, J. and R.J. Herring (1983): *The Lender-of-Last-Resort Function in an International Context*, Essays in International Finance, No. 151, Princeton, N.J., Princeton University, International Finance Section

Guttentag, J. and R.J. Herring (1986a): *Disaster Myopia in International Banking*, Essays in International Finance, No.163, Princeton, N.J., Princeton University, International Finance Section

Guttentag, J. and R.J. Herring (1986b): *Innovations and the Financial Safety Net*, The Wharton Program in International Banking and Finance, University of Pennsylvania, Philadelphia

Guttentag, J. and R.J. Herring (1987a): Emergency Liquidity Assistance for International Banks, in Portes, R. and A.K. Swoboda (editors): *Threats to International Financial Stability*, Cambridge University Press, Cambridge, pp. 150-186

Guttentag, J. and R.J. Herring (1987b): *Restructuring Depository Institutions*, International Banking Center, the Wharton School, University of Pennsylvania

Guttentag, J. and R.J. Herring (1988): *Prudential supervision to manage systemic vulnerability*, Federal Reserve Bank of Chicago

H

Haas, Er. (1980): Why collaborate? Issue-linkage and international regimes, *World Politics*, 3, No. 2, April, pp. 357-405

Haberman, G. (1987): Capital requirements of commercial and investment banks: contrasts in regulation, *Federal Reserve Bank of New York Quarterly Review*, Autumn, pp. 1-10

Hadjiemmanuil, Ch. (2006a): Economic and Monetary Union, in Chalmers, D., Hadjiemmanuil, Ch., Monti, G. and A. Tomkins (editors): *European Union Law*, Cambridge University Press, Cambridge, New York, Melbourne, Madrid, Cape Town, Singapore, São Paolo, Chapter 12, pp. 506-560

Hadjiemmanuil, Ch. (2006b): Financial Services, in Chalmers, D., Hadjiemmanuil, Ch., Monti, G. and A. Tomkins (editors): *European Union Law*, Cambridge University Press, Cambridge, New York, Melbourne, Madrid, Cape Town, Singapore, São Paolo, Chapter 18, pp. 781-829

Hagan, S. (2010a): Enhancing the IMF's regulatory authority, *Journal of International Economic Law,* Vol. 13, Number 3, September, Oxford University Press, Oxford, pp. 955-968

Hagan, S. (2010b): Reforming the IMF, in Giovanoli M. and D. Devos (editors): *International Monetary and Financial Law: The Global Crisis*, Oxford University Press, Oxford-New York, pp. 40-68

Hannoun, H. (2010a): *Towards a Global Financial Stability Framework*, speech at the 45th SEACEN Governor's Conference, Siem Reap province, Cambodia, February 26-27, at: http://www.bis.org/speeches/sp100303.htm

Hannoun, H. (2010b): *Information Gaps: What has the Crisis Taught us?*, opening remarks at the conference The financial crisis and information gaps, prepared for G20 Finance Ministers and Central Bank Governors, Basel, April 8-9

Hartkamp, A.S., Heelnik, M.W., Hondius, E. Joustra, C. and E. du Perron (1998): *Towards a European Civil Code*, 2nd edition, Kluwer Law International, The Hague

Hasan, I. and L.J. Mester (2008): *Central Bank Institutional Structure and Effective Central Banking: Cross-Country Empirical Evidence*, April 8, at: http://www. philadelphiafed.org/econ/wps

Hausmann, Y. (1995): *Die Eigenmittelvorschriften des schweizerischen Bankengesetzes im Vergleich zu den Bestimmungen der Europäischen Union und des Basler Ausschusses für Bankenbestimmungen und -überwachung*, Schweizer Schriften zum Bankrecht, Band 31, Schulthess Polygraphischer Verlag, Zürich

Herdegen, M. (2008): *Internationales Wirtschaftsrecht*, 7, Auflage, Verlag C.H.Beck, München

Herring, R.J. (2011): *The Capital Conundrum*, Financial Institutions Center, Wharton, Working Paper Series, 11-70

Herring, R.J. and J. Carmassi (2008): The Structure of Cross-Sector Financial Supervision, *Financial Markets, Institutions & Instruments*, Vol. 17, No. 1, February

Herring, R.J. and J. Carmassi (2010): The Corporate Structure of International Financial Conglomerates: Complexity and its Implications for Safety and Soundness, in Berger, A.N., Molyneux, P. and J. Wilson (editors), *Oxford Handbook of Banking*, Chapter 8, Oxford University Press, Oxford-New York, pp. 195-229

Herring, R.J. and R.E. Litan (1995): *Financial Regulation in the Global Economy*, The Brookings Institution, Washington D.C.

Herring, R.J. and J. Safra (2008): *Risk Management and Its Implications for Systemic risk*, Testimony before the United States Senate Banking, Housing, and Urban Affairs Subcommittee on Securities, Insurance and Investment, July

Herring, R.J. and A.M. Santomero (1991): *The Role of the Financial Sector in Economic Performance*, Center for Business and Policy Studies, part of the Kingdom of Sweden's Productivity Commission, Stockholm

Herring, R.J. and A.M. Santomero (2000): *What is Optimal Financial Regulation?*, Financial Institutions Center, Wharton, Working Paper Series, 00-34

Hesselink, M.W. (2007): European contract law: A matter of consumer protection, citizenship, or justice?, *European Review of Private Law 3*, p. 232 ff.

Hildebrand, Ph.M. (2008): *Is Basel II Enough? The Benefits of a Leverage Ratio*, Financial Markets Group Lecture, London School of Economics, London, December

Hills, S. (2004): Explaining the Credit Risk Elements in Basel II, in M.K. Ong (editor): *The Basel Handbook: A Guide for Financial Practitioners*, Risk Books, Incisive RWG, London, pp. 31-47

Hirtle, B.J., Schermann, T. and K.J. Stiroh (2009): *Macroprudential Supervision of Financial Institutions: Lessons from the SCAP*, Federal Reserve Bank of New York Staff Reports, No. 409, November

Hoenig, Th. (2008): Central Banks: Changing mandates, Speech at the Central Bank of Argentina 2008 Money and banking Conference *Financial Turbulence – Impact on Developed and Emerging Economies*, Buenos Aires, September 1

Howells, G. and S. Weatherill (2005): *Consumer Protection Law*, second edition, Ashgate, England, USA

Huang, X., Zhou, H. and H. Zhu (2009): *A Framework for Assessing the Systemic Risk of Major Financial Institutions*, Bank for International Settlements, Working Papers, No 281, Basel, April

Huertas, T.F. and R.M. Lastra (2011): The Perimeter Issue: To What Extent Should *Lex Specialis* be Extended to Systemically Significant Financial Institutions? An Exit Strategy from too Big to Fail, in Lastra, R.M. (editor): *Cross-Border Bank Insolvency*, Oxford University Press, Oxford-New York, pp. 250-280

Hufbauer, G. and D.D. Xie (2010): Financial stability and monetary policy: need for international surveillance, *Journal of International Economic Law,* Vol. 13, No. 3, September, Oxford University Press, Oxford, pp. 939-953

Hull, J.C. (1997): *Options, Futures, and other Derivatives*, International Edition, Prentice Hall International, London

Hüpkes, E. and D. Devos (2010): Cross-border Bank Resolution: A Reform Agenda, in Giovanoli, M. and D. Devos (editors): *International Monetary and Financial Law: The Global Crisis*, Oxford University Press, pp. 359-377

I

Ingves, St. (2008): *Financial Turbulence, Monetary Policy and Inflation*, Speech to SACO, the Swedish Confederation of Professional Associations, Stockholm, September

International Banking Federation Working Group on Macro-Prudential Supervision (2010): *Preliminary Consideration for Macro-Prudential Supervisory Framework*, International Banking Federation, D1187A, June

International Monetary Fund (2010): *Global Financial Stability Report. Meeting New Challenges to Stability and Building a Safer System*, IMF, Washington D.C., April

International Monetary Fund, Bank for International Settlements, and Financial Stability Board (2009): *Guidance to Assess the Systemic Importance of Financial Institutions, Markets and Instruments: Initial Considerations*, report to the G-20 Finance Ministers and Central Bank Governors, October

Ippolito, R.A. (2005): *Economics for Lawyers*, Princeton University Press, Princeton and Oxford

Iyer R. and J.-L. Peydro (2010): *Interbank Contagion at Work. Evidence from a Natural Experiment*, European Central Bank, Working Paper Series, No. 1147, January

J

Jackson, H.E. and E.L. Symons, Jr. (1999): *Regulation of Financial Institutions*, American Casebook Series, West Group, St. Paul, Minnesota

Johnson, Ch.A. and R.S. Steigerwald (2007): Legal and Policy Aspects of the Central Bank's Role in the Payment System: Some Costs and Benefits of the Choice of Settlement Asset, Seminar on *Current Developments in Monetary and Financial Law*, Washington D.C., October

K

Kane, Ed. (1985): Strategic planning in a world of regulatory and technological change, *Handbook for Banking Strategy*, Wiley, Chichester-New York-Brisbane-Toronto-Singapore, pp. 725-743

Kane, Ed. (1987): Competitive Financial Regulation: an International Perspective, in Portes, R. and A.K. Swoboda (editors): *Threats to International Financial Stability,* Cambridge University Press, Cambridge, pp. 112-129

Kapstein, E.B. (1989): Resolving the regulator's dilemma: international coordination of banking regulations, *International Organisation*, 43, No. 2, pp. 323-345

Kapstein, E.B. (1991): *Supervising International Banks: Origins and Implications of the Basle Accord*, Essays in International Finance, No. 185, International Finance Section, Department of Economics, Princeton University, Princeton, New Jersey

Kapstein, E.B. (1992): Between power and purpose: central bankers and the politics of regulatory convergence, *International Organisation*, 46, No.1

Kapstein, E.B. (1994): *Governing the Global Economy: International Finance and the State*, Harvard University Press, Cambridge, Massachusetts – London, England

Karsten, J. and G. Petri (2005): Towards a handbook on European contract law, *Journal of Consumer Policy 28*, p. 31 ff.

Kaufmann C. and R.H. Weber (2010): The role of transparency in financial regulation, *Journal of International Economic Law,* Vol. 13, No. 3, September Oxford University Press, Oxford, September, pp. 779-797

Key, S.J. (1993): Is National Treatment Still Viable? U.S. Policy in Theory and Practice, in H. Genberg and A.K. Swoboda (editors): *World Financial Markets after 1992*, edited by The Graduate Institute of International Studies (Geneva), Kegan Paul International, London and New York, pp. 89-126

Key, S.J. and H.S. Scott (1991): *International Trade in Banking Services: A conceptual Framework*, The Group of Thirty, Occasional Papers No.35, Washington D.C.

Kiff, J. and P. Mills (2007): *Money for Nothing and Checks for Free: Recent Developments in U.S. Subprime Mortgage Markets*, IMF Working Paper, WP/07/188, International Monetary Fund

Kim, T. (1993): *International Money & Banking*, Routledge, New York

Knight, M.D. (2007): The Current Credit Market Turmoil: Financial and Macroeconomic Implications, Group of Thirty International Banking Session on *The Evolving Structure of the World Economic System*, Washington D.C., October

Knight, M.D. (2008a): *Now you See It, Now you Don't; The Nature of Risk and the Current Financial Turmoil*, Speech at the Ninth Annual Risk Management Convention and Exhibition of the Global Association of Risk Professionals, New York, February

Knight, M.D. (2008b): Some Reflections on the Future of the Originate-to-distribute Model in the Context of the Current Financial Turmoil, Speech at the Euro 50 Group Roundtable on *The Future of the Originate and Distribute Model*, London, April

Knight, M.D. (2008c): Weaknesses Revealed by the Market Turmoil: Where do we go from here?, Keynote address at the Chatman House Event *The New Financial Frontiers*, London, April

Koekkoek, K.A. (1988): Trade in Services, the Developing Countries and the Uruguay Round, *The World Economy*, Vol. 11, Number 1, pp. 151-155

Kokkola, T. (2010): *The Payment System: Payments, Securities and Derivatives, and the Role of the Eurosystem*, European Central Bank

Kokott, J. (2000): Finanzdienstleistungen nach dem Fünften Protokoll zum GATS/WTO-Übereinkommen, *Aktuelle Rechtsprobleme des Finanz- und Börsenplatzes Schweiz,* Band 8, Stämpfli Verlag, Bern, pp. 209-229

Kondeas, A.G., Caudill, S.B., Gropper, D.M. and J.E. Raymond (2008): Deregulation and productivity changes in banking: evidence from European unification, *Applied Financial Letters 4*, Routledge, pp. 193-197

Köndgen, J. (2009): *Certificates from an Investor Protection Perspective: Can the Courts do the Job or do we Need Regulation*, power point presentation presented at the Free University of Bozen-Bolzano CRELE, November

Kuritzkes, A., Schuermann, T. and S.M. Weiner (2003): *Risk Measurement, Risk Management and Capital Adequacy in Financial Conglomerates*, Wharton Business Scool, Financial Institutions Center, Working Papers Series, No. 2, at: www.wharton. upenn.edu/fic/papers/03.html

L

Laeven, L. and F. Valencia (2008): *Systemic Banking Crises: A New Database*, IMF Working Paper, WP/08/224, September, at: http://www.imf.org/external/pubs/ft/wp/ 2008/wp08224.pdf

Laeven, L. and F. Valencia (2012): *Systemic Banking Crises Database: An Update*, IMF Working Paper, WP/12/163, June, at: http://www.imf.org/external/pubs/ft/wp/ 2012/wp12163.pdf

Lambert, T.A. (2010): A middle ground on insider trading, *Regulation*, Winter 2009-2010, pp. 44-49

Lando, O. and H. Beale (2000): *Principles of European Contract Law, Parts I and II*, Kluwer Law International, Hague

Lando, O., Clive, E., Prüm, A. and R. Zimmermann (2003): *Principles of European Contract Law, Part III* , Kluwer Law International, Hague

Langevoort, D.C. (2010): Global securities regulation after the financial crisis, *Journal of International Economic Law,* Vol. 13, No. 3, September, Oxford University Press, Oxford, pp. 799-815

Lasosiére Report (2009): *The High-Level Group on Financial Supervision in the EU, Chaired by Jacques de Larosière, Report*, Brussels, 25 February, available at: ec.europa.eu/commission_barroso/president/pdf/statement_20090225_ en.pdf.

Lastra, R.M. (2000): The Role of the European Central Bank with Regard to Financial Stability and Lender of Last Resort Operations, in C.A.E. Goodhart (editor): *Which Lender of Last Resort for Europe?*, Central Banking Publications, London, pp. 197-212

Lastra, R.M. (2001a, editor): *The Reform of the International Financial Architecture*, International Banking, Finance and Economic Law Series, Kluwer Law International, The Hague - London - New York

Lastra, R.M. (2001b): The Bretton Woods Institutions in the XXIst Century, in Lastra, R.M. (editor): *The Reform of the International Financial Architecture*, International Banking, Finance and Economic Law Series, Kluwer Law International, The Hague - London - New York, pp. 67-90

Lastra, R.M. (2006): *Legal Foundations of International Monetary Stability*, Oxford University Press, Oxford-New York

Lastra, R.M. (2011, editor): *Cross-Border Bank Insolvency*, Oxford University Press, Oxford – New York

Lastra, R.M. and G. Wood (2010): The crisis of 2007-2009: nature, causes and reactions, *Journal of International Economic Law,* Vol. 13, Number 3, September, Oxford University Press, Oxford, pp. 531-550

Lenza, M., Pill, H. and L. Reichlin (2010): *Monetary Policy in Exceptional Times*, Working Paper Series, No. 1253, European Central Bank – Eurosystem, October

Levich, R.M. (1992): The Euromarkets after 1992, in Dermine J. (editor): *European Banking in the 1990s*, 2nd edition, Blackwell Business, Cambridge, pp. 391-421

Liechtenstein, C. (2000): International Jurisdiction over International Capital Flows and the Role of the IMF, in M. Giovanoli (editor): *International Monetary Law: Issues for the new millennium*, Oxford University Press, Oxford-New York, pp. 61-80

Liechtenstein, C. (2010): Lessons for 21st Century Central Bankers: Differences between Investment and Depositary Banking, in Giovanoli M. and D. Devos (editors): *International Monetary and Financial Law: The Global Crisis*, Oxford University Press, Oxford, pp. 217-233

Louis, J.-V. (2009): L'Union européenne et sa monnaie, in Commentaire J. Megret : *Integration des marchés financiers*, 3e édition, Institut d' Etudes Européennes, Editions de l' Université de Bruxelles, Bruxelles, pp. 91-148

Louis J.-V. (2010): The implementation of the Larosière report: a progress report, in Giovanoli, M. and D. Devos (editors): *International Monetary and Financial Law: The Global Crisis*, Oxford University Press, Oxford – New York, pp. 146-176

Lowenfeld, A.F. (2003): *International Economic Law*, International Economic Law Series, paperback, Oxford University Press, Oxford - New York

Lowenfeld, A.F. (2010): The International Monetary System: A look back Over Seven Decades. *Journal of International Economic Law,* Vol. 13, Number 3, September, Oxford University Press, Oxford, pp. 575-595

M

Macht, C. (2007): *Der Baseler Ausschuss für Bankenaufsicht und Basel II – Bankenregulierung auf einem internationalen level paying field*, Studien zum Bank- und Börsenrecht, Band 64, Nomos Verlagsgesellschaft, Baden-Baden

Martinson, M. and J.V. Houpt (1989): Transfer risk in US banks, *Federal Reserve Bulletin*, pp. 255-258, April

Mauerhofer, G. (1998): *Die Wertpapierdienstleistungsrichtlinie*, Schriften zum gesamten Europarecht, Manzsche Verlags- und Universitätsbuchhandlung, Wien

McCauley, R., McGuire, P. and G. von Peter (2010): The architecture of global banking: From international to multinational, *BIS Quarterly Review,* March

McCormick, R. (2006): *Legal Risk in the Financial Markets*, Oxford University Press, Oxford-New York

McKnight, A. (2008): *The Law of International Finance*, Oxford University Press, Oxford-New York

Meng, W., Ress, G. and T. Stein (2011, Hrsg.): *Europäische Integration und Globalisierung*, Festschrift zum 60-jährigen Bestehen des Europa-Instituts, Schriften des Europa-Instituts der Universität des Saarlandes – Rechtswissenschaft, Band 84, Nomos Verlagsgesellschaft, Baden-Baden

Mercuro, N. and S.G. Medema (2006): *Economics and the Law, From Posner to Post-Modernism and Beyond*, second edition, Princeton University Press, Princeton and Oxford

Meyer, C. (1996): *Die Bankbilanz als Finanzielles Führungsinstrument*, Bank- und Finanzwirtschaftliche Forschungen, Band 96, Verlag Paul Haupt, Bern-Stuttgart-Wien

Mikesell, R.F. (1994): *The Bretton Woods Debates: A Memoir*, Essays in International Finance, No. 192, Princeton University, Department of Economics

Mishkin, F.S. (2007): *The Economics of Money, Banking and Financial Markets*, 8th edition, The Addison-Wesley series in economics, Pear Education Inc., Boston

Moessner, R. and W. Allen (2010): *Banking Crises and the International Monetary System in the Great Depression and now*, BIS Working Papers No. 333, Monetary and Economic Department, Bank for International Settlements, December

N

Nielsen L. (2011): *Classification of Countries Based on Their Level of Development. How it is Done and How it Could be Done*, IMF Working Paper, WP/11/31 (at: http://www.imf.org/external/pubs/ft/wp/2011/wp1131.pdf)

Nier, Er.W. (2009): *Financial Stability Frameworks and the Role of Central Banks: Lessons form the Crisis*, IMF Working Paper, WP/09/70, International Monetary Fund, April, at: http://www.imf.org/external/pubs/ft/wp/ 2009/wp0970.pdf

Nobel, P. (2010): *Schweizerisches Finanzmarktrecht und Internationale Standards*, dritte Auflage, Stämpfli Verlag, Bern

Norberg, J. (2009): *Financial Fiasko: How America's Infatuation with Homeownership and Easy Money Created the Economic Crisis*, Cato Institute, Washington, D.C.

Norton, J.J. (1995): *Devising International Bank Supervisory Standards*, Graham & Trotman / Martinus Nijhoff, London - Dordrecht - Boston

Norton, J.J. (2001): *Pondering the Parameters of the 'New International Financial Architecture': A legal Perspective*, in Lastra R.M. (editor): The Reform of the International Financial Architecture, International Banking, Finance and Economic Law Series, Kluwer Law International, The Hague - London - New York, pp. 3-46

Noussia, K. (2010): The 'good bank-bad bank' concept: A model solution?, *Journal of International Banking Law and Regulation*, Vol. 25/8, Sweet and Maxwell, pp. 401-411

Nyberg, L. (2007): *The Financial Market Turmoil*, Speech to the Riskdag Committee on Finance, Stockholm, November

O

Organisation for Economic Co-operation and Development (1983): *The Internationalisation of Banking - The Policy Issues*, OECD, Paris

Organisation for Economic Co-operation and Development (1987): *Prudential Supervision in Banking*, OECD, Paris

Organisation for Economic Co-operation and Development (1993): *Financial Conglomerates*, OECD, Paris

Ong, M.K. (2004): *The Basel Handbook: A Guide for Financial Practitioners*, Risk Books, Incisive RWG, London

Oser, D. (2008): *The UNIDROIT Principles of International Commercial Contracts: A Governing Law?*, Brill Academic Publishers, Leiden

P

Padoa-Schioppa, T. (1994): *The Road to Monetary Union in Europe - The Emperor, the Kings and the Genies*, Clarendon Press, Oxford

Padoa-Schioppa, T. (2000): EMU and Banking Supervision, in C.A.E. Goodhart (editor): *Which Lender of Last Resort for Europe?*, Central Banking Publications, London, pp. 13-29

Padoa-Schioppa, T. (2004): *The Euro and Its Central Bank*, The MIT Press

Panetta, F., Faeh, Th., Grande, G., Ho, C., King, M., Levy, A., Signoretti, F.M., Taboga, M., and A. Zaghini (2009): *An Assessment of Financial Sector Rescue Programmes*, BIS Papers No. 48, Monetary and Economic Department, Bank for International Settlements, July

Papademos, L. (2007): *The Financial Market Turmoil, the European Economy, and the Role of the European Central Bank*, Speech at an event organized by the European Institute, New York, September

Papademos, L. (2008): *Financial Stability Review*, European Central Bank, Frankfurt am Main, December

Papademos, L. (2009): *Tackling the Financial Crisis: Policies for Stability and Recovery*, Speech at the Annual Dinner of the Society of Business Economist, London, February

Park, Y.Ch and Ch. Wyplosz (2010): The future of the IMF and of regional cooperation in East Asia, in Wyplosz, Ch. (editor): *The New International Monetary System - Essays in honor of Alexander Swoboda*, Routledge International Studies in Money and Banking, Rutledge, USA - Canada, pp. 29-43

Patrikis, E. (1999): Role and Functions of Authorities: Supervision, Insolvency Prevention and Liquidation, in M. Giovanoli and G. Heinrich (editors): *International Bank Insolvencies – A Central Bank Perspective*, International Banking, Finance and Economic Law Series, Kluwer Law International, United Kingdom, pp. 283-292

Persaud, A. (2000): *Sending the Herd off the Cliff Edge: The Disturbing Interaction between Herding and Market – Sensitive Risk Management Practices*, Institute of International Economics, Washington

Petrovic, Ana and Ralf Tutsh (2009): *National rescue measures in response to the current financial crisis*, ECB Legal Working Paper Series, No. 8, July

Piedelièvre S. (2008): *Droit de la Consommation*, Economica, Paris

Pitshas, Ch. (2003): Allgemeines Űbereinkommen über den Handel mit Dienstleistungen (GATS), in H.J Priess and G.M. Berrisch (editors): *WTO-Handbuch - World Trade Organisation*, pp. 495-564

Polak, J.J. (1991): *The Changing Nature of IMF Conditionality*, Essays in International Finance, No. 184, Princeton University

Portes, R. and A. Swoboda (1987): *Threats to International Financial Stability*, Cambridge University Press, Cambridge

Posner, R.A. (2010): *The Crisis of Capitalist Democracy*, Harvard University Press, Cambridge-Massachussets-London, England

Poveda, E.C. and S. Dröge (1997): International trade in financial services: An assessment of the GATS, *Aussenwirtschaft,* 52, pp. 603-635

Proctor, Ch. (2005): *Mann on the Legal Aspect of Money*, sixth edition, Oxford University Press, Oxford-New York

Proctor, Ch. (2010): *The Law and Practice of International Banking*, Oxford University Press, Oxford-New York

R

Rajan, R.G. (2010): *Fault Lines: How Hidden Fractures Still Threaten the World Economy*, Princeton University Press, Princeton University Press

Ramsay I. (1997): Models of Consumer Bankruptcy: Implications for Research and Policy, *Journal of Consumer Policy 20*, p. 269 ff.

Rasmusen, Er. (1989): *Games and Information*, Basil Blackwell, Oxford

Reddy, Y. (2001): Issues in implementing international financial standards and codes, *BIS Review 62/2001,* p. 21 ff.

Reich, N. (2005): A European contract law, or an EU contact law regulation for consumers?, *Journal of Consumer Policy*, 28, p. 383 ff.

Reinhart, C.M. and K.S. Rogoff (2008): *The Time is Different: A Panoramic View of Eight Centuries of Financial Crises,* NBER Working Paper Series, Working Paper 13882, National Bureau of Economic Research, at: http://www.nber.org/papers/w13882

Robinson, St.W. (1972): *Multinational Banking: A Study of Certain Legal and Financial Aspects of the Postwar Operating of the United States Branch banks in Western Europe*, Sijthoff, Leyden

Rosenthal, D. (2002): *Consumer Credit Law and Practice*, Butterworths, London

Ruding, H.O. (2002): *The Transformation of the Financial Services Industry*, Financial Stability Institute, Occasional Paper, No. 2, BIS, Basel, March

S

Sanio, J. (2011): Die Zukunftssorgen der Vorwegnehmer, *die Bank*, Zeitschrift für Bankpolitik und Praxis, Nr. 4, April, pp. 36-40

Santomero, A.M. and P. Hoffman (1998): *Problem Bank Resolution: Evaluating the Options*, Financial Institutions Center, Wharton, Working Paper Series, 98-05-B

Santos J.C. (1998): *Commercial Banks in the Securities Business: A Review*, BIS Working Papers No. 56, Bank for International Settlements, Basel, June

Saunders, A. (1987): The Interbank Market, Contagion Effects and International Financial Crises, in R. Portes and A.K. Swoboda (editors): *Threats to International Financial Stability*, Cambridge University Press, Cambridge, pp. 196-232

Saunders, A. and I. Walter (1994): *Universal Banking in the United States, What could we gain? What could we lose ?,* Oxford University Press, New York-Oxford

Schreiber, V. (2005): *International Standards: Neues Recht für die Weltmärkte*, St. Galler Studien zum Privat-, Handels- und Wirtschaftsrecht, Haupt Verlag, Bern-Stuttgart-Wien

Schwander-Auckenthaler, K. (1995): *Missbrauch von Bankgeschäften zu Zwecken der Geldwäscherei,* Institut für Schweizerisches Bankwesen der Universität Zürich, Verlag Paul Haupt, Bern, Stuttgart, Wien

Schwarcz, S.L. (2008): *Systemic Risk*, Duke Law School Legal Studies, Research Paper Series, No. 163, March, at: http://ssrn.com/abstract=1008326

Schwartz, A.J. (2009): Origins of the financial market crisis of 2008, *Cato Journal*, Vol. 29, No.1, Cato Institute, Winter

Schwarze, J. (2007): *Europäisches Wirtschaftsrecht*, Nomos, Baden-Baden

Schwarzenberger, G. (1966): The principles and standards of international economic law, *Recueil des Cours de l'Académie de droit international de la Haye*, Vol. 117 (I), pp. 95-320

Schwintowski, H.-P. and F.A. Schäfer (2004): *Bankrecht: Commercial Banking – Investment Banking,* Carl Heymanns Verlag KG, Köln-Berlin-Bonn-München, 2. Auflage

Scott, H.S. (2010): Reducing systemic risk through the reform of capital regulation, *Journal of International Economic Law,* Vol. 13, No. 3, Oxford University Press, Oxford, pp. 763-778, September

Seelig, S. and Al. Novoa (2009): *Governance Practices at Financial Regulatory and Supervisory Agencies*, IMF Working Paper WP/09/135, at: http://www.imf.org/external/pubs/ft/wp/2009/wp09135.pdf.

Sekolec, J. (1999): The UNCITRAL Model Law on Cross-Border Insolvency, in M. Giovanoli and G. Heinrich (editors): *International Bank Insolvencies*, International Banking, Finance and Economic Law Series, Kluwer Law International, The Hague- London-Boston

Sele, C. (1995): *Standortkonkurrenz zwischen Finanzplätzen unter besonderer Berücksichtigung des Offshore-Geschäfts – Der Fall Liechtenstein*, Bank- und Finanzwirtschaftliche Forschungen, Band 203, Verlag Paul Haupt Bern, Bern-Stuttgart-Wien

Servais, D. (2007): *Integration des Marchés Financiers*, Commentaire J. Megret, Institut d' Etudes Européennes, Editions de l' Université de Bruxelles, Bruxelles

Shin, H.S. (2010): *Financial Intermediation and the Post-crisis Financial System*, Bank for International Settlements, Working Papers, No 304, Basel, March

Siegwart, H., Caytas, I.G. and J.I. Mahari (1989): *Global Political Risk*, Helbing and Lichtenhahn, Basle and Frankfurt am Main

Sigrist, D. (2006): Basel II – kurz erklärt, in W. Wiegand (Herausgeber): *Basel II: die rechtlichen Konsequenzen*, Institut für Bankrecht an der Universität Bern, Berner Bankrechtstag, Band 12, Stämpfli Verlag, Bern

Sinkey, J.F. (1992): *Commercial Bank Financial Management*, MacMillan Publishing Company, New York, fourth edition

Slaughter, A.M. (2000): Governing the Global Economy through Government Networks, in M. Byers (editor): *The Role of Law in International Politics*, Oxford University Press, Oxford-New York

Slovik, P. and B. Cournède (2011): *Macroeconomic Impact of Basel III*, OECD Economics Department Working Papers No. 844, OECD Publishing, at: http://www. oecd.org/eco/Workingpapers

Smaghi, L.B. (2008): Restarting a Market; The Case of the Interbank Market, Speech at ECB Conference on *Global financial Linkages, Transmission of Shocks and Asset Prices*, Frankfurt, December

Smaghi, L.B. (2009a): *Macro-prudential Supervision*, speech at the CEPR/ESI 13th Annual Conference on Financial Supervision in an Uncertain World, European Banking Center at Venice International University, Venice, September

Smaghi, L.B. (2009b): *Regulation and Supervisory Architecture: Is the EU on the Right path?*, Speech at 2009 ECON meeting with national parliaments, Brussels, February 12

Smaghi, L.B. (2010): *The Role of Regulators when Markets Fail*, speech at the conference on the Squam Lake Report: Fixing the Financial System, New York City, June

Smits, R. (1997): *The European Central Bank - Institutional Aspects*, Kluwer Law International, The Hague

Smits, R. (2010): European Supervisors in the Credit Crisis: Issues of Competence and Competition, in Giovanoli, M. and D. Devos (editors): *International Monetary and Financial Law: The Global Crisis*, Oxford University Press, Oxford – New York, pp. 305-328

Snyder, F. (2011): EMU – Integration and Differentiation: Metaphor for European Union, in P. Craig and G. de Búrca (editors): *The Evolution of EU Law*, Oxford University Press, Oxford (2nd edition), pp. 687-716

Sousi–Roubi, B. (1995): *Droit bancaire européen*, Dalloz, Paris

Spulber, D. (1989): *Regulation and Markets*, The MIT Press, Cambridge, Massachussets, London

Staikouras, P.K. (2012): A Theoretical and Empirical Review of the EU Regulation on Credit Rating Agencies: In Search of Truth, Not Scapegoats, *Financial Markets, Institutions & Instruments*, New York University Salomon Center and Wiley Periodicals, Inc, pp. 71-155

Steil, B. (1994): *International Financial Markets Regulation*, Wiley Publishers, Chichester-New York-Brisbane-Toronto-Singapore

Steil, B. (2002): *Changes in the Ownership and Governance of Securities Exchanges: Causes and Consequences*, February

Stein, T. and Ch. von Buttlar (2009): *Völkerrecht*, 12. Auflage, Academia Iuris, Carl Heymanns Verlag, Köln-München

Steinberg, M.I. (1999): *International Securities Law: A Contemporary and Comparative Analysis*, International Banking, Finance and Economic Law Series, Kluwer Law International, The Hague - London - New York

Stephanou, C. (2012): European Responses to the Sovereign Debt Crisis, in C. Stephanou and C.V. Gortsos (ediotrs): *Containing the Sovereign Crisis: European and Greek Responses*, ECEFIL Working Paper Series, No. 2012/4, pp. 9-44, May at: http://www.ecefil.eu//UplFiles/wps/WORKING%20PAPER%20SERIES%202012_4.pdf

Stephanou C. and C.V. Gortsos (2012): *Containing the Sovereign Crisis: European and Greek Responses*, ECEFIL Working Paper Series, No. 2012/4, May at: http://www.ecefil.eu//UplFiles/wps/WORKING%20PAPER%20SERIES%202012_4.pdf

Stiglitz, J. (2002): *Globalisation and its Discontents*, Penguin Books, London

Stillhart, G. (2002): *Theorie der Finanzintermediation und Regulierung von Banken*, Bank- und finanzwirtschaftliche Forschungen, Verlag Paul Haupt, Bern-Stuttgart-Wien

Strahan, Ph.E. (2008) *Liquidity production in 21st Century Banking*, Boston College, Wharton Financial Institutions Center & NBER, January

Strauss-Khan, D. (2010): Building a Crisis Management Framework for the Single Market, Keynote speech at the European Commission conference on *Crisis Management Arrangements for a European Banking System*, Brussels, March

Swoboda, A. (2008): *Restoring International Financial Stability: Five Guidelines for Regulatory Reform,* paper prepared for the conference: Building an International Monetary and Financial System for the 21st Century: Agenda for Reform, The Reinventing Bretton Woods Committee, New York, November

T

Tarashev, N., Borio, C. and K. Tsatsaronis (2009): The systemic importance of financial institutions, *BIS Quarterly Review*, September

The Department of the Treasury (2008): *The Department of the Treasury Blueprint for a Modernized Financial Regulatory Structure,* The Department of the Treasury, Washington D.C., March

The Financial Crisis Inquiry Commission (2011): *The Financial Crisis Inquiry Report*, Official Government Edition, U.S. Government Printing Office, Washington D.C.

The Joint Forum (2010): *Review of the Differentiated Nature and Scope of Financial Regulation: Key Issues and Recommendations*, Bank for International Settlements, January

The World Bank (1989): *World Development Report: Financial Systems and Development*, Oxford University Press, Oxford-New York, pp. 49-61

The World Bank (2001): *Progress Report: International Financial Architecture: An Update on World Bank Activities*, November, World Bank, Washington

Thévenoz, L. (2010): The Rescue of the UBS, in Giovanoli M. and D. Devos (editors): *International Monetary and Financial Law: The Global Crisis*, Oxford University Press, Oxford-New York, pp. 378-391

Tietje, C. and M. Lehmann (2010): The role and prospects of international law in financial regulation and supervision, *Journal of International Economic Law,* Vol. 13, No. 3, September, Oxford University Press, Oxford, pp. 663-682

Tirole, J. (2010): Lessons from the Crisis, in M. Dewatripont, Rochet, J.-Ch. and J. Tirole (editors): *Balancing the Banks: Global Lessons from the Financial Crisis*, Princeton University Press, Princeton and Oxford, chapter 2, pp. 10-77

Toniolo, G. (2005): *Central Bank Cooperation at the Bank for International Settlements, 1930-1973*, Cambridge University Press, Cambridge

Trachtman, J.P. (2010): The international law of financial crisis: spillovers, subsidiarity, fragmentation and cooperation, *Journal of International Economic Law,* Vol. 13, Number 3, September, Oxford University Press, Oxford, pp. 719-742

Trichet, J.C. (2008a): Reflections on the Current Financial Markets Correction, Keynote address at the OESD Forum 2008: *Climate Change, Growth, Stability*, Paris, June

Trichet, J.C. (2008b): Some Lessons from the Financial Market Correction, Speech at the *European Banker of the Year 2007* award ceremony, Frankfurt am Main, September

Trichet, J.C. (2009a): A Paradigm Change for the Global Financial System, Roundtable at the International Colloquium *Nouveau Monde, Nouveau Capitalisme*, Paris, January

Trichet, J.C. (2009b): *Hearing at the Economic and Monetary Affairs Committee of the European Parliament*, Speech, Brussels, January

Trichet, J.C. (2009c): *Remarks on the Future of the European Financial Regulation and Supervision*, Keynote address at the Committee of European Securities Regulators (CESR) February

Trichet, J.C. (2009d): *The ECB's Response to the Crisis*, Statement at the European American Club, Paris, February

Trichet, J.C. (2009e): *Systemic Risk*, Clare Distinguished Lecture in Economic and Public Policy organized by the Clare College, University of Cambridge, Cambridge, December

Trichet, J.C. (2010a): *Macro-prudential Oversight and the Future European Systemic Risk Board*, Keynote address at the European Banking Congress, Frankfurt an Main, November

Trichet, J.C. (2010b): *The Great Financial Crisis: Lessons for Financial Stability and Monetary Policy*, Introductory remarks at the Colloquium in honour of Lucas Papademos, Frankfurt am Main, May

Tridimas, T. (2011): EU Financial Regulation: Federalization, Crisis Management, and Law Reform, in Craig, P. and G. de Búrca (editors): *The Evolution of EU Law*, Oxford University Press, Oxford (2nd edition), pp. 783-804

U

UNCITRAL (2007): *Modern Law for Global Commerce,* Proceeding of the Congress of the United Nations Commission on International Trade Law Held on the Occasion of the Fortieth Session of the Commission, at: http://www.uncitral.org/pdf/english/ congress/09-83930Ebook.pdf

V

Van den Bossche, P. (1999): *The Legal Texts – The Results of the Uruguay Round of Multilateral Trade Negotiations,* Cambridge University Press, Cambridge

Van den Bossche, P. (2008): *The Law and Policy of the World Trade Organisation: Text, Cases and Materials*, 2nd edition, Cambridge University Press, Cambridge

Vicuña, A.S. (2008): *Regional Monetary Unions*, International Law Association, Rio de Janeiro Conference, Report of the Committee on International Monetary Law (MOCOMILA), section I, at: http://www.ila-hq.org

Vicuña, A.S. (2010): An Institutional Theory of Money, in Giovanoli M. and D. Devos (2010, editors): *International Monetary and Financial Law: The Global Crisis*, Oxford University Press, Oxford-New York, pp. 517-532

Vinals, J. (2010): *Macro-prudential Regulatory Policies: The New Road to Financial Stability?*, welcoming remarks at the IMF/Federal Reserve Bank of Chicago International Banking Conference, September

von Bogdandy, A. and J. Windsor (2008): Annex on Financial Services, Second Annex on Financial Services, Second Protocol to the GATS, Fifth Protocol to the GATS, Understanding on Commitment in Financial Services, in R. Wolfrum, P.T. Stoll and C. Feinäugle (editors): *WTO – Trade in Services*, Max Planck Commentaries on World Trade Law, Martinus Nijhoff Publishers, Leiden-Boston, pp. 618-666

W

Wagner, K. (1982): *Die internationale Tätigkeit der Banken als aufsichtsrechtliches Problem*, Nomos Verlagsgesellschaft, Baden-Baden

Walker, G.A. (2001): *International Banking Regulation: Law, Policy and Practice*, International Banking, Finance and Economic Law Series, Kluwer Law International, The Hague - London - New York

Weber, A. (2008): *Financial Markets and Monetary* Policy, Deutsche Bundesbank, Eurosystem, June

Weber, R.H. (1999): *Elektronisches Geld: Erscheinungsformen und rechtlicher Problemaufriss*, Schweizer Schriften zum Bankrecht, Band 58, Schulthess Polygraphischer Verlag, Zürich

Weber, R.H. (2010): Multilayered governance in international financial regulation and supervision, *Journal of International Economic Law,* Vol. 13, No. 3, September, Oxford University Press, Oxford, pp. 683-704

Wellink, N. (2008a): *Basel Committee Initiative in Response to the Financial Crisis*, Remarks before the Committee on Economic and Monetary Affairs of the European Parliament (ECON), Brussels, March,

Wellink, N. (2008b): *Recent Market Turmoil-Implications for Supervisors and Risk Managers*, Remarks at the GARP 2008 9th Annual Risk Management Convention & Exhibition, New York, February

Wellink, N. (2008c): *Responding to Uncertainty*, Remarks at the International Conference of Banking Supervisors, Brussels, September

Werner, W. (1996): Liberalisierung von Finanzdienstleistungen: Atlantische Positionen und Konzepte auf dem Weg zur Interimslösung im multilateralen Dienstleistungsabkommen (GATS), *Aussenwirtschaft*, 51, pp. 327-357

White, B. and D. Vittas (1986): Barriers in International Banking, *Lloyds Bank Review*, July, pp. 19-31

White, W.R. (1996): *International Agreements in the Area of Banking and Finance: Accomplishments and Outstanding Issues*, Bank for International Settlements, Basel

White, W.R. (2008a): International Governance for the Prevention and Management of Financial Crises, Dinner Speech at the Bank of France International Monetary Seminar on *Liquidity Crisis, Capital Crisis*?, Paris, June

White, W.R. (2008b): Past Financial Crises, the Current Financial Turmoil, and the Need for a New Macrofinancial Stability Framework, speech at the LSE Financial Markets Group and Deutsche Bank Conference *The Structure of Regulation: Lessons from the Crisis of 2007*, London, March

Wicker, E. (2000): *The Banking Panics of the Great Depression*, paperback, Cambridge University Press, Cambridge

Williamson, J. (2000): *A more focused IMF*, Conference on the Future of the Bretton Woods Institutions: The European Contribution on the debate on the New Financial Architecture, Paris, France, at: http://www.iie.com/papers/currency.htm

Wood, P.R. (1995a): *International Loans, Bonds and Securities Regulation*, Law and Practice of International Finance, Volume 3, Sweet & Maxwell, London

Wood, P.R. (1995b): *Title Finance, Derivatives, Securitisations, Set-off and Netting*, Law and Practice of International Finance, Volume 5, Sweet & Maxwell, London

World Trade Organization (1999): *Guide to the Uruguay Round Agreements,* Kluwer, The Hague

Wray, L.R. (2010): *What do Banks do? What should Banks do?*, Levy Economics Institute of Bard College, Working Paper No. 612, August

Wyplosz, Ch. (**2010**, editor): *The New International Monetary System - Essays in honor of Alexander Swoboda*, Routledge International Studies in Money and Banking, Rutledge, USA - Canada

Y

Yokoi-Arai, M. (2002): *Financial Stability Issues: The case of East-Asia*, International Banking, Finance and Economic Law Series, Kluwer Law International, The Hague - London - New York

Z

Zamil, R.S. (2009): Too big to fail, *Finance and Development*, December, International Monetary Fund, pp. 41-44

Zerey, J.C. (**2010,** Hrsg.): *Finanzderivate - Rechtshandbuch*, 2. Auflage, Nomos Verlag, Baden-Baden - facultas.wuv Verlag, Wien - Helbing & Lichtenhahn Verlag, Basel

INTERNET ADDRESSES

Bank for International Settlements (www.bis.org)
Basel Committee on Banking Supervision (www.bis.org/bcbs)
Committee on Payment and Settlement Systems (www.bis.org/cpss)
Committee on the Global Financial System (www.bis.org/cgfs)
Dissemination Standards Bulletin Board (dsbb.imf.org)
Financial Action Task Force (www.fatf-gafi.org/pages)
Financial Stability Board (www.financialstabilityboard.org)
International Accounting Standards Board (www.iasc.org.uk)
International Association of Deposit Insurers (www.iadi.org)
International Association of Insurance Supervisors (www.iaisweb.org)
International Auditing Practices Committee (www.ifac.org/iapc)
International Federation of Accountants (www.ifac.org)
International Monetary Fund (www.imf.org)
International Organization for Securities Commissions (www.iosco.org)
Joint Forum (www.bis.org/bcbs/jointforum.htm)
Organization for Economic Cooperation and Development (www.oecd.org)
World Bank (www.worldbank.org)
World Trade Organisation (www.wto.org)